Front cover:

Edward D. Wood, Jr. (right) signs up some financing for *Bride of the Monster* (1955) as his only bankable star, Bela Lugosi, looks on approvingly – from How high was his brow? Albert Lewin, his critics and the problem of pretension by Susan Felleman (page 452).

This issue:
Auteurism Revisited

Edited by Richard Koszarski

This issue is dedicated to William K. Everson 1929–96

Editorial office:

Richard Koszarski
American Museum of the Moving Image
36-01 35th Avenue
Astoria, NY 11106
USA

Publishing office:

John Libbey & Company Ltd
13 Smiths Yard
Summerley Street
London SW18 4HR
UK
Telephone: +44 (0)181-947 2777
Fax: +44 (0)181-947 2664

Other offices:

John Libbey Eurotext Ltd,
92120 Montrouge, France
John Libbey - CIC s.r.l.,
00161, Rome, Italy

Printed in Great Britain by
Biddles Ltd, Guildford, UK

CH00496089

An International Journal

Volume 7, Number 4, 1995

This issue:
AUTEURISM REVISITED

Film History, Volume 7, pp. 355–357, 1995. Copyright © John Libbey & Company
ISSN: 0892-2160. Printed in Great Britain

Auteurism revisited

The very notion of revisiting auteurism some-how suggests a nostalgic trip back to the old home town, with everything looking slightly worn and considerably smaller than remembered.

But American auteurism, although so much a part of 1960s cinema culture, can hardly be read as a mere artifact of the historical forces blowing across the Atlantic at the end of the studio era. From the days of D.W. Griffith, many of those seeking to view the cinema as an art saw film criticism as necessarily artist-centred, and identified the direc-tor as the necessary artist.

Although lacking a book, a teacher, or even a catchy title, this informal critical school had de-veloped a '*politique des auteurs*' all its own, quite internationally, and well before Andre Bazin had ever put pencil to paper. '[I]n the final analysis it is to the director we look as the creative artist, as the unifying mind; the completed picture must be his personal interpretation of the theme'. Andrew Sarris didn't write this. It's the final sentence of Eric Rideout's introduction to *The American Film*, an exhaustive 1937 study which sought to reduce an entire national cinema to the work of a few selected Hollywood directors[1].

In 1915 Ernest Dench had put it even more bluntly in *Making the Movies*, a survey of production practice released just two years after Griffith's no-torious '... producer of all Biograph successes' pro-nouncement:

'Good actors, authors and photographers are indispensable, but unless they are guided by a talented director, results will be disappointing. The director is the man. The movie director has command of everything'[2].

Frank Capra might have called him 'the name above the title'.

Of course, such orthodoxy turned into wall-paper very quickly, an unspoken assertion lurking behind all serious discourse. And because it was an orthodoxy it soon attracted its own school of revi-sionists. Tamar Lane, a wonderful Hollywood gadfly, roasted silent-era auteurists in his 1923 vol-ume, *What's Wrong With the Movies?*:

'The director is the pampered pet and spoiled child of the motion picture world. He is also the silent drama's champion magician, bunco man and hokus-pokus merchant. His reputation is gained by 80 per cent bluff and 20 per cent ability ... The average puttied gentleman has only the slightest idea what the scene he is directing is going to look like when it is finally flashed upon the screen. But he is a good bluffer ... The rest of the photoplay crew are usually forgotten. They may come in at times for a small amount of notice, but it is the megaphone gent who hogs all the honours.'[3]

Tamar Lane's position had it's own following, of course, most prominently in American news-paper film reviewing. These reviewers, whose po-sition in the journalistic hierarchy was on a par with that of obituary writers, tended to avoid the whole notion of art when discussing Hollywood movies, and so focussed their attentions elsewhere. But for every Ward Marsh or Bosley Crowther there was always a Richard Watts, Jr. or Harriette Underhill. Those with the luxury of longer deadlines, like Agee, Ferguson or Farber, typically turned to the director when discussing the screen's artistic highspots.

What happened in the post-World War II period, first in Paris, but then wherever a repertory cinema existed, was the imposition of a broad his-torical framework over what had previously been little more than a gut critical response. When chal-lenged to defend its paternity (by reviewers like Pauline Kael), auteurism sometimes described itself as 'a theory', other times as 'an updated film his-tory'[4]. This may have been a helpful strategy at the time, but the loose application of such loaded ter-minology left the whole position open to a series of endless attacks from what *The Oxford Companion to Film* chose to call 'more rigorous and analytical critical approaches'[5].

These approaches, often borrowed wholesale from older and more respectable disciplines, were able to make mincemeat of any claims to academic rigour on the part of the surviving auteurists. For the past twenty-five years, disciples of one or another of these schools have generally dominated those Anglo-American cinema departments created (ironically) in the aftermath of the original auteurist impulse of the 1960s. The whole notion of authorship became highly suspect, and any reference to specific directors might easily be dismissed as 'great man theory'. Tamar Lane would have approved wholeheartedly.

Unfortunately, none of these subsequent critical approaches had any degree of success outside academia. Out in the 'real world' of the multiplexes, slick new movie magazines, and 'Sneak Previews'-style television commentaries, it might as well be 1968. Today, terms like *mise-en-scène* are casually tossed around at all levels of popular criticism, and most televised reviewers will discuss every sequel to *Porkies* or *Halloween* in terms of its director's larger *oeuvre*.

To quote an American political axiom, 'You can't beat somebody with nobody'. No matter how tattered, subjective and impressionistic the old *politique*, no alternative has demonstrated the same degree of staying power, or the same appeal to so wide a segment of the filmgoing public. That this conclusion has finally wafted up to the more rarified levels of film study has steadily become more clear over the past decade. One can see the change coming even in so traditionally academic a work as Roberta Pearson's study of performance style in D.W. Griffith's Biograph films. Self described as one of 'a generation of film scholars trained to debunk auteurism,' she spends several pages of her introduction apologetically justifying a focus on the great man's work[6]. But the body of the text avoids the continuing comparisons with the work of other studios or directors that would have clearly marked this closely reasoned study as something other than neo-auteurism.

The crux of the matter was stated quite simply in a 1990 issue of *CineAction! A Magazine of Radical Film Criticism & Theory*. Writing in the introduction to a special issue entitled 'Rethinking Authorship', the editors observe, in part:

> One can acknowledge an artist's *intention* and *awareness* without negating the influence of ideology and cultural norms. We do think, however, that the concept of authorship is useful in terms of aesthetics and politics. Aside from discussions of style, the term implies that people are responsible for the works they create and that art can investigate critically, and make reference to social concerns. Art does not reproduce automatically the current vagarities (sic) of the dominant ideology[7].

We concur. While there is certainly no need for a wholesale return to the 1960s, it seems obvious that a complete debunking of auteurism ignores one of the most powerful tools in the critical arsenal. Combined with insights gleaned from the more successful post-auteurist methodologies, author-based criticism must play a significant, perhaps central, role in understanding those achievements which make cinema so attractive a subject of inquiry in the first place.

In adding our own fuel to this rekindled fire, *Film History*'s contribution is less critical or theoretical than traditionally historical. So the point of departure must be Andrew Sarris, who graciously accepted our request to return once more to the original scene of the crime. Suggesting how a new style of author-centred criticism might inform more recent analytical strategies, Robert Spadoni dissects the creation of *Grand Hotel* through materials unavailable to 1968 scholars. But the bulk of the issue is devoted to those forgotten or marginalized 'subjects for further research' who never quite made the original pantheon: Susan Woal on Romaine Fielding, Charlene Regester on Oscar Micheaux, Susan Fellemann on Albert Lewin, Robert Birchard on Edward D. Wood, and a previously unpublished interview with this issue's candidate for the director most in need of further research: Joseph Lerner.✪

Richard Koszarski

Notes

1. Eric Rideout, *The American Film* (London: The Mitre Press, 1937), 2.

2. Ernest Dench, *Making the Movies* (New York: Macmillan, 1915), 1.

3. Tamar Lane, *What's Wrong with the Movies* (Los Angeles: The Waverly Company, 1923), 56–58.

4. Sarris often made the claim that auteurism was a 'theory', but in *The American Cinema* (New York: Dutton, 1968) he described it as 'an updated film history' (p. 15) as well as 'a theory of film history' (p. 19).

5. Liz-Anne Bawden (ed.), *The Oxford Companion to Film* (New York: Oxford University Press, 1976), 45.

6. Roberta Pearson, *Eloquent Gestures* (Berkeley: University of California Press, 1992), 10–16.

7. Florence Jacobowitz and Richard Lippe, 'Rethinking Authorship', *CineAction! A Magazine of Radical Film Criticism & Theory* No. 21–22 (Summer/Fall 1990), 1–2.

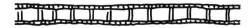

Film History, Volume 7, pp. 358–361, 1995. Copyright © John Libbey & Company
ISSN: 0892-2160. Printed in Great Britain

Notes of an accidental auteurist

Andrew Sarris

O n my visit to the 1995 Sydney Film Festival in June to receive the second Sydney Salute, the first having been awarded to director Ken Russell in 1994, I was repeatedly urged to dredge up all my memories of the Sarris-Kael controversies from the 1960s as if it were yesterday. (Michel Ciment of *Positif* was on hand with his own fix on the issues involved, though he was somewhat distracted by an outbreak of Australian Francophobia over Jacques Chirac's decision to resume underground nuclear testing in the pacific). The words 'auteur theory' and 'auteurist' kept popping up in all sorts of contexts. I was asked if I had regretted anything I had written. I responded by quoting Mario Puzo to the effect that if he had known so many people were going to read *The Godfather*, he would have written it better. For my part, if I had known people would still be talking about the 'auteur theory' a continent away more than three decades later, I would have become paralysed with a writer's block, and never have written the article that, thanks to Pauline Kael, lifted me overnight from obscurity to notoriety without passing GO.

A superciliously cinephobic book reviewer for *The New York Review of Books* recently speculated that Kael had omitted her famous anti-auteurist article, 'Circle and Squares', from her latest collection of pieces because she preferred to look forward rather than backward. My own suspicion is that in the present climate of political correctness, she may have been nervous about a coyly homophobic passage such as the following: 'Isn't the anti-art attitude of the *auteur* critics both in England and here, implicit also in their peculiar emphasis on virility? (Walsh is, for Sarris 'one of the screen's most virile directors'. In *Movie* we discover: 'When one talks

about the heroes of *Red River*, or *Hatari*: one is talking about Hawks himself ... Finally everything that can be said in presenting Hawks boils down to one simple statement; here is a man'.) ... The *auteur* critics are so enthralled with their narcissistic male fantasies (*Movie*: 'Because Hawks's films and their heroes are so genuinely mature, they don't need to announce the fact for all to hear') that they seem unable to relinquish their schoolboy notions of human experience ... Can we conclude that, in England and the United States, the *auteur* theory is an attempt by adult males to justify staying inside the small range of experience of their boyhood and adolescence – that period when masculinity looked so great and important but art was something talked about by poseurs and phonies and sensitive-feminine types'?

At the time, Kael had never met any of us alleged 'narcissistic male' auteurists, an epithet which in that nervously coseted period suggested a poor wretch like Sal Mineo's Plato with his beef-cake pin-up of Alan Ladd hung in his high-school locker in Nicholas Ray's *Rebel Without a Cause*. Kael's clucking mother-hen disapproval of us bad boys was at least for me, very difficult to answer in kind. How *do* you answer a woman who questions your manhood without sounding both ridiculous and misogynous. If you start sputtering that you are indeed manly because you are married with five mistresses and ten children, your female tormentor simply narrows her eyes and sweetly, but demandingly inquires, 'What are you trying to prove, and what are

Andrew Sarris, author of *The American Cinema, Directors and Directions 1919–1968*, is film critic for the *New York Observer* and Professor of Film at Columbia University. Correspondence c/o 19 East 88th Street, New York, NY 10128, USA.

you tring to hide in the closet'? In 1963 I was not married, I didn't have five mistresses or ten children, and I lived with my mother in Queens. In my own mind therefore, I was a sitting duck for Kael's insinuations. Why, however, was the New York cultural establishment so ready to cheer Kael in her curious crusade despite her rhetorical excess? I have always suspected that her non-movie champions saw her attack as a way of putting down movies and people who took them at all seriously. When Kael's early champions discovered that she, too, was a movie enthusiast, they began turning on her as well.

I find it ironic that Quentin Tarantino has expressed admiration for both Hawks and Kael. He can't have it both ways. He must choose one or the other. Perhaps, he is taking out insurance against Kael and her coterie beginning to speculate about *his* sexual inclinations.

Of all the anti-auteurists arrayed against me in the 1960s the one I most respected was the late Dwight MacDonald. I could only chuckle at his witty rejoinder, 'Homer nods, but Hitchcock never'.

I once almost stumbled over Kael and Jacques Rivette of *Cahiers du Cinema* and the *Nouvelle Vague* conversing amiably on a staircase at a multi-cultural cocktail party. When they recognized me, they broke apart with seemingly conspiratorial guilt as if I had caught them in *flagrante delicto*. Recently, another *Cahiers* fossil named André Labarthe declared a bit too vehemently that Peter Bogdanovich was the only American who both understood and properly applied the *Politique des Auteurs*. If the *Cahiers* critics were indeed my spiritual parents, I was orphaned at an exceptionally early age. It can't all be attributed to my insufficient appreciation of Jerry Lewis.

People have asked me if I intend to update my categories in the American Cinema Compilations of 1963 and 1968. The answer is no. My Pantheon directors are secure. If I could go back in time I would add Leo McCarey, Preston Sturges and Billy Wilder. I would add a new category for dissonant, against-the-grain temperaments like John Huston, William Wellman, Stanley Kubrick, Robert Altman, Sam Peckinpah. In the polemical 1960s I under-

rated more directors than I overrated. I am more interested in having conversations with people who think I underrated something or someone than with people who think I overrated something or someone. Yet, my decades of experience as a reviewer tells me that people become more enraged over things I profess to like than things I profess to dislike. People are always more intimidated by pans of movies they enjoy than by raves over movies they despise. Another new category if I could go back in time: The *Objet d'Art* Directors: William Wyler, Carol Reed, Rouben Mamoulian, Jack Clayton, Rene Clair, Rene Clement, David Lean.

I am critically and theoretically the product of everything I have read, and every conversation in which I have engaged. I discovered Freud belatedly through auteurism, and have recommended his essays on Leonardo Da Vinci and William Shakespeare to my students. My revisionist stance labelled 'auteurism' was always as much about genres as about directors, and as much about subtexts as about contexts. Hence, my eternal indebtedness to André Bazin and Northrop Frye: Bazin for unlocking the key to the sublime stillnesses and silences of the cinema; Frye for his seminal statement that since the *Iliad*, the fall of an enemy is regarded as a tragic rather than a comic event.

In my polemical Francophile period in the 1960s I gave insufficient credit to such American journalistic influences as Gilbert Seldes, Meyer Levin, George Jean Nathan, Burton Rascoe, Frank Nugent, Otis Ferguson, Manny Farber, James Agee, Seymour Peck and, above all, Louis Kronenberger, the closest stylistic equivalent of Oscar Wilde in America.

Some of my detractors mistakenly supposed that I did not value the greatest foreign-language directors as highly as the greatest Hollywood directors. Nothing could be further from the truth. I began my career as a foreign art-film snob, and still have traces of the virus in my system. Max Ophuls's *Madame de ...* is still number one on my all-time list, and not far behind are Kenji Mizoguchi's *Ugetsu*, Jean Renoir's *La règle du jeu*. Carl Dreyer's *Ordet*, Luis Bunuel's *Belle de jour*, F.W. Murnau's *Sunrise*, Roberto Rossellini's *Flowers of St. Francis*, Robert Bresson's *Au Hasard Balthazar*, Claude Chabrol's

Fig. 1. Screenwriter Harold Pinter, critic Andrew Sarris, and director Joseph Losey at a panel in New York in connection with the opening of *Accident* (1967).
[Photo by Fred W. McDarrah, 505 LaGuardia Place, New York, USA]

Les Bonnes Femmes, Eric Rohmer's *A Tale of Spring-time, et al.* My heresy at the time of the *auteur* wars in the 1960s was in the suggestion that John Ford's *The Searchers* and Alfred Hithcock's *Vertigo* fully belonged on that same lofty plateau.

My easiest and most paradigmatic directors to teach: Alfred Hitchcock and Buster Keaton. My hardest: John Ford and Jean Renoir.

I prefer Michael Powell's *The Life and Death of Colonel Blimp* to Orson Welles's *Citizen Kane*. I prefer Welles's *The Magnificent Ambersons* to *Kane*. Why? The respective treatments of women.

I would argue that Ava Gardner surpassed Marilyn Monroe as an icon of sensuality in their respective motion pictures in the 1950s. Monroe has triumphed in death over Gardner purely through the medium of still photography.

Among my critical vices is a weakness for dialectics that lead me into oversimplifications and shakey comparisons, *vide* my writings on Chaplin and Kea-

ton, Hitchcock and Welles, Cecil B. De Mille, and Frank Lloyd, Ford and Hawks. Yet even at my worst, I consider it preferable to look for stylistic differences in movies than to look for thematic similarities in the manner of the sociologists of yesterday, and the semioticians of today.

I have tried to give screenwriters their due whenever I could in good conscience, but as a tribe they still loathe me for allegedly demeaning their role in cinematic creation even more than the studio satraps had done in the past. Joseph L. Mankiewicz attempted to smooth things over by designating every screenplay a directed movie, and every directed movie a screenplay, but then he was successful as writer, director and producer, and could afford to be civilized about the subject.

Kael attacked me in *Circles and Squares* for using a word like 'soul' to describe however tentatively what I was trying to define in auteurism. In our largely secular circle it was an easy point for her to score, but I was only beginning my often lonely quest for a way of combining Aristotelian elitism with Christian mercy in broadening the moral range of movie reviewing. Thus the apparent paradox, if not outright contradiction, involved in Luchino Visconti's cinematographic rendering in *La Terra Trema* of poor Sardinian fishermen as if they were Renaissance princes. The cinema thus united the two divergent strands of classical narrative: Homer and the Bible.

My first temporizing formulations of auteurism led me inexorably to the still tantalizing mysteries of movies themselves, and to the mystical realm of *mise-en-scène*, a concept articulated most expressively and most eloquently by Alexander Astruc through his analysis of the art of the late Kenji Mizoguchi: 'But Mizoguchi knows well that, after all, it is not very important for his film to turn out well; he is more concerned with knowing whether the strongest bonds between himself and his characters are those of tenderness or contempt. He is like the viewer who sees the reflection of pleasure in the features of the one he watches, even though he also knows quite well that it is not this reflection alone which he is seeking but perhaps quite simply the tedious confirmation of something he has always known but cannot refrain from verifying. So I consider *mise-en-scène* as a means of transforming the world into a spectacle given primarily to oneself – yet what artist does not know instinctively that what is seen is less important than the way of seeing, or a certain way of needing to see or be seen'.

I had never really thought about it before, but re-cently I began to realize that auteurism started out unconsciously as merely a means to an end, that end being the common experience some of us shared in Paris, London, New York, and other cosmopolitan centres, of being on the outside looking in, victims of failed careers seeking to justify the hours and hours of addictive gazing at the screen for some shred of insight into the human condition. It had to be somewhere beneath the too often vulgar and banal surface. We could not be such fools as to be taken in completely by the Hollywood snake-oil salesmen. Kael's school-marm diatribes *did* strike a nerve in this regard. Her prose reminded many of us of old dates from hell where manipulative young women responded to our clumsy pawing by asking us sarcastically if we were ready to grow up and accept responsibility. This was before the 1960s when men learned to become permanent adolescents by proudly refusing to make commitments. Most of our movies these days reflect this permanence of male adolescence, and I would be the last person to suggest that this is a welcome development. The fact remains that what auteurism did for me was to make me culturally viable and legitimate, and for that I shall be eternally grateful to the accidental or intuitive decision to bring the word 'auteur' bawling and screaming into the English language. The rest is refinement of expression, expansion of relevance, accumulation of associations, and the continuing investigation of the means by which the movies continue to project their magic.⊘

Film History, Volume 7, pp. 362–385, 1995. Copyright © John Libbey & Company
ISSN: 0892-2160. Printed in Great Britain

Geniuses of the systems: Authorship and evidence in classical Hollywood cinema

Robert Spadoni

Introduction

I f a text should be discovered in a state of anonymity', Michel Foucault writes, 'whether as a consequence of an accident or the author's explicit wish – the game becomes one of rediscovering the author'[1]. Subsequent directions taken in the writing of history – academic histories of Hollywood's studio era as far as this essay considers – have introduced a new probable cause for the state of a text's anonymity. They have also made the game of rediscovering the author more fun or more urgent, depending on one's idea of a game. In either case, the game is harder to play now than when Peter Wollen wrote that auteur theory 'implies an operation of decipherment; it reveals authors where none had been seen before'[2].

On the smooth gray surface of the classical Hollywood cinema, a bulge of anonymity rises at MGM in the 1930s. This force left no signature on any film but left its mark on many. It shaped them like a set of determinative norms. It constrained and guided the choices of the craftspersons and artists who worked on them, like a paradigm. The right piece of evidence could help turn this force into a person. In The Genius of the System, Thomas Schatz bases his account of the development of Grand Hotel (1932) on such a piece of evidence – on

transcribed pages of six story development conferences. But since when is Irving Thalberg a figure papered over by film history?

Thalberg was a darling of press and public in his time and canonized not long afterwards[3]. Today a billion people can still hear his name spoken with solemnity and reverence during the odd Academy Awards telecast[4]. Surely a historian could find a needier beneficiary. Still, while Thalberg might not be teetering on the edge of oblivion, neither has he nor any other studio producer achieved the star status that auteur theory accorded to some studio directors – many of whom enjoy continued favour in film studies today. A good deal of scholarship has, in one way or another, gone around Irving Thalberg. What would it take to shift Thalberg's status within film studies, from film manager to film artist? Why bother? This essay comes at these questions from a few angles and suggests answers based, partly, on the Grand Hotel evidence that Thomas Schatz examined.

This essay considers less Schatz's treatment of

Robert Spadoni, who developed this paper at the New York University Cinema Studies Department, now studies film at Northwestern University. Correspondence c/o Dept. of Radio/TV/Film, 1905 Sheridan Road, Northwestern University, Evanston, Illinois 60208, USA.

the evidence than the evidence itself, less *Grand Hotel* than ways it can be written about, less Irving Thalberg than the idea of the film author. We will work toward a historical trace, not in a historical mode, but through metadiscourse intended to bring into line some ideas about film history and theory. Our inquiry will stick close to the idea of the film author and touch down on the *Grand Hotel* evidence, I hope, before making too much of generalizations. The conference transcripts will bring us to our main purpose, which is to ask how historical evidence might get behind a challenge to an influential conception of Hollywood studio cinema and, in the bargain, point an old theory in some new directions.

Two approaches and their findings

Schatz describes auteur theory's sharp limitations in a few places[5]. In another he articulates an alternative to organizing and understanding Hollywood studio films – namely, through genre study[6]. Elsewhere still, Schatz exhibits a belief in film authors. He exhibits it in his discussion of *Grand Hotel*'s development, and in the first pages of *The Genius of the System: Hollywood Filmmaking in the Studio Era*. In his introduction, below the heading 'The Whole Equation of Pictures', Schatz slips a mission statement between two quotes. The first quote simultaneously evokes Thalberg and a calculus in which individuals like Thalberg do not cancel out of Hollywood studio history. The comment is Scott Fitzgerald's, that 'not a half dozen men have been able to keep the whole equation of pictures in their heads'[7]. The second quote follows a general admonition not to credit too much to producers. It is André Bazin's condemnation of auteurist pantheons and his call for recognition of 'the genius of the system'[8].

The genius of the system, then, is calculated by the whole equation of pictures, which slots producers in among its constants and variables. Surely this is not a remarkable formula for a history of Hollywood studio-era filmmaking. Surely a variation of it must figure into any such history. A formula fitting the description figures into David Bordwell, Janet Staiger and Kristin Thompson's *The Classical Hollywood Cinema: Film Style and Mode of Production to 1960*. However, in that formula, producers

are littler variables and they fall in among many more. Fitzgerald's 'half dozen men' tips us off that Schatz's system is not one that moves people, technology and movies around with Marxian determinism – at least it never did that to certain individuals.

Schatz's stated mission is 'to calculate the whole equation of pictures, to get down on paper what Thalberg and Zanuck and Selznick and a very few others carried in their heads'[9]. These very few men drop out of Schatz's formula and, from below it, they *dream* the formula. 'The chief architects of a studio's style were its executives'[10], Schatz writes early on and, later, that 'Thalberg hit his stride in the early 1930s, and his studio machine turned out a steady supply of quality hits'[11]. Does this Great System theory have Great Men at its core, pulling the knobs and spinning the dials?

The authors of *The Classical Hollywood Cinema* do not swerve from an approach that seldom stops on individuals (such as Thalberg) for much longer than a mention. Schatz, on the other hand, finds that certain moments at certain studios call for attention to certain individuals. At these conjunctures, he finds, these individuals had the run of the show. In such chapters as 'MGM and Thalberg: Alone at the Top'[12], Schatz argues that understanding an identifiable piece of the system (and its output) as largely controlled (and shaped) by the hand of one person is not an unhelpful way of understanding these historical conjunctures. While it might seem that no history could chart a course through the studio era without stopping to consider Thalberg significantly, there are other routes: Bordwell, Staiger and Thompson plough through the same time and place with only a cursory mention of the man[13]. Whereas their work draws power from its striking consistency of approach, Schatz demonstrates strength in a capacity to shift gears – to find Great Men emerging, at times, and making great differences. Each approach, as practiced, holds implications for how and where authors might figure into Hollywood history.

Not long before the 1988 appearance of *The Genius of the System*, a shift in the dominant conception of what constituted Hollywood studio cinema, and how films were made there, and who (or what) needs to be understood as having made them, rewrote some major ground rules for writing Hollywood studio history. This shift's principal

Fig. 1. Irving Thalberg – the genius of the system?
[Marc Wanamaker/Bison Archives.]

tion or result of a desire for something 'good' or something 'different' permits a history to proceed with minimum – and minimizing – attention to individual personalities and contributions. Magnifying this tendency of effect is the BST optic's blindness to masterpieces, since focusing on an individual film for too long invariably brings individual persons into focus as well[15]. The preface states: 'The Hollywood mode of film practice constitutes an integral system, including persons and groups but also rules, films, machinery, documents, institutions, work processes, and theoretical concepts. It is this totality that we shall study'[16]. BST sees through a film unless it is one of their 100 randomly selected films or fits one of their definitions of a 'limit case'[17]. Films falling into neither category fall by default between the wide borders of this ascriptive, descriptive history. On closer examination, the smooth gray surface of the classical cinema is filigreed with rules, films, machinery, documents, work processes, theoretical concepts, and the shifting masses of groups observed from far distances. But, try as one might, it is hard to make out very many persons. BST negates most biographical approaches to threading a historical narrative through studio Hollywood.

Schatz's attention to studio producers, and some other factors we are about to consider, suggest that conditions are favourable for the launching of a new biographical approach. But why producers and not directors? And why history and not theory? Let's back up and approach some answers through the work of auteurist V.F. Perkins.

architects were Bordwell, Staiger and Thompson, and its blueprint was *The Classical Hollywood Cinema* (hereafter 'BST'). Here is an aspect of the new wave that makes it hard for historians with even slightly auteurist leanings to traffic in its wake.

One way BST constructs a cinema definitively shaped by norms and neatly packed into a ruling paradigm, and one way the authors smooth 500 pages into something startlingly uniform and unified, is to sort a great heap of atomized source data into but two bins. The impulses that shaped Hollywood industry and output were toward standardization and differentiation. (*Standardization*, Staiger explains, means both uniformity and a 'criterion, norm, degree or level of excellence'[14].) Tagging every inclination and action as the reflec-

New wave authors

Perkins writes in *Film as Film* that 'we can sustain the belief that a good film is necessarily an expression of one man's vision, a communication from the director to his audience, only if we can demonstrate a difference in kind and effect between the personal film and the factory movie'[18]. There is another option: forget directors and lock on to producers. Suddenly the imperative to distinguish factory movies from personal films disappears. Factory movies become the personal films of factory bosses. Schatz uses this approach to study some lengths of some strands of the studio era and suggests that, in studies training their focus on just these lengths, a producer-centred approach might be appropriate. Schatz suggests that it might not be falling back into the worst habits of yesterday's historians to refer, as he does, to 'Thalberg's production system'[19], or to claim (after laying down qualifiers) that 'the controlling force, of course, was Irving Thalberg'[20], or even to state outright that 'the force of his personality and his will had shaped MGM'[21]. The years just preceding *The Genius of the System* made author-centred approaches among the more dangerous kind to attempt, but they also made some new varieties possible.

After many nods to the work's coherence and to collaboration and pure accident as decisive factors in studio production, Perkins places all bets on the director: 'He is in charge of what makes a film a *film*'[22]. But on his way to this conclusion, Perkins writes that 'whatever the function he performs and the privileges he enjoys, his status must under normal circumstances be that of an employee'[23]. Perkins elsewhere brushes a little harder against the producer-as-author idea[24]:

> The film industry is largely controlled by men who not only claim to be able to predict a picture's prospects by reference to its ingredients (story, cast, setting, etc.) but who also 'know probably less about the process of making films than the manufacturers of any other consumer product in the world'.

So, while producers exercise considerable control over the selection of a picture's ingredients, what they lack in creative vision and practical knowledge is sufficient to void all arguments that might profitably proceed from claims to this control. Perkins is not the first to express this view. Above he quotes Joseph Losey. In *Hollywood the Dream Factory*, Hortense Powdermaker presents an array of

producer types, including Mr. Mediocre, Mr. Kow-tow, Mr. Schizo and Mr. Good Judgment. The rare exception, Mr. Good Judgment 'does not think of himself as a creative genius, but has confidence that he knows a good story when he sees one, and that he has the ability to pick people, such as writers and directors, who can carry it through'[25]. Similar ideas about producers colour much auteurist thinking, including Peter Wollen's, who writes that 'a great many features of films analysed have to be dismissed as indecipherable because of 'noise' from the producer'[26]. Knee-jerk disparagements and dismissals like these helped for decades to mask off a loaded vein of opportunity, one that Schatz didn't tap until after some other historians had exposed it.

BST tracks the rise of the central-producer system and, with it, the rise of the central producer. The authors show how producers came to be cardinal to studio production in ways that run against the cherished cliché: 'This system introduced a new set of top managers – producers such as Thomas Ince and later Irving Thalberg who meticulously controlled the making of their firm's films ... [The producer] was responsible for the output of a specific number of quality films produced within carefully prepared budgets; the producers selected and coordinated the technical experts '[27] – including the director. Thanks in some measure to BST, Schatz's 'strong conviction that these producers and studio executives have been the most misunderstood and undervalued figures in American film history'[28] is less audacious than he makes it sound. His efforts figure into a wider movement toward new understandings of producers, one that reached a new level of clarity and definition in 1993, when Tino Balio wrote that 'the rise in status of the producer came at the expense of the director. Having lost much of their autonomy, directors became cogs in a wheel, relegated essentially to the task of staging the action'[29].

A second bias that had to be dislodged separates the *auteur* from the *metteur-en-scène*. Wollen makes the difference between them clear where he writes that 'the meaning of the films of an *auteur* is constructed *a posteriori*'[30]. Perkins seems at first to be prefiguring a part of Schatz's author-finding strategy when he writes that, 'in outline at least, the shape of a picture is controlled by the construction of its script'[31], but then goes on to reflect Wollen's view when he clarifies his own: 'Far from creating a finished work, [the script writer] offers an outline open to an infinite variety of treatments'[32]. The ban on considerations of preproduction activity had to be lifted before authors could credibly be located in script-development conferences.

Again BST is seen to clear away theoretical deadwood and open up a space for new propositions and treatments. BST describes how the script's function changed with the coming of the central producer system: 'Planning the work and estimating production costs through a detailed script became a new, extensive, and early step in the labor process ... The script became a blueprint detailing the shot-by-shot breakdown of the film'[33]. The script became as open to an infinite variety of treatments as the blueprint for a house is – that is, not very open. Schatz takes this thread and interweaves it with the new centrality of the central producer, then personalizes the result, writing that Thalberg 'shepherded each story property as it went through script development and into final preparation before shooting, then monitored production itself through written reports and the screening of dailies, then oversaw the postproduction process of editing, previews, retakes and reediting'[34].

A short answer to the question 'Why producers'? is that, since 1985 (the year BST 'established the foundation for any serious study of American film history'[35]), producers have made safer bases for author-centred assertions than directors have. Schatz describes producers at work[36]:

> These men – they were always men – translated an annual budget handed down by the New York office into a program of specific pictures. They coordinated the operations of the entire plant, conducted contract negotiations, developed stories and scripts, screened 'dailies' as pictures were being shot, and supervised editing until a picture was ready for shipment to New York for release.

The course of a producer's typical workday put him in regular contact with events and terms that help sidle a historical narrative comfortably close to BST's 'economic aims and principles of the Hollywood mode of production'[37]. And yet, while one's narrative rings with all the right words, it retains a hero with passions, dreams, personal triumphs and tragic flaws. Traditional conceptions and figurations of studio Hollywood – some as insightful today as they once were on film history's cutting edge – survive by means of a transference of attention, from directors to producers.

Another short answer is that producers were businessmen and, as such, they generated lots of paperwork, and paperwork – bundled, boxed and forgotten – turns into historical evidence. Any time when scholars of classical cinema are well advised to venture an opinion only after (quoting Schatz) 'digging through several tons of archival materials from various studios and productions companies'[38] is a good time to construct a narrative around a studio producer.

Still, while his book contains what I interpret as seeds, signposts and precursors, Schatz more explicitly tears down existing auteurist pantheons than erects any new ones. His project is not to design an author built to withstand the censure that would likely rush to meet any serious attempt to claim an individual as originating important shifts in classical film styles and production modes. What would these objections be and how might the transcripts assist in an effort to meet them? For answers we must look through Schatz to one of his primary sources, and turn our attention more fully to the project at hand.

The author inside

By the end of the 1970s, writes Edward Buscombe, the concept of authorship, 'the vantage point from which many of the most coherent maps had been drawn, had been severely undermined'[39]. Another to cite auteur theory's strengths as a set of heuristics and its barrenness as a set of ideas in the same sentence is Stephen Crofts: 'The principle's critical success, however, belies its theoretical bankruptcy'[40]. When Perkins wrote that 'the notion of the director as sole creator, uniquely responsible for a picture's qualities, defects, impact and meaning, must be approached with at least some caution'[41], he was taking his own advice and edging his way, cautiously, toward propounding that very notion. The going was only to get rougher as the decade wore on.

But it would be unfair to single out auteur theory for having fallen out of favour. Theory in general had acquired a bad reputation by the end of the decade. 'The 1970s in film studies were, self-consciously, a decade of theory'[42], writes Buscombe, who joins others in hailing the rise of film history as salve and salvation to a discipline in need of both. Of the 1970s, when new theories ousted reigning ones practically overnight, 'knowledge was power, the power to declare who was in the vanguard and who had been left behind on the scrapheap'[43]. A rock-solid faith seems implicit in this use of the past tense, in the effects of film history on film studies. Compared to a world where 'semiotics played havoc' and 'the gusty squalls of psychoanalysis'[44] whipped through unexpectedly and often, a field dominated by history is calmer and more stabilized. As clear seems to be the dividing line between history and theory. History brings with it a whiff of credibility and a title of authority that, by the end of the 1970s, inconstant theory had lost. Theoretical knowledge was power, the power to bully and jockey – to turn fickle tides with a little inference, some rhetoric, and a good handle on the right jargon. Historical knowledge is something different. Truth maybe.

The rise of film history has not similarly delighted auteur theorists, who now most likely write auteur history. Semiotics and psychoanalysis loom smaller than they did before but, as Buscombe explains, now auteurists have other problems: 'The notion that film history, like history on a wider scale, is essentially to be understood as the aggregation of the actions of great men, has been largely expelled from the discourse of contemporary film studies'[45]. The day's big thinkers, those individuals whose tastes and agendas determine where the vanguard is, and who is on the scrapheap, bar history from proceeding in its most comfortable tradition and make the present as inhospitable a time as any to peddle an auteurist viewpoint.

```
            "GRAND HOTEL"          December 9, 1931

                        STORY CUTTING CONFERENCE:

                        THOSE PRESENT WERE:
                        Irving Thalberg
                        Paul Bern
                        Edmund Goulding
                        Frank Partos

Mr. Bern:      My first cut is pages 36 to 40.

Mr. Thalberg:  Most of my suggestions come toward the latter part
               of the story.

Mr. Bern:      Yes, Irving - so far as actual story construction
               comes. Why don't we listen to Irving first.

Mr. Thalberg:  In the play, Witte entered didn't he? -- He came
               in. Pimenov doesn't come in now, does he?

Mr. Goulding:  No.

Mr. Thalberg:  I'm trying to analyze the feeling of excitement
               I felt in the gambling scene, which is now lacking.

Mr. Goulding:  The beginning of the scene starts on page 128.

        NOTE: It was discussed whether to jump from one
              scene to another or to start from the be-
              ginning of the script. It was agreed upon
              to start from the beginning of the script,
              however, this intention was not carried out.

Mr. Goulding:  I want Irving's feeling of this, page by page.
               Three meetings would take us through the script.

Mr. Bern:      Eddie's intention is to have the camera, from
               certain distance away, on a face and move from one
               face to another. We are making a terrible mistake
               if we don't shoot it two ways.

Mr. Thalberg:  You mean two cameras at one time? That's a cinch.
               I am with you there. My idea was that the person
               is in the picture and as they finish talking -- be-
               hind him in double exposure is the next person
               talking - so you hear two voices -- there is never
               a lapse of a second -- there is a slight confusion
               as you get the double effect -- there is a feeling
               of new people piling in. I see the people coming
               in from all directions. The figures shooting from
               different angles talking might give a terrific
               feeling of excitement.

Mr. Goulding:  That's a trick.

Mr. Thalberg:  It's a very exciting trick -- you can get the audience
               to the point where they say: "Jesus!"
                                                CONTINUED:
```

Fig. 2 (and next page). Two pages from Maxine Beeson's story conference transcripts. USC Cinema-Television Library. [Used by Permission Turner Entertainment Co., All Rights Reserved.]

The last decade's academic histories of Hollywood studio cinema have been so influenced by what I have called the BST approach, and others 'the Wisconsin project'[46], that it is not easy to write on the subject without traversing some part of this collective formalist discourse – even if to roundly disagree. History is not by its essence inclined to serving formalist ends, though. Years before film scholars would be obliged to engage the problematics (and potentials) of arguing a case through film history, Perkins wrote[47]:

Criticism itself is a public activity, concerned only with what can be communicated. I may *feel* a picture to be coherent but unless I can

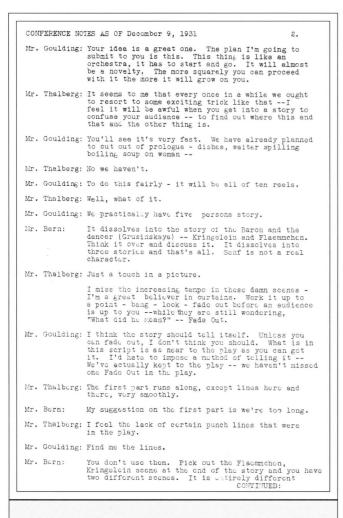

Fig. 2 (continued from previous page).

explain the nature of its coherence my feeling carries no greater critical weight than my response to the colour of the hero's tie.

And, of course, pressure to supply critical weight bears not just on writers of film criticism. Film theorists know this pressure equally well. Moreover, because *weight* suggests a stuffing that can be packed, as and where necessary, into most any structure, it seems to me as appropriate a property to assign to historical evidence as to the persuasive matter in any piece of academic writing. Rhetors seed their discourses with critical weight, and whether they do it in footnotes to Derrida or a dog-eared issue of *American Projectionist*, they do it for

much the same reason – to sell something. Proponents of the old history/theory duality sometime downplay this most basic similarity.

BST plays this similarity up. The preface states, 'This book thus stands out not only as a history of the Hollywood cinema but also as an attempt to articulate a theoretical approach to film history'[48]. Some histories just demonstrate – and don't articulate – their theoretical approaches, but no history is without them. Buscombe writes that 'history is necessary to theory'[49], which might be true in a time when history is the mandated mode for film scholars; but more like it is that history is *useful* to theory. In either case, Buscombe's claim stops short of one BST makes of itself, and one we might make of any less forthright (and/or less self-knowing) history as well – that history *is* theory. Research and development into a new theory of authorship might begin with a look at the critical weights holding down many of the most influential theories of the day.

Bordwell writes that 'in mass-production cinema, which has traditionally involved collaborative labor, scholars have found it difficult to assign authorship to any individual'[50]. Perkins similarly describes a gap that 1970s auteurists, himself included, could only work around: 'Intentions and creative processes are invisible. At best we guess them or are given external, often suspect, information about them'[51]. Bordwell pinpoints this same obstacle – though with an opposite intention to surmounting it – when he cites 'problems of attribution, authentication, the relevance of biographical data and statements of intention, etc.'[52]. Here we see one of the biggest problems the auteurist faces taking shape in the form of a hole that historical evidence can fill. Foucault frames a broader but related problem: 'We try, with great effort, to imagine the general condition of each text, the condition of both the space in which it is dispersed and the time in which it unfolds'[53].

Imagining a text's unfolding and dispersal at the moment of its inception figures centrally into any auteurist game plan. Anything that might flesh out the image and dignify it with some critical weight carries use value. BST's source material, as far-gathered and voluminous as it is, represents but a paper-thin and delicately constituted slice of the accumulable data. A similarly gifted set of *auteur* historians might loot the same repositories and discover the basis for another story, one built on as impressively much data and likewise forged to satisfy the latest dictates of historiographical correctness. Some historians have, to date, turned up traces limning but fragments of the new narratives that might spring up. Schatz happened upon such a trace in his research into *Grand Hotel*.

On 17 November 1931, Irving Thalberg and Edmund Goulding met for the first of six story conferences[54]. Their goal was to turn William Drake's screenplay – based on his Broadway adaptation of Vicki Baum's *Menschen im Hotel* – into a final draft, then, in the final sessions, to turn Goulding's shot footage into a finished picture. Conference reporter Maxine Beeson transcribed all six sessions. Today the transcripts are in the USC Cinema-Television Library, in one of several MGM collections in the United States. These transcripts are packed with details. They are not the patient and meticulous reconstruction of an event their writer never witnessed, but Maxine Beeson's on-the-fly reconstruction of an event as it unfolded around her. The text bristles with the extemporaneity of moments in the making, creators creating, conversations unrehearsed, and vigorous discharges of inspiration and anger. The transcripts do not reveal who paused for effect, where and for how long, or what the attendees were wearing or thinking, but one cannot help but glimpse unique personalities circulating in them[55]. One cannot help but read this document and watch the hotly contested sphere of the classical Hollywood cinema transform into a workaday world that has, refreshingly, never heard of the classical Hollywood cinema. This world is animated in real-time and, as yet, no late-20th century scholar's heavily interpretive cast has covered every last inch of it.

Goulding to Thalberg: 'Don't forget that foot-

age is our great problem – we have one hundred and fifty pages and have to cut it down to one hundred and twenty-five or thirty'. Thalberg to Goulding: 'First we want to get our story and then cut it down. Have you got the play here. To me the play was so far better, Eddie. In my humble opinion'[56]. It's arguable that Goulding is here pushing for standardization (standard running time) and that Thalberg is pushing for standardization in BST's second sense of the term (story quality) and that, in the end, both will be achieved in a resolution of tensions within and by the classical paradigm. I have already suggested that this reasoning, while it shakes a descriptive theory into line from the bottom up, constitutes questionable grounds when it is applied too liberally. BST might have an answer for every instance of distinctly authorial intervention on the transcripts document, but 'That's standardization' and 'That's differentiation' might start to wear thin after the first few citations. Full of specificity and density and colour, a record of spontaneous human activity churning out standardized and differentiated product, the transcripts challenge any theory that would so foreground practices (and background practitioners) almost untheorized, almost by themselves.

But the transcripts do not exist in published form anywhere. Their real value, as it happens, lies in what can be done with them. The transcripts oblige writers with the right historical narratives to construct because, with no help from any writer except Maxine Beeson, the transcripts are a historical narrative. They lend themselves to excerpting, condensing, splicing and all other manner of creative incorporation into accounts chronicling the development of *Grand Hotel* or the life of Irving Thalberg. The parallels that assert themselves, between this record of six moments in a process (these 77 pages of mostly dialogue) and the record of a later moment in the same process (the script), are ripe for rhetorical musing. And, while transcript excerpts do not tax a history's credibility the way anecdotes can, they produce the same enlivening effects. The transcripts rough out the screenplay for a biopic that was never made. Paradoxically, advantageously, this is certifiable evidence *and* the stuff of romance. Schatz exploits their dual nature[57]:

The dynamics of the Thalberg-Goulding interplay demonstrated Thalberg's talent and confidence but also his knack for diplomacy – he knew when to stroke Goulding and when to bear down. During an early session, for example, they disagreed over the revision of a scene. 'Have you got the play here?' Thalberg asked Goulding. 'To me the play was so far better, Eddie. In my humble opinion'. Such diplomacy vanished when Goulding pushed too hard, as he did while defending a certain cut ...

More valuable than spice is critical weight, however, and in this the transcripts prove how valuable they are. When Bordwell observes that 'both the author as empirical agent and as institutional trademark stand outside the texts themselves'[58], he echoes Foucault's claim that 'the text points to this "figure" that, at least in appearance, is outside it an antecedes it'[59]. Authenticating and even locating this outside and anteceding figure has proved difficult. Switching focus to the transcripts brings into view an author standing *inside* the text – at least in appearance. One way to understand this appearance – of these figures' intratextuality – is to listen to the voices speaking through the pages of this document. Foucault writes[60]:

> In a novel narrated in the first person, neither the first-person pronoun nor the present indicative refers exactly either to the writer or to the moment in which he writes, but rather to an alter ego whose distance from the author varies ... It would be just as wrong to equate the author with the real writer as to equate him with the fictitious speaker; the author function is carried out and operates in the scission itself, in this division and this distance.

Foucault plants an author function in the space between a biological author and the first-person singular pronouns in a text, if any. (The transcripts are filled with them.) Shrink this space and it follows that one shrinks the author function proportionately to both restoring authorship to the real writer and establishing a shorter and less problematic link between him or her and those pronouns. Wollen writes that 'the word "fun" crops up constantly in Hawks's interviews and scripts. It masks his despair'[61]. Mapping the 'fun' in an interview or film text onto a biological person represents the sort of spindly conjectural limb onto which auteurists have habitually ventured[62]. The discursive fields of film history are thick with alternative routes.

Perhaps this intratextuality is not just in appearance[63]:

> Thalberg: I think you can still cut it.
>
> Goulding: I know what I'd like to do with that fellow – I would make it, if you had Beery playing it – Could you compromise on this –
>
> Bern: Irving thinks we can cut this down.
>
> Goulding: What would you lose if you come to Presying's booth, without Mulle, or the shaving set or anything – just an ordinary business man.
>
> Bern: That's the only time you introduce his wife.
>
> Thalberg: Awfully important.

The space between the transcribed Thalberg and the man at the conference table, while it can never be argued to nothing, is certainly smaller than the one between a film text's pronouns and its biological author. Moreover, in interviews, where celebrities can be models of insincerity, this space is almost surely larger than the one between the biological Thalberg and his transcription. The biological Thalberg was working with his sleeves rolled up (maybe literally), among hired staff, for hours. One exchange after another demonstrates his unremitting attention to nuts-and-bolts questions and problems. (Once, when Goulding got off the subject to complain about studio politics, Thalberg's response was, 'We're discussing this scene'[64].) All the unglamorous shoptalk encourages our impression that this group was not pitching its remarks to a recording device and not thinking about the eyes of posterity. Finally, any text can only get so close to the person(s) who generated it. Thalberg might have reviewed Beeson's transcripts and made significant changes before they went out to Goulding and whomever else. Beeson might have been sloppy and inattentive. Who knows what Thalberg said to Goulding in the washroom? Maybe Thalberg kept his most brilliant intentions to himself. A caliper measure of the distance is less to the point

Fig. 3. Joan Crawford studies her script on the *Grand Hotel* set.

conference transcripts become fair game. In this respect, Foucault joins BST, and Schatz, in marking out a course for a new auteurism – one that looks outside the borders of film texts for works that circumscribe (and point to) authors. Foucault asks, 'If an individual were not an author, could we say that what he wrote, said, left behind in his papers, or what has been collected of his remarks, could be called a "work"[66]? 'No', the auteur historian might reply, 'but if the individual *were* an author ...' and then plough ahead with a working corollary.

To the question, 'To whom should authorship of the transcripts be attributed?' two (personified) contenders lead: Beeson, who *wrote* the work; and Thalberg, whose talk in large measure *produced* it. But the transcripts index other works and so call up other ranges of possible authors. Who wrote the screenplay and the film? These ranges include more people: Vicki Baum, who takes credit on the film's title screen; William Drake, who adapted her play for Broadway and wrote a draft of the screenplay; Frances Marion, who worked on the screenplay (and got no credit for it) with Drake[67]; Goulding, who turned the results of each session into the next draft; and Thalberg. If we credit Thalberg and not Beeson with authorship of the transcripts (they *are* mostly his words) and recognize in his dominance of the proceedings that he, at least as much as anyone else, orchestrated the creation of this film, then we find the transcripts coming forward to assist the auteur historian by simultaneously positing Thalberg as the author of three works.

than the fact that it can be *theorized* as smaller than ones that have haunted many auteurists' most basic claims.

The foregoing has avoided considering the *Grand Hotel* screenplay and film as works in favour of considering the transcripts as one – a minor proposition, possibly, but not an invalid one. Transcripts can be designated as works, just as Wollen can tacitly designate a Hawks interview as a work when he finds authors and meanings in it. When Foucault asks, 'How can one define a work amid the millions of traces left by someone after his death'[65]? he fingers a problem – the slipperiness of a definition – that grants semantic leeway wherein

Meaning unmade and remade

> Mr. Goulding: I want Irving's feeling of [sic]
> this, page by page.
> – Transcript of 9 December 1931, page 1

Demonstrating Thalberg's authorship of the transcripts, a work discovered a few years ago by one historian and – passed along in the form of narrativized snippets – by his readers, is not going to take the auteur historian far enough. Following BST's deployment of the source data *it* favours, a new approach might fit the transcripts into a discursive trajectory that ranges ahead of its more easily demolished forerunners. Again, forerunner V.F. Perkins provides our starting point.

According to Perkins, Perkins is no auteurist[68]:

> If as connoisseurs we wished to place the picture in the context of Tourneur's work and beliefs it would be important to find out how far *Night of the Demon* embodies a sincere attitude to the occult. But so long as we are concerned, as critics, with the meaning and quality of this particular movie such information remains irrelevant.

Critics are different from connoisseurs because they can, at will and when appropriate, abandon consideration of the director's intentions. Perkins makes a point of demonstrating this willingness a few times, here for example: 'It is quite possible that on some intensely personal, private level those lions were seen by Eisenstein as a coherent, even essential, part of his film's pattern. However, that is not relevant to our assessment'[69].

Critics know when to take the hard line on directorial intentions. However, Perkins reveals himself to be the auteurist that he is when he discusses film meanings. These he tracks coming through films[70]. Noël Carroll describes Perkins's 'anti-intentionalism: the meaning available on the screen is what is important, rather than possible authorial meanings'[71]. But how did the meanings get on the screen? Who or what made them available? What gives Perkins away is his assumption that meanings are there to be read. Meaning so fixed is the front anchor of an author construct, even if the rear anchor goes unnamed (or its intentions are declared irrelevant). Foucault writes, 'We are used to thinking that the author is so different from

all other men, and so transcendent with regard to all languages that, as soon as he speaks, meanings begin to proliferate, to proliferate indefinitely'[72]. From whence do Perkins's meanings proliferate?

They proliferate from the work. But the work as a handy theoretical concept is far from the safe bet it used to be. Foucault writes influentially that 'it is not enough to declare that we should do without the writer (the author) and study the work itself. The word *work* and the unity that it designates are probably as problematic as the status of the author's individuality'[73]. BST, stopping to consider films only when they are randomly selected or instructively transgressive, freights this undermining notion of the work into film studies. BST designates as important a collection of films that are, of themselves and as a group, not especially important. Meanwhile, the classical paradigm gets final cut on all works rolling off the Hollywood assembly line – and makes many suggestions along the way, too, for 'so powerful is the classical paradigm that it regulates what may violate it'[74]. BST is about the constraining of authors and works.

But sweeping works into the margins and over the edges of one's discourse does not prevent meanings from proliferating from works that other discourses screw into their centres. Nor does demoting film artists to artists who paint by numbers silence discourses that celebrate these same artists as something more special. Meaning as Perkins theorizes it remains a problem. Meanings must be unloosed from film texts and shown to originate in places that do not coincide, overlap, or index film authors. Meanings must coalesce independently from works. The connection between intentions (contemplated during production) and impressions (collected during consumption) must be cut before the film author can be pronounced dead.

Two zones wherein film meanings register are circumscribed and transformed by two books, both Bordwell's. *Narration in the Fiction Film* (mainly) addresses meanings 'typical' film viewers encounter, and *Making Meaning* tackles meanings turned up by academic critics. While an attempt to consider either book adequately and fairly here would yield flimsy results, I mean to suggest a couple of pertinent links between them and BST.

Narration in the Fiction Film buries the film author under an electric haze of cognitive activity.

'No trait we could assign to an implied author of a film could not more simply be ascribed to the narration itself'[75], Bordwell writes, then – opting for the simpler description – effectively boxes the implied author (and the biological author who might be attached) out of the discussion. The very notion of an implied author is 'anthropomorphic fiction'[76]. Reader comprehension is what makes meaning, not a work's coherence and not an author's intentions. Meanings are still constrained under this view, just not by works or authors anymore. Now they change as their manifold sources do. Now 'comprehension of films changes through time as we construct new schemata'[77]. Bordwell joins Buscombe and Crofts in recognizing the worthwhile results that auteur theories have produced, but finds the approach misapplied in analyses of classical narration: 'Nor is this to say that a film produced within the protocols of one mode cannot be construed according to the protocols of another; we saw this occurring with Hollywood films at the hands of auteur critics'[78].

Making Meaning: Inference and Rhetoric in the Interpretation of Cinema slides the spotlight from the spectator's mind to the critic's page. There Bordwell finds critical inference over textual implication and craft of rhetoric over truth of ideas. The subtitle alone is enough to set this theory in clear contradistinction to Perkins's *Understanding and Judging Movies*. In a sense, Bordwell's metacriticism is fervent with assertions of authorship, only now the authors are critics. With respect to film authors, *Making Meaning* has much the same effect as *Narration in the Fiction Film*; that book describes the classic communication diagram, wherein 'a message is passed from sender to receiver' – to which Bordwell adds: 'I suggest, however, that narration is better understood as the organization of a set of cues for the construction of a story. This presupposes a perceiver, but not any sender, of a message'[79]. *Making Meaning* likewise presupposes no sender.

Bordwell rankles more than a few peers with his claim that the dominant conceptual framework into which they set their practice is faulty: 'The artwork or text is taken to be a container into which the artist has stuffed meanings for the perceiver to pull out ... Comprehension and interpretation are assumed to open up the text, penetrate its surfaces, and bring meanings to light'[80]. Bordwell offers another model entirely for relating film comprehension

and interpretation to film meanings. *Making Meaning* is part of an ambitious project. As Bill Nichols writes, 'Neo-formalism may not simply contest the meanings that a feminism, say, might find, but contest the very grounds on which meaning rests'[81]. *Making Meaning* and *Narration in the Fiction Film* unstop a new wellspring for the meanings Perkins sees coming through the film text. Together they join BST in a convergence on the film author.

Of the three phalanxes, only one is expressly history[82]. A long contemplation of the evidence BST marshals seems to lead straight to that book's conclusions. But what about, for example, the *Grand Hotel* transcripts, the likes of which get effectively sidelined by the BST approach? Much of the assault I just described can be concentrated into a single anti-auteurist charge to which the transcripts voice an answer.

Crofts sketches a taxonomy of author conceptions, two of which are 'author as expressive individual' and 'author as thematic and stylistic properties impressionistically and unproblematically read off from the film or films'[83]. These he numbers 1 and 2.1, respectively. Bordwell's two books widen and fill the breach between these conceptions – moments, respectively, of production and consumption – and problematize readings of type 2.1 to near extinction. Crofts calls the conflation of these moments 'the terms of auteurism, the conventional mode of Authorship'[84], then explains the problem[85]:

> What is elided in this process is consideration of any potential difference in assumptions between, on the one hand, the biological individual and, on the other, the reader's construction of the author from the film(s) ... a wild leap of faith from the moment of production to the moment of reading.

The faulty claim, then, is that the author authors what the reader reads. But what if some validity could be argued back into this old claim? Judiciously mapping 2.1 onto 1 might come to seem less like a wild leap and more like a navigable option. Crofts's pronouncement that 'the author is in fact created by the reader'[86] might come to seem as patently one-sided as the hoariest and most unenlightened auteurist counterclaim.

The transcripts broaden the basis of the tradi-

Fig. 4. Edmund Goulding, behind the sofa, lining up another shot with 'the camera ... floating all over the place'.

tional auteurist stance, which has been a vulnerable one because auteurism has stood, traditionally, on one foot – the film text or, just as shaky, the film oeuvre. 'Auteur criticism has relied almost completely upon thematic interpretation'[87], Bordwell writes and – although auteur critics worked wonders with their idea of *mise-en-scène* – as Buscombe points out, 'Well before the 1980s arrived it had become evident that simply staring at the text wasn't enough'[88]. The transcripts provide a place to stare that is, relative to the film text, elsewhere. This is useful because it permits emplotments that link moments of film production to cues on film texts to moments of film reading. It permits claims about a film to be braced up in discursive trajectories that are fired from a point in time and space *through* the text and out to another point. One or two such passes is not enough to moor a discourse, but examples set by some film-studies best sellers of the past ten years suggest a robust practice that is.

An emplotment I find especially worth explor-

ing proceeds backwards through time and begins by asking a question that is central to the historical poetics Bordwell compellingly proposes at the end of *Making Meaning*: 'What *effects* and *functions* do particular films have'[89]? Working up answers necessitates 'the reconstruction of earlier acts of comprehension[90]' and leads to another question, which (I suppose) is mine: What *caused* the effects? An advantage to reasoning backwards is that it leaves what auteurism's attackers find most objectionable – authorial intentions – for the end of the argument. Few are likely to complain that a critic's description of an audience reaction (or of his or her own) is inadmissible. Such a description represents but one humble moment of comprehension.

Mordaunt Hall wrote in his review of Grand Hotel:[91]

> And later, wearing a chinchilla coat, she is gay and light-hearted, for love has beckoned to the temperamental dancer. Grusinskaya leaves

the screen hopeful of meeting the Baron at the railroad station, but the audience knows that the good-natured and sympathetic thief has met his doom.

Less important (and verifiable) than the accuracy of Hall's gauge on what the audience knows as they watch this scene is what Hall knows. This is the only one of the dancer's moments he mentions, and one of only two moments in the whole film he mentions at all.

The moment has made an impression on Mordaunt Hall. The transcripts indicate that the moment was transplanted from the play at Thalberg's insistence. Goulding's latest changes to the script have altered the feeling of Grusinskaya's last exit (as Thalberg remembers it playing on Broadway). Thalberg describes the lost feeling to Goulding: 'Just as Grusinskaya went out of the hotel, everybody realized that she didn't know the Baron had been killed. It left a pall of death on everybody'[92]. Thalberg saw to it that the same moment left the same pall on (at least) one viewer.

The determinative play of an author's intentions across a text can be charted with reasonable confidence and described in some detail with the help of documents such as the transcripts. Such documents can take guesswork out of reporting what an author must have thought or decided or said during the course of a film's development. The transcripts pinpoint *degrees* of intentionality, 'Personally my slight one tenth of one per cent preference would be concentrating it in a room'[93]; *concentrations* of intentionality, 'Most of my suggestions come toward the latter part of the story'[94]; and even *absences* of intentionality, 'I don't think it makes a damn bit of difference'[95]. The raw potential of the document is plainest in exchanges such as this one, in which Goulding asks, 'What is your intention with the Baron'? and Thalberg answers, 'My intention is this ...'[96] An alternative to casting doubt on the relevance of all statements of intention, etc. and then moving on to one's preferred relevances would be to pick out a statement – such as the one above – and seeing if it is not possible to anchor one or more causal chains with it.

The transcripts make it clear how completely the *auteur/metteur-en-scène* distinction breaks down on a Thalberg project. Elements of *mise-en-*

scène are seen here to issue straight from Thalberg's mouth: 'My idea was that the person is in the picture and as they finish talking – behind him in double exposure is the next person talking – so you hear two voices'[97]. Another time, after viewing some footage, Thalberg comments, 'The scene is a great scene until the point where the camera starts floating all over the place where it starts following her over to the pearls. Get a closeup of her'[98]. Elsewhere he makes his wishes clear to another *a posteriori* artist, editor Blanche Sewell, where he 'showed Blanche on the reports where he wanted her to cut'[99]. Interestingly, Thalberg at one point expresses something of the opposite of the bias that, for decades, helped to keep him out of (the auteurist's) sight: 'Directors, on the whole, are not clever enough to get contrast out of dialogue'[100].

Thalberg coaches Garbo from the conference room: 'Eliminate her saying: "I'm *so* tired". Have her say: "I'm so tired" very simply. There are certain things that can not be over-played and be sincere. And one of them is a person feeling sorry for herself'[101]. Elsewhere he sends vaguer and more sweeping directions into Goulding's territory: 'The writing is all right but the playing of it has got to be different from the impression you get from the script'[102]. Thalberg even exerts mindful influence on our intake of a costume design: 'When Grusinskaya comes out into corridor to meet Suzette and Pimenov pick it up a little later – lose some of that terrible hat'[103]. On whether the *auteur/metteur-en-scène* distinction is worth retaining at all in an estimation of this ubiquitous, hands-on author, the transcripts back a claim, vividly and for a project's duration, that Schatz makes more generally – regarding 'one of Thalberg's basic tenets of studio filmmaking – namely, that the first cut of any picture was no more than the raw material of the finished product'[104].

For Thalberg, mapping 1 on to 2.1 was not nearly as problematic as Crofts would have us believe. In fact he did it all the time. Here he paints a scene between the Baron and Grusinskaya, demonstrating expertise in his attention to the scene's impacts on viewers: 'She wants to give him money – he doesn't take it, but says he'll be on the train. You get suspense against hope, against hope that when he tries to steal Kringelein's money you don't blame him. You are pulling for the Baron but don't want her mood destroyed'[105]. Actually, Thalberg here isn't envisioning reactions of moviegoers but – as he does throughout the sessions – recollecting reactions of theatregoers (including his own) on the day he attended a matinee performance[106]. The transcripts thus introduce a complication not anticipated by Crofts, or Bordwell, in which receptions *precede* intentions, and in which theatre-bound receptions – both as witnessed and experienced – serve as a film author's blueprint.

'I see it clearly', he tells Goulding and the others[107]. 'The curtain went up. Senf comes in saying: "Jesus, no baby yet"'[108] and on goes Thalberg with another page-long description of a Broadway-staged scene. Thalberg consistently bases instructions to Goulding (and some to Sewell and the actors) on recollections of how the stage melodrama worked its audience. At one point, after describing the feel of a scene as it played on stage – and before expressing dissatisfaction with Goulding's rewrite of it – Thalberg says: 'We can't lose that mood of [Grusinskaya's] in the play of this terribly dejected creature who went around saying how terrible life is and then completely changes. It was so beautiful'[109]. Elsewhere he lays it on the line for Goulding: 'I've seen the other scene played, it's a great scene and I've read yours and it reads like hell'[110] and, here, he does it again[111]:

Thalberg: Lousy fade out.

Goulding: It is a cut.

Thalberg: Lousy cut. In the play it was better.

Another time he simply dictates: 'Scene two, act two – love scene, page seventy one of script. Create transposition from play in it'[112]. All this is enough to suggest, to me, the strong possibility of reading Thalberg's authorship into another wrinkle in this film text – into the closeness in feel and actual dialogue to the Broadway play that more than one critic noticed. One praised the studio for 'filming the play practically unaltered in form'[113]. Another played up for his readers the apprehension he felt on the day he attended the film[114]:

It was with much uneasiness that I ventured the other day to visit the picture version of 'Grand Hotel', fearing that it had been desecrated by the impious showmen of Hollywood. What a

chance, thought I, for havoc and delirious rebuilding, for laying waste and for indiscriminate replacement ... It is a disappointment, therefore, to report to similarly sceptical theatregoers that 'Grand Hotel' is as excellent a play when performed by machinery as it is when done by human actors.

(Schatz might be quick to add that what made the difference here was *whose* machinery was doing the performing.) With the transcripts supplying the vital linking term, signs of fidelity to the Broadway source material become signs of the Hollywood producer[115].

Bill Nichols writes that 'Bordwell invokes style (unusual camera angles or movement, odd editing patterns, disjunctive sounds) as the narrative's mechanism for calling attention to itself. This schema neatly isolates the narrational process from reference to anything beyond itself'[116]. Moments of self-conscious narration do call attention to narration, but they call attention to more than that. After recommending a bit of flashy camera work for a scene, Thalberg adds: 'It seems to me that every once in a while we ought to resort to some exciting trick like that'[117]. What Bordwell calls a moment of self-conscious narration, Thalberg calls an exciting trick. Where Bordwell claims that 'the intermittence of authorial presence works to reaffirm classical norms'[118], we might claim that the intermittence of authorial presence (as Bordwell defines it, as moments of self-conscious narration) actually affirms the *continuous* presences of subtler authors. To restrict all signs of authorship to moments of flashy filmmaking is to give free reign, over the vast remainder of the text, to codified norms. Another way to see it is that Hollywood's best authors knew that too many unusual camera angles or odd editing patterns or disjunctive sounds would get in the way of a moviegoer's good time. The magician is on stage for the whole show, even when she or he is not performing some exciting trick. Bordwell's view is, perhaps, not less or more correct than mine. The difference is one of emphasis, opinion and agenda.

Tino Balio writes that 'the so-called "one locale" setting of MGM's *Grand Hotel*, which provided the basis for interweaving several unrelated narrative threads, inspired such pictures as Columbia's *American Madness*, which is set in a bank,

Fig. 5. Lewis Stone in *Grand Hotel*'s unitary locale, the work of [uncredited] unit art director Alexander Toluboff.

Warners' *Employees' Entrance*, which is set in a department store, and Paramount's *Big Broadcast*, which is set in a radio station'[119]. Judith Crist observed the film's persisting influence in 1970[120]:

> The *Grand Hotel* formula has served moviemakers (and playwrights) well through the decades, with a variety of folk from all walks of life brought into brief conjunction to love a little, gag it up a bit and then part, each to his own reward. We've encountered these little cross sections at bus stops, aboard ship, on doomed planes, at lonely inns, at the mercy of the elements, gunmen or the clock.

Twenty-five years later this one-locale, multi-thread formula is still with us[121]. Who knew it might endure so? Thalberg told a reporter a year before the film's release[122]:

> I don't mean that the exact theme of 'Grand Hotel' will be copied, though this may happen, but the form and mood will be followed. For instance, we may have such settings as a train, where all the action happens in a journey from

one city to another; or action that takes place during the time a boat sails from one harbor and culminates with the end of the trip. The general idea will be that, of drama induced by the chance meeting of a group of conflicting and interesting personalities.

Thalberg also knew this formula did not demand 'story quality'. Story quality might even get in this formula's way. He told Goulding, 'To me this is a lousy play that only succeeded because it is lousy. It's full of life – a painted carpet upon which the figures walk – audiences love those damn things, if they are properly done'[123]. Critic William Boehnel agreed, writing[124]:

> 'Grand Hotel' is a melodrama which in literary design is undistinguished. But so craftily has it been put together and so entertainingly has it been directed that it seems better than it actually is. More than that, it shows how vividly characters can be drawn and how electric situations may become when treated with intelligence and understanding.

To what extent does the craftiness, vividness, electricity, intelligence, understanding, and even the direction all praised here point – through the transcripts – to one human source[125]? Surely to some extent that attests to the collaborative nature of studio filmmaking, but surely not to one that justifies the short shrift that Thalberg and many others have been handed by some prevailing accounts.

Grand Hotel is no limit case, not to popular historian Ethan Mordden – who ballyhoos the film as 'surely the most glamorous, possibly the most entertaining, and arguably the definitive Hollywood movie'[126] – and not to the current mainstream of academic film history. The cover of the fifth installment in the History of the American Cinema series features a photograph, from the film, of Garbo and John Barrymore in a romantic embrace. The photograph appears under the title *Grand Design*. What can a rhetor make of the transcripts and all they disclose about the sources of the effects and functions of this, 'perhaps all Hollywood's most typical film'[127]? She might make a case for the bonafide authorship of a consummately classical Hollywood film.

Out of a complex of effects and causes, one or more authors might emerge[128]. While the approach can and should lead to causes *besides* authors, one of its distinctive and determinative features will be that it begins by assuming that such outcomes are conceivable. (Bolder practitioners might begin by mentioning that such outcomes are *desirable*, but this is a matter of style.) The pairing of an effect with an *opposite* intention steers the open-minded auteur historian toward considerations of, for example, tensions between Studio Relations Committee guidelines and Thalberg's desire to turn out a hit. Or a discordant pairing might point to factors associated with *Grand Hotel*'s stars or MGM's (and Hollywood's) star system. Mordden claims that 'the auteur of *Grand Hotel* was MGM's star system'[129]. The claim all by itself is problematic but it might – together with the conventional modes of Authorship and the BST approach – point toward more complete answers than have yet ben articulated. Surely, and as importantly, a combining of approaches will lead to questions that have yet to be asked.

Whenever the line between intention and reception bends or breaks – attributable perhaps to Bordwell's mental sets and schemata, or the Produc-

tion Code, or Goulding's intervention, or Freudian psychosexual forces, or the fact that sound had come to films only four years before the first conference – will provide occasion to depart from the classic communication diagram. Bordwell writes that 'by situating matters of meaning within the framework of effects, a poetics need not adopt the communication model of sender-message-receiver'[130]. It need not, but sometimes – and maybe often – a poetics worth its salt will need to adopt precisely this model in order to get the effects and causes scrupulously correlated. Sometimes, when evidence and instinct point that way, a film author's intentions will be shown to determine a film cue's effects. Sometimes Foucault's claim that 'these aspects of an individual which we designate as making him an author are only a projection'[131] will seem incomplete. Sometimes meanings will come through.

Conclusion

Changes in regard for one type of critical weight over another can give rise to narratives that outfit old objects with new emphases and meanings. The season's fashionable discursive mode can cause total revisions to upsurge where formerly there had been nothing new to say. Increased interest in conceptions of economic systems as determinants of film styles and modes of production, shifts in attention – from some moments and agencies of film production to some others – and the currently soaring market value of 'interoffice memos, corporate correspondence, and other general records, along with the budgets, schedules, story conference notes, daily production reports, [and] censorship files'[132] have all made the time right for the discovery of a new film author. But isn't film studies only just now pulling clear of all the old film authors?

Cases for reintroducing the film author to film studies are to be found in blind spots in the BST optic, which is trained at too short a distance from its (selected) primary sources to register an object as large as *Grand Hotel*, and which simultaneously surveys from too great a distance to register an object so small. Buscombe describes film history's alignment with the most serious and best that historiographic tradition has to offer[133]:

The historian focused either on the far distance, paying attention to what Braudel called the *longue durée,* the slow-moving but massive shifts in human conditions of existence, or on what was immediately under his or her nose: changes in the previously unregarded brute realities of human life – food, sexual practices, methods of warfare.

Such an approach allows a historian to crunch and spray data into smooth curves that nicely limn this or that thesis, but seminal films and influential persons fall through cracks that, between practiced microscopy and macroscopy, are wide.

Authors abound in every approach we have considered here. Foucault writes[134]:

> [The author] is a certain functional principle by which, in our culture, one limits, excludes and chooses; in short, by which one impedes the free circulation, the free manipulation, the free composition, decomposition, and recomposition of fiction. In fact, if we are accustomed to presenting the author as a genius, as a perpetual surging of invention, it is because, in reality, we make him function in exactly the opposite fashion.

So it goes for directors in Perkins, a half-dozen producers intermittently in Schatz, and the classical paradigm continuously in BST. That BST constructs a system of constraint is certain. It just happens that the massive object under construction there is not a personified genius but, through that figure's radical diminution, a system that enforces a set of constraints all its own. Jane Gaines writes that 'it is the genius of criticism to will its own position into being so effectively that the discourse of the object of analysis fits the discourse of the method like a glove'[135]. Such a fit would suggest that limitations an approach finds in the object it approaches might point, most emphatically, to limitations in the approach itself. It would suggest that claims to 'a limit to authorial uniqueness in Hollywood'[136] might trace, most precisely, a limit of perception. The last sentence of *The Classical Hollywood Cinema* vibrates with the doubleness Gaines refers to, 'by which the object is made to order by the criticism'[137]. Here the discourses of method and object fit each other so perfectly that it is not clear whether,

in this last sentence, this discourse of method is referring to the object or to itself: 'The historical and aesthetic importance of the classical Hollywood cinema lies in the fact that to go beyond it we must go through it'[138]. The genius of the BST system lies in the barely concealed second sense, still vibrating after eleven years, just behind this resolute finish.

Bordwell's claim that 'conceptions of authorship enable us to appreciate the richness of the classical cinema'[139] is equally defensible with its terms switched; conceptions of the classical cinema (might) enable us to appreciate the richness of authorship (if we let them). Another assertion that runs as smoothly in reverse is one that 'authorial presence in the Hollywood cinema is usually consonant with classical norms'[140]. BST opts to put quotes around *author* and to leave them off *norm,* but, by arguing for authorship's inverse, isn't BST just arguing for another kind? Foucault predicts[141]:

> I think that, as our society changes, at the very moment when it is in the process of changing, the author function will disappear, and in such a manner that fiction and its polysemous texts will once again function according to another mode, but still with a system of constraint – one which will no longer be the author.

Foucault's and BST's interpreters can decide whether, in the world of film studies, BST marks the inception of such a mode, or whether that system might as easily be termed an author construct as its replacement. Gone is the individual but, when one examines some of the shortfalls and shortcuts bound up through BST, one wonders whether the individual was really at the root of auteurism's problems in the first place. And besides, whether producers, directors or norms get the last word – and whether BST liberates film studies from the author or merely reconstitutes that figure out of a powder of data – there is another way to evaluate a theory.

Perkins writes that 'the most telling argument for a critical belief in the 'director's cinema' is that it has provided the richest base for useful analyses of the styles and meanings of particular films'[142]. BST recognizes as much, that 'auteur critics are right; like "film noir", the category of "authorship" does locate important differences within the classical style'[143]. And these differences remain important. As Robert Sklar writes[144]:

Not every Hollywood hero of the *Cahiers du Cinéma* critics has achieved cinematic immortality, nor have the critics' thematic concerns necessarily persisted. But to a remarkable degree, the figures in whom they were interested – rather than, for example, 1950s winners of Academy Awards for directing – are those who have continued to hold critical attention over the years.

And these figures keep holding our attention, while encircling approaches and their attendant manifestos and terminologies keep coming and going[145].

Can discourses of contemporary film studies afford to expel the notion that great persons figured importantly into the development of Hollywood cinema? Or should we temper, refine, reign in, and hold on to that notion? In a final analysis that probably won't be possible until the paradigm wars themselves are history, a half-dozen producers might turn out to provide as usefully constraining a system as a 'few dozen heroic directors'[146] – and the classical paradigm might (I think it will) turn out to contribute immensely to new understandings of classical Hollywood's individual film artists. We see something of the latter happening already in, for example, Bordwell and Thompson's chapter in *Grand Design: Hollywood as a Modern Business Enterprise, 1930–1939*[147]. BST covers a much longer stretch than this books' mere nine years, but even with the narrower scope factored in, Thalberg is simply larger in this whole equation of pictures. Bordwell and Thompson's chapter on Technological Change and Classical Film Style enriches a book that brings other approaches, and emphases, to bear on its subject[148].

Why pick one totalizing approach when braiding and swapping in as many as are necessary – and as can be kept under control in a single discourse – enables a scholar to move ever closer to the particularities of the moments and places under examination? Schatz's single-author venture demonstrates a switch-hitting ability that suits the study of an era that broke down by period, and by studio, and – he shows – sometimes quite usefully by persons in charge. The past, even a classically ordered one, is more myriad and inconsistent than any one unswerving approach can ever provide access to.

But it is not just the course of past events that follow various natures and bend, uniquely, according to local circumstances. Perkins winds toward his conclusion with a comment that is, I think, more pertinent today then when he made it[149]:

> The temptation is to deny the validity of judgement altogether and to confine criticism to a descriptive role with no claim to be able to evaluate. But this position turns out to be a sham. Even description depends upon forms of evaluation which are no less 'subjective' than judgement. A descriptive analysis will need at the least to make claims about the distribution of the film's emphasis; and emphasis is as subjectively perceived, relies as much on a personal response, as judgement.

Dignified and documented, history is description with judgement folded into it. Critical weight, no matter how heavy and no matter how scientific the methods by which we process it, is grist for the mill – whatever mill a historian happens to be working in. The *Grand Hotel* transcripts are not unique in their versatility. Like almost any trace, they could accommodate almost any thesis. They lend themselves to plugging many sorts of holes, steering readers toward a variety of predetermined conclusions and, most importantly, to creating the impression of assiduous research. The transcripts hold out the promise that framing these luminous objects of truth is an ever-so-thin margin of space wherein a historian has room to invent or lie. Bridging a decade of film theory to one of film history, Buscombe writes that history is necessary to theory. The deference is gracious but misleading. History is useful to theory. History is a very popular flavour of theory. As such it is prone to all the same failures, and demands of us all the same vigilances. History is also – just as all those flavours that nobody ever samples anymore were in their day – a piquant means by which to persuade other people to come over to one's beliefs. A recent work of historical scholarship figures James Cagney, Humphrey Bogart and John Garfield as authoring forces[150]. Another refigures D.W. Griffith as a genius after all[151]. A chapter in *Grand Design* 'suggests that powerful department heads, such as MGM's Cedric Gibbons and Paramount's Hans Dreier, and individual artists, such as Anton Grot, William Cameron Menzies, and Gregg Toland, exerted an enormous influence over the look of a picture'[152]. Individuals are resurfacing. Authors are surging back into film studies and crashing the gates of the film studios.○

Notes

1. Michel Foucault, 'What is an Author'? *The Foucault Reader*, ed. Paul Rabinow (New York: Pantheon Books, 1984), 109.

2. Peter Wollen, *Signs and Meaning in the Cinema*. (London: BFI, 1972), 77.

3. For a description of Thalberg's public image during his lifetime and afterwards, see Richard Koszarski, *An Evening's Entertainment: The Age of the Silent Feature Picture, 1915–1928* History of the American Cinema, vol. 3 (Berkeley, Los Angeles, London: University of California Press, 1994), 251–253. See also Thomas Schatz, *The Genius of the System: Hollywood Filmmaking in the Studio Era* (New York: Pantheon Books, 1988), 123.

4. The Irving Thalberg Award was awarded eleven times between (and including) 1969 and 1994. (Fact obtained from a call by the author to the Academy of Motion Picture Arts and Sciences.)

5. For example, Schatz writes near the start of *The Genius of the System* that 'auteurism itself would not be worth bothering with if it hadn't been so influential, effectively stalling film history and criticism in a prolonged stage of adolescent romanticism' (5).

6. See Thomas Schatz, *Hollywood Genres: Formulas, Filmmaking, and the Studio System* (New York: McGraw-Hill, Inc., 1981). Also in this book, Schatz describes how genre-based and author-centred approaches are not mutually exclusive (7–10).

7. Schatz, *The Genius of the System*, 8. Schatz slightly misquotes this line from *The Last Tycoon*: 'Not half a dozen men have ever been able to keep the whole equation of pictures in their heads'. F. Scott Fitzgerald, *The Last Tycoon* (1941; New York: Collier Books, Macmillan Publishing Co., A Scribner Classic, 1986), 3.

8. Ibid., 8.

9. Ibid.

10. Ibid., 7.

11. Ibid., 108.

12. Ibid., 98–124.

13. The authors bring Thalberg into the picture when they describe, in a paragraph, how he organized associate supervisors below him and how his approval was required on their major decisions. The main purpose seems to be to show how Thalberg exemplifies the strong central producer. Thalberg later returns, as briefly, in a description of how L.B. Mayer took advantage of Thalberg's absence (due to illness) to make changes in MGM management hierarchy and personnel. David Bordwell, Janet Staiger and Kristin Thompson, *The Classical Hollywood Cinema: Film Style and Mode of Production to 1960* (New York: Columbia University Press, 1985), 320 and 327.

14. Bordwell, Staiger and Thompson, 96.

15. Names of films widely considered masterpieces occasionally do come up in BST, although consistently in contexts and for purposes that tend to undercut – or at least to overlook – their recognized status somehow. For example, *Citizen Kane* receives attention as Bordwell endeavors to show that, in it, Gregg Toland's experiments in deep-focus cinematography exceeded conventional boundaries. Bordwell then shows, in an examination of subsequent work, that Toland came back within classical boundaries after *Kane* and stayed there (345–352). *Kane* stands out, therefore, as a limit case, an instance in which an artist temporarily managed to violate classical codes before the system corrected his behaviour.

16. Bordwell, Staiger and Thompson, xiii.

17. BST's unspecified sample is introduced on page 10 and listed in Appendix A (388).

18. V.F. Perkins, *Film as Film: Understanding and Judging Movies* (New York: Da Capo Press, 1972), 173.

19. Schatz, *The Genius of the System*, 36.

20. Ibid., 105.

21. Ibid., 175. The reference is to Thalberg.

22. Perkins, 184 (original emphasis).

23. Ibid., 160.

24. Ibid., 164. Another to toy briefly with this idea is Raymond Durgnat. He writes that William Dieterle's 'style may have come closest to Selznick's ideas, or he may best have understood and translated certain of Selznick's intentions (whether the second way of putting things would imply that he isn't an auteur is a nice point; it would imply that Selznick was)'. Raymond Durgnat, 'King Vidor, Part II,' *Film Comment* 9:5 (September/October, 1974), 17. Durgnat takes the possibility no further.

25. Hortense Powdermaker, *Hollywood the Dream Factory* (Boston: Little Brown and Company, 1951), 129.

26. Wollen, 104.

27. Bordwell, Staiger and Thompson, 136.

28. Schatz, *The Genius of the System*, 8.

29. Tino Balio, *Grand Design: Hollywood as a Modern Business Enterprise, 1930–1939* History of the American Cinema, vol. 5 (New York: Charles Scribner's Sons, 1993), 9.

30. Wollen, 78.

31. Perkins, 179.

32. Ibid., 185.

33. Bordwell, Staiger and Thompson, 135. Staiger shows that scripts were serving as film blueprints well before the advent of the central producer system in Janet Staiger, 'Blueprints for Feature Films: Hollywood's Continuity Scripts', *The American Film Industry*, ed. Tino Balio (Madison and London: The University of Wisconsin Press, 1976), 173–192.

34. Schatz, *The Genius of the System*, 108.

35. Balio, viii.

36. Schatz, *The Genius of the System*, 7.

37. Bordwell, Staiger and Thompson, xv.

38. Schatz, *The Genius of the System*, 8.

39. Edward Buscombe, 'Film History in the 1980s', *The Velvet Light Trap* No. 27 (Spring 1991), 3.

40. Stephen Crofts, 'Authorship and Hollywood,' *Wide Angle* 5:3 (1983), 17.

41. Perkins, 158.

42. Buscombe, 3.

43. Ibid.

44. Ibid.

45. Ibid., 5.

46. See for example, Bill Nichols, 'Form Wars: The Political Unconscious of Formalist Theory,' *Classical Hollywood Narrative: The Paradigm Wars*, ed. Jane Gaines (Durham and London: Duke University Press, 1992), 55.

47. Perkins, 189–190 (original emphasis).

48. Bordwell, Staiger and Thompson, xv.

49. Buscombe, 4.

50. Bordwell, Staiger and Thompson, 77.

51. Perkins, 172. Durgnat provides an example of the sort of groundless guessing that has characterized

some auteurism: 'Unless the film, at certain stages, looked altogether different from the release version, I can only surmise that Vidor felt these killings to have (like Zeke's, or his Billy the Kid's) some sort of emotional justification' (17–18).

52. Bordwell, Staiger and Thompson, 77.

53. Foucault, 104.

54. The six session dates: I, 17 and 18 Nov. 1931; II, 9 December 1931; III, 10 December 1931; IV, 26 December 1931; V, 17 March 1932; and VI, 18 March 1932.

55. Schatz takes dramatic license and inserts a pause – and motivates it – where Thalberg insists on the addition of a line for Kringelein (Lionel Barrymore's character): '"It doesn't matter that life be long, but that one feel it entirely – drain it to the last. Then collapse". Thalberg waited for the effect to sink in. "That scene alone can make a picture", he said' (117).

56. Transcript of 17 November 1931, 2. All references are to page numbers as marked. Used by Permission Turner Entertainment Co. All rights reserved.

57. Schatz, *The Genius of the System*, 111.

58. Bordwell, Staiger and Thompson, 78.

59. Foucault, 101.

60. Ibid., 112.

61. Wollen, 84.

62. Crofts describes 'the director of the film, that self-same person who sometimes fools obsequious interviewers as to his/her "real intentions"' (17). Crofts would likely argue that reading an opposite meaning into an interviewee's statement, as Wollen does, is no less naive than taking the statement at face value.

63. Transcript of 26 December 1931, 3.

64. Ibid., 6.

65. Foucault, 104.

66. Ibid., 103.

67. See Balio, 185.

68. Perkins, 174–175.

69. Ibid., 189.

70. Ibid., 185.

71. Noël Carroll, *Philosophical Problems of Classical*

Film Theory (Princeton: Princeton University Press, 1988), 175.

72. Foucault, 118.

73. Ibid., 104.

74. Bordwell, Staiger and Thompson, 81.

75. David Bordwell, Narration in the Fiction Film (Madison: The University of Wisconsin Press, 1985), 62.

76. Ibid. The charge is not the same as a repudiation of the biological author, but it helps account for the biological author's conspicuous absence in this theory of narration.

77. Ibid., 310.

78. Ibid., 335.

79. Ibid., 62.

80. David Bordwell, Making Meaning: Inference and Rhetoric in the Interpretation of Cinema (Cambridge, Massachusetts and London England: Harvard University Press, 1989), 2.

81. Nichols, 54.

82. However, in both Making Meaning and Narration in the Fiction Film, Bordwell skillfully mixes flavours, feels, and attributes of all three modes. Of Narration in the Fiction Film, Nichols writes that 'Bordwell's analysis of narrational process has many strengths, not least among them its supple blend of theory, criticism, and, to a more limited extent, history' (55).

83. Crofts, 17.

84. Ibid.

85. Ibid., 18.

86. Ibid., 17.

87. Bordwell, Staiger and Thompson, 80.

88. Buscombe, 3.

89. Bordwell, Making Meaning, 263 (original emphasis).

90. Ibid., 266.

91. Mordaunt Hall, rev. of Grand Hotel, New York Times 13 Apr. 1932: 23.

92. Transcript of 9 December 1931, 4.

93. Transcript of 17 November. 1931, 2.

94. Transcript of 9 December 1931, 1.

95. Transcript of 10 December 1931, 1.

96. Transcript of 17 November 1931, 16.

97. Transcript of 9 December 1931, 1.

98. Transcript of 17 March 1932, 4. The camera's reserve was noticed by critic Percy Hammond: 'One expects, from past experiences with the camera, to see Miss Baum's narrative amplified by spectacular photography, showing the characters as unlimited in the scope of their movements as they are in the novel. There is not much of this pageantry, however'. Percy Hammond, 'The Cinema Again Atones,' New York Herald Tribune 15 May 1932: sect. 7, 1.

99. Transcript of 18 March 1932, 4.

100. Transcript of 26 December 1931, 6.

101. Transcript of 17 March 1932, 2 (original emphasis). According to some tastes, Thalberg might have coaxed Garbo a little further along these lines. The Variety critic wrote that 'Garbo gives the role of the dancer something of artificiality, risking a trace of acting swagger, sometimes stagey'. Rush. (full name not given), rev. of Grand Hotel, Variety 19 April 1932: 14.

102. Transcript of 18 November 1931, 13.

103. Transcript of 18 Mar. 1932, 5.

104. Schatz, The Genius of the System, 37.

105. Transcript of 18 November 1931, 12–13.

106. An interview Thalberg gave a year before the film's release places the performance close to 3 May 1931. 'Producer Discusses Pictures,' New York Times 3 May 1931: sect. 8, 6.

107. Two others in regular attendance were Paul Bern and Frank Partos.

108. Transcript of 9 December 1931, 3.

109. Transcript of 18 November 1931, 13.

110. Transcript of 26 December 1931, 12.

111. Transcript of 17 November 1931, 5.

112. Ibid., 3.

113. Rush. (full name not given), rev. of Grand Hotel, Variety 19 April 1932: 14.

114. Percy Hammond, 'The Cinema Again Atones', New York Herald Tribune 15 May 1932: sect. 7, 1.

115. These signs of fidelity might impel another critique of BST as well. If this, 'perhaps all Hollywood's most typical film' (Ethan Mordden, The Hollywood Studios: House Style in the Golden Age of the Movies (New York: Alfred A. Knopf, 1988), 105), came

together under the authority of a man pushing to capture the moods and effects of a stage play, then might the transcripts testify in a case in which norms, codes, and practices which are *extrinsic* to classical cinema are piped into a classical film – more-or-less directly through its producer – from a Broadway melodramatic antecedent? Rick Altman writes that 'Bordwell and Thompson pay little attention to the possible contribution of melodramatic material to the classical paradigm' (Rick Altman, 'Dickens, Griffith and Film Theory Today', *Classical Hollywood Narrative: The Paradigm Wars*, ed. Jane Gaines (Durham and London: Duke University Press, 1992), 25) and, elsewhere, he asks: 'Of what current tendencies and stresses within film theory is the neglect of cinema's debt to melodramatic stage adaptations symptomatic'? (14) The answering of this broad and far-reaching question might begin with the asking of some smaller ones, such as ours.

116. Nichols, 66. Bordwell demonstrates the validity of Nichols's charge here: 'When in *Psycho* Norman Bates climbs the stair to his mother's room, the camera tentatively follows him up and cranes back to a bird's-eye view just outside the doorsill, self-consciously displaying its deliberate withholding of information. By exploiting certain polar possibilities of the classical schemata of narration, Hitchcock's authorial persona oscillates between being modest and omnicommunicative within very narrow limits (i.e. presenting a single character's point-of-view) and flaunting its omniscience by suppressing crucial information' (Bordwell, Staiger and Thompson, 79). At least as plausible as Bordwell's explanation is Hitchcock's: 'I didn't want to cut, when he carries her down, to a high-shot because the audience would have been suspicious as to why the camera has suddenly jumped away. So I had a hanging camera follow Perkins up the stairs, and when he went into the room I continued going up without a cut ... Meanwhile, I had an argument take place between the son and his mother to distract the audience and take their minds off what the camera was doing' (Francois Truffaut, *Hitchcock* (New York, London, Toronto, Sydney, Tokyo, Singapore: Simon and Schuster, Inc., 1983), 276). So, far from *flaunting* omniscience is Hitchcock's attempt (if we can take the director at his word) to call as little attention to it as possible. Bordwell's explanation fore-grounds, merely, narration; Hitchcock's, the operation of a crafty author.

117. Transcript of 9 December 1932, 2.

118. Bordwell, Staiger and Thompson, 80.

119. Balio, 101. For more references to *Grand Hotel* as originating a formula and providing inspiration, see Balio 164, 185, 187, 230–231, 268, 272, 279, 287 and 297.

120. Judith Crist, *The Private Eye, the Cowboy and the Very Naked Girl* (New York: Paperback Library, 1970), 20.

121. Critic Richard Watts, reporting on the buzz surrounding the film's release, suggests that the formula's (optional) all-star element had no precedent: 'Then comes the debate as to the wisdom of the Metro-Goldwyn group in providing the screen followers with such a wasteful banquet. There is a strong faction which ... feels that the film manufacturers went too far. Audiences that have been shown a film containing a large proportion of the Hollywood hierarchy will not, it is held, be satisfied to go back to the days of the one-star films'. Richard Watts, Jr., *New York Herald Tribune* 24 April 1932: sect. 7, 3.

122. 'Producer Discusses Pictures,' *New York Times* 3 May 1931: sect. 8, 6. Falling on the line between Thalberg and Crist is critic William Boehnel, who wrote: 'And before you leave [the Grand Hotel] you have met and learned to love and admire, hate and sympathize with the little group whose destinies the author has skillfully woven into a thrilling and exciting melodrama'. William Boehnel, rev. of *Grand Hotel*, *New York World Telegram* 13 April 1932: 14.

123. Transcript of 9 December 1931, 5.

124. Boehnel, 14.

125. A film encyclopaedia notes that Goulding 'lacked a distinctive personal style' (Ephraim Katz, *The Film Encyclopedia* (New York: Harper and Row, 1979), 496), and another, of his films, that 'it is generally assumed that such films were primarily authored by the studio and the stars' (Samantha Cook, ed., *The International Dictionary of Films and Filmmakers – 4: Writers and Production Artists* (Detroit, Washington DC and London: St. James Press, 1993, 343). None of this, however, is to suggest that Goulding – no matter how heavy Thalberg's influence (or light his own) – did not bring an especial quality to this film. The encyclopaedist writes: 'We must give Goulding credit for the exceptionally involved choreography of faces, voices, and bodies in *Grand Hotel* when we look at the same stars in other movies of the period ... We need only see Garbo as directed by Clarence Brown or George Fitzmaurice to appreciate the contribution of Edmund Goulding. He is exceptionally sensitive to the time it takes the actress to register thought through her mere act of presence' (343). While *how much* credit Goulding is due for such details as shot lengths becomes clearer on examination of the transcripts, that credit is due is not contested here.

126. Mordden, ii.

127. Ibid. 105.

128. The range and number of sources from which a film's effects may be harvested and across which they may be cross-referenced – suggest the potential sweep of the auteur historian's compass. Effects may be reported by reviews concurrent with a theatrical release (or rerelease, or video release); or confected by the densest 1970s symptomatic criticism; or inferred through the latest advances in the study of historical film reception. Mining for causes can, unexpectedly, refract into a metacritical investigation of, for example, Barthes's ruminations on the face of Garbo (Roland Barthes, *Mythologies* (New York: The Noonday Press, 1972), 56–57), and provide fresh angles from which to interrogate effects this viewer claims some films have (and have had) on ideal (and presumably historical) spectators.

129. Mordden, 14.

130. Bordwell, *Making Meaning*, 270.

131. Foucault, 110.

132. Schatz, *The Genius of the System*, 9.

133. Buscombe, 3–4.

134. Foucault, 119.

135. Jane M. Gaines, 'Introduction: The Family Melodrama of Classical Narrative Cinema,' *Classical Hollywood Narrative: The Paradigm Wars*, ed. Jane Gaines (Durham and London: Duke University Press, 1992), 1.

136. Bordwell, Staiger and Thompson, 78.

137. Gaines, 2.

138. Bordwell, Staiger and Thompson, 385.

139. Ibid., 81.

140. Ibid., 78.

141. Foucault, 119.

142. Perkins, 185.

143. Bordwell, Staiger and Thompson, 77.

144. Robert Sklar, *Film: An International History of the Medium* (New York: Harry N. Abrams, Inc., 1993), 351.

145. Bordwell's dead-on comment here about film criticism applies to – and across – all three official arms of film studies: 'The history of film criticism is largely that of predecessors ignored or forgotten, ships passing in the night, people talking at cross-purposes, wholesale dismissals of prior writers' work, and periodic cycles of taste' (Bordwell, *Making Meaning*, 39).

146. Schatz, *The Genius of the System*, 5.

147. Balio, 109–141.

148. Moreover, *within* Bordwell and Thompson's chapter are signs of divergency from the approach as practiced in 1985. While basic tenets remain the same, the authors have modified their rhetorical style in ways that impact the presentation. The first sentence of their section titled 'Sources of Innovation' reads, 'While technological and artistic innovation can usually be attributed to individuals, those individuals operate within a broader context' (119). Focus on broader contexts – studios, firms, and professional organizations – is softened here, in the introductory subordinate clause of this sentence, with a reference to individuals. This tendency – of individuals to pop up in the beginnings of sentences that are really about broader contexts – exhibits itself a few times. 'For all his autonomy', the authors claim about the executive head of Technicolor, 'Kalmus was obliged to work with related service firms' (129). Elsewhere, following a quote that describes two ways a director might choose to begin a scene, the authors comment, 'While Michael Curtiz uses neither tactic at the start of the specimen scene [described earlier in the chapter], he does obey Cromwell's suggestion in other sequences' (127). Here, as in BST, the classical paradigm imposes limits on individuals, but in an instance whose implications are allowed to let stand, this individual's options are not fully circumscribed by stated limits. (If an unstated limit hemmed Curtiz in at the start of the specimen scene, the authors – notably – seem content to leave it that way.) The general relaxation of policy permits a paragraph about a technological innovation to end on a note that would have been uncharacteristic in 1985: 'The boom won Arnold an Academy Technical Award' (128).

149. Perkins, 191.

150. Robert Sklar *City Boys: Cagney, Bogart, Garfield* (Princeton: Princeton University Press, 1992).

151. Tom Gunning *D.W. Griffith and the Origins of American Narrative Film: The Early Years at Biograph* (Urbana and Chicago: University of Illinois Press, 1994).

152. Balio, 10.

Film History, Volume 7, pp. 386–400, 1995. Copyright © John Libbey & Company
ISSN: 0892-2160. Printed in Great Britain

How high was his brow? Albert Lewin, his critics and the problem of pretension

Susan Felleman

When you've spent years of your life researching, contemplating and analysing the work of one artist, you naturally come to assign him or her a place, no matter how small, in a canon of your own devising. This remains the case even if your subject is a filmmaker and you reject a strictly auteurist view of cinema. This conviction does not require a hagiographic or heroic view of the artist, a belief in his or her genius, or even a commitment to any particular canon. It relies simply on the undeniable fact of your subject having engaged your intellectual energies so thoroughly. Naturally, too, since you not only find your subject interesting, but have, or at least attempt to have, a modicum of self respect and ambition, you think that the fruits of all your labour – in my case a dissertation on the director Albert Lewin[1] – ought to be published, especially if they constitute – as did mine – the first major study of the subject. Such were my largely unexamined feelings and assumptions when I sent an inquiry to the editor (hereafter referred to as 'Editor X') of a prominent series of monographic studies on film directors.

I thought the match might be auspicious. The series included books on a number of directors who, like Lewin, attempted in their careers to balance the 'artistic' with the 'commercial'. Most of these were neither the most independent, nor the most institutionally ensconced of directors, neither the most avant-garde nor the most popular. Rather, they were an eclectic mix of individuals working along the margins of the commercial cinema, in the USA and abroad, including, among others, Joseph Losey, Vincente Minnelli, Woody Allen, Paul Morrissey and Wim Wenders. I was therefore hopeful that Editor X would think Lewin a suitable addition to these ranks when I sent my inquiry and was rather shocked to receive, in the return post, a hastily hand-written reply, which, after a quick swipe at me and my worthiness (or lack thereof) as a potential author, proceeded to reject my proposed book vituperatively:

> ... I am only including directors whose work achieves a degree of *excellence* far beyond Lewin's. There are *many* publishing projects nowadays devoted to popular, influential, exotic, or commercially successful filmmakers, but only this series alone – to my knowledge at

Susan Felleman has taught Art History at a number of colleges, including Hampshire College, the College of Staten Island, and the School of Visual Arts. She has published widely on art and film. Correspondence c/o 352a 14th Street, Brooklyn, New York, NY 11215, USA.

Fig. 1. The always impeccably dressed Albert Lewin in his New York City apartment, lounging beneath a portion of a 19th-century Swedish folk painting representing the parable of the wise and foolish virgins, reading *Transition Forty-Eight* (no. 2, 1948), a short-lived reprise of Eugene Jolas's pre-war Journal, and absorbing the aura of a pile of art books, topped by a monograph on the self-taught African-American painter, Horace Pippin [Cinema-Television Library, University of Southern California.]

– right. I was offered a contract by the second publisher to which I applied – a relief to me, but proof, no doubt, to Editor X, of the shocking loss of standards in contemporary publishing. But reflecting on this correspondence, wondering what line this beleaguered warrior for excellence was holding all by himself, where, why, and against what or whom, I came face to face again with a problem that has dogged me throughout my work on Lewin and that I have left unresolved – the problem of his reception.

Known as one of Hollywood's few resident intellectuals, Albert Lewin (1894–1968) was the director in the 1940s and 1950s of six literary, artful, exotic and odd films. First a student (B.A., NYU, 1915; M.A. Harvard, 1916), then teacher (U. Missouri, 1917–18) and doctoral student (Columbia, 1918–22) of English Literature, and then a film and theatre critic (*The Jewish Tribune*, 1921–22), Lewin decided to enter films after seeing *The Cabinet of Dr. Caligari* in 1921. Having swiftly worked his way up the ranks at the Goldwyn and Metro studios, he became indispensable to Irving Thalberg as a writer, then head of the story department and, finally, production supervisor on such prestige MGM films as *Mutiny on the Bounty* (1935) and *The Good Earth* (1937). It was not until 1942, five years after Thalberg's death and Lewin's subsequent departure from MGM that he released his first directorial project, from his own adaptation of Somerset Maugham's *The Moon and Sixpence*, for the independent production company he had started with his friend, David Loew.

least, devoted [sic] to *uncompromised artistic merit*. Therefore, I really feel I must hold the line. Because art is included in a work, needless to say doesn't mean that the work is itself 'art' – it is much more likely (as I believe these films to be – at least those of the 1940s) to be *kitch* [sic]. *Many* series are devoted to such fake/pop/schlock 'art' – so you will, I hope, have no trouble placing your ms. elsewhere [emphasis his].

As it turned out, he was – in at least one respect

Nearly fifty years old, Albert Lewin had begun

his strange career as an 'auteur', writer and director of six films so eccentric and self-conscious that they bear little witness to his long tenure under Thalberg[2]. Lewin commissioned original art works, songs and dances for his films, packed them with metaphors and metonyms, signs and symbols, and, always convinced that the talking film had diminished the visual power of cinema, endeavoured to develop methods of staging and filming that defied the conventions which had evolved around synchronous dialogue. Lewin characterized himself as an 'equilibrist'[3] and described his ambition 'to make a few pictures which will be both commercial and artistic, and which will have enough originality and distinction to be remembered for a little while'[4]. The highly stylized, self-reflexive and intellectually layered results of this endeavour were uneven by almost any standards, as was the reception of Lewin's oeuvre; even *The Picture of Dorian Gray*, the most internally consistent and highly regarded of Lewin's films, met with mixed responses at the time of its release and has since.

If the novel of ideas is rarely successful commercially and even more rarely well-received critically, then the film of ideas is even less so on both counts, especially in Anglo-American culture. This is one of the main problems of Albert Lewin's directorial oeuvre. Ideas were much of the stuff of which Lewin's films were made and thus constitute a focal problem in his reception. Often deemed by his (Anglo-American) critics 'middlebrow', disparagingly, or 'highbrow', sarcastically, Lewin himself hardly hesitated to wield these same ultimately futile and dismissive terms, whose etymological history underscores their suspect value as classifications.

> 'Highbrow', first used in the 1880s to describe intellectual or aesthetic superiority, and 'lowbrow', first used shortly after 1900 to mean someone or something neither 'highly intellectual' or 'aesthetically refined', were derived from the phrenological terms 'highbrowed' and 'lowbrowed', which were prominently featured in the nineteenth-century practice of determining racial types and intelligence by measuring cranial shapes and capacities[5].

Though certainly already current by mid-century, these terms seem to have achieved their greatest visibility, ironically, from Russell Lynes' rather

damning article of 1949, 'Highbrow, Lowbrow, Middlebrow'. According to the criteria Lynes outlines, Lewin, as well as most, if not all, of his critics, and, indeed, Lynes himself, all firmly qualify as 'Upper Middlebrows', along with other 'principal purveyors of highbrow ideas' including '[m]any publishers ... most educators, museum directors, movie producers, art dealers, lecturers, and the editors of most magazines which combine national circulation with an adult vocabulary'[6]. One would think this not particularly shameful company to keep. But highbrows, exemplified in Lynes' article by Clement Greenberg and positions staked out by him in the *Partisan Review*, hold middlebrows in fearful contempt, blaming them for 'devaluating the precious, infecting the healthy, corrupting the honest, and stultifying the wise'[7]. Lynes is pretty hostile to such elitist rhetoric, even going so far as to imply it is totalitarian (and, ironically, it does sound suspiciously like some of the vitriol that the Nazis spewed in their attacks on modern art[8]), but he defends some highbrows on the grounds that not all 'are so intolerant or desperate as this, or so ambitious for authority'[9]. It is very much a Greenbergian vein of highbrowery that my Editor X manifested in his dismissal of Lewin's work as 'fake/pop/schlock', and, especially, 'kitsch' which inevitably recalls one of Greenberg's most famous tracts, 'Avant-Garde and Kitsch' of 1939[10].

One would think, too, that someone in Lewin's position – consciously camped out on the border between high and popular cultures – would be loathe to cast this particular type of aspersion, but in fact, he was as ready as the next guy to sling 'brow' slurs. He was outraged by James Agee's review of *The Picture of Dorian Gray* (1945) and seven years later was still fuming:

> The middle-brow critic has the notion that it is his function to serve as a bridge between the artist and his public. He is not a bridge at all, but a road-block ... James Agee ... is one of the middle-brows I refer to who consider themselves stupendous highbrows. He said in his review that he had to thank me for making him read the Oscar Wilde book. He admired the book and despised the picture. While preparing the picture, I happened to have read the contemporary criticisms of Wilde's book. It

was furiously attacked by people just like James Agee, who said things about the book not unlike things he said about the picture ...[11].

It may well be true that a critic admitting to having been introduced to a minor classic of literature by a motion picture was leaving himself open to such derision, but Agee was far from alone in his dislike of Lewin's film. In fact, his review was much more sympathetic to Lewin's aims than many, and faulted the film more for its execution than its approach:

> A good movie might have been made from *The Picture of Dorian Gray*. Albert Lewin's version is respectful, earnest, and, I am afraid, dead ... the movie is just a cultured horror picture, decorated with epigrams and an elaborate moral, and made with a sincere effort at good taste rather than with passion, immediacy, or imagination[12].

Agee didn't despise *Dorian Gray* so much as pity it. He misconstrued Lewin's purposes in his fastidious evocation of *fin-de-siècle* aestheticism, mistaking for effortful taste an archaeological and psychological sense of milieu. *The Picture of Dorian Gray* meant to be a horror picture, and achieved this (arguably perhaps) in no small part through its rather chilling, formal rigour. Agee missed this, too, but he was neither a philistine nor a snob.

Other critics and viewers, though, did *really* despise Lewin's film. 'The Picture of Dorian Gray is reminded of nothing so much as a Grosset and Dunlap edition of the Oscar Wilde

work, editorially fumigated by Lloyd C. Douglas, and ornamented with illustrations from the brush of Maxfield Parrish', wrote Herb Sterne, invoking the most invidious tendencies of 'middlebrow' culture[13]. Actually, if any illustrator should be invoked as an influence on Lewin's sets, it is not Parrish, but Aubrey Beardsley, illustrator of the volume of Mallory's *Morte d'Arthur* (1893) which is shown open to an illustration of 'How Sir Tristan drank of the love drink' in Dorian Gray's library[14]. Lewin indeed sometimes achieves a cinematic equivalent in his film of what one might call Beardsley's 'post-Pre-

Fig. 2. *The Picture of Dorian Gray,* 1945 (Peter Lawford and Donna Reed). Critics found the film effortfully 'tasteful', but Lewin had more deliberate uses for style. Many scenes use flat, linear, black-and-white compositions to evoke the look associated with Wilde's *fin-de-siècle* decadence and to foreground the dialectic between good and evil.
[Cinema-Television Library, University of Southern California.]

Raphaelitism', and uses the style to further both internal (i.e. the atmosphere associated with Wildean decadence) and external (a kind of narrative dissociation from the story's amorality and perversity) demands of his scenario. But these sorts of visual meanings either eluded or offended too many of Lewin's viewers. Producer Val Lewton, who saw the film in 1945 with Mark Robson, thought it 'a disgustingly pretentious piece of poopishness'[15], and his was not a unique reaction.

Lewin characterized the reception of *The Picture of Dorian Gray* himself in an unsent response to James Agee: 'The divergence of opinion regarding my film ... is violent. Harry Hansen, Alton Cook, Howard Barnes, Eileen Creelman, Kate Cameron, and a number of others, approve of it with varying degrees of enthusiasm. At the same time it is a subject of amusement, contempt or condemnation by Bosley Crowther, John Mason Brown, the *New Yorker*, *Time*, P.M., and by you in the *Nation*'[16]. And If American response was split about *The Picture of Dorian Gray*, it was increasingly unanimous in its low opinions of Lewin's later films. Characterized by an odd combination of tragedy and irony, spectacle and ritual, pomposity and play, these had a particularly 'un-American' mien. Andrew Sarris sums up many an American critic's response to films that aspire to sophistication or literacy in his evaluation of Lewin and the other directors whom he places in his 'Strained Seriousness' category of American directors, composed of 'talented but uneven directors with the mortal sin of pretentiousness. Their ambitious projects tend to inflate rather than expand'[17].

If there is any epithet more damning than 'middlebrow', in our culture at large, and in the microcosm of American film, it must be 'pretentious', an often unexamined and misused, but even more often effective, pejorative. It may fail to distinguish between genuine and feigned knowledge, expertise or literacy, and level its dismissal at *any* person or product that manifests or aspires to these qualities. Albert Lewin, whatever his failings as a writer and director, was not a pretender to the worlds of arts and letters – he was, as a scholar and critic, a graduate of these worlds. That has not stopped a majority of his American critics from characterizing his films as vulgar and naive and condemning him as pretentious and snobbish[18].

Aside from a few writers, perhaps, not many people in Hollywood, especially in the classic period, were likely to be greeted with epithets such as these. Most European émigrés, even the well educated, seem to have been to some extent exempted from charges of pretension and snobbery, no doubt for a complex variety of reasons, including the often tacit assumption on the part of many Americans that Europeans are more 'cultured' than us, but also because they tended not to make blatantly 'arty' or 'intellectual' films, and because they were all too often isolated from the rest of the community. John Russell Taylor in his *Strangers in Paradise* characterizes Lewin as one of the only Hollywood denizens 'who appreciated the special qualities of the émigrés ... whose strange devotion to European culture made them almost as much outsiders as if they were European non-joiners themselves'. Taylor goes on to display the ambivalence or scepticism that is so ubiquitous in discussions that must deal with intellect and American movie makers in the same breath:

> Lewin ... had been a professor before being lured into movies – a fact that always enormously impressed those around, particularly Irving Thalberg ... Lewin was always very consciously and obviously an odd-man-out in Hollywood: it was in a sense his gimmick. With his Savile Row suits, his collection of Pre-Columbian artifacts (years before they were fashionable), his disdain (real or apparent) for commerce, his obsession with surrealism and his host of European friends, he was absolutely what then passed in Hollywood – and probably still would – for an intellectual[19].

Lewin was, by almost any definition of the term, in fact an intellectual. That was the crux of his problem. The anti-intellectualism revealed by criticism such as was often levelled at Lewin may have been unnecessary and unusual in Hollywood, but was and is, however, hardly unusual in American culture at large. Richard Hofstadter has written the definitive study, *Anti-Intellectualism in American Life*, identifying and analysing this persistent animus in the American body politic, which often harbors the suspicion, he argues, that intellectuals 'are pretentious, conceited, effeminate, and snobbish; and very likely immoral, dangerous, and subversive'[20].

As an intellectual, Lewin was not so cloistered as to be protected him from charges of middle-browery from 'above' or from charges of pretension from 'below'. This fact, I believe, goes far in explaining the vicissitudes of his reception. The anti-intellectualism Lewin encountered in Hollywood was motivated from within and without. Not only did the industry cater to a 'know-nothing' public, but it was itself fraught with anti-intellectualism. This is beautifully illustrated by an anecdote about his battles with MGM during production of *The Picture of Dorian Gray*:

> The film went forward, not without difficulties since it ran over schedule and budget. Once [Pandro S.] Berman spent most of the day watching Lewin set up just one characteristically complex shot: that which starts on Dorian, inclined to be contrite for ill-using poor innocent Angela Lansbury [Sibyl] and writing her a letter, then moves over to George Sanders [Lord Henry Wotton], who turns and walks away from the camera to deliver the crucial information that the girl has killed herself, then turns back at last, cynically, to observe the effect of his words. Berman watched all this with some mystification, then took Lewin aside. 'Al, I don't see why you're complicating things for yourself. This guy's telling his friend the very sad and tragic news that his girl has died. Why don't you do it in a nice two-shot on the sofa, with over-shoulder close-ups?' Lewin felt there wasn't much point in explaining at length, so he said, 'Well, Pan, that's my style, you see'. Berman was puzzled. 'Style, style, people are always talking about style. What is this style'? Lewin explained that it was the quality which told you at once that a Lubitsch film was by Lubitsch, or if you turned on a radio to Wagner made sure you knew at once it wasn't Mozart or Bach. Berman reflected. 'Oh, so that's style. Well, I don't want it in any of my movies'[21].

If Berman's is the quintessential anti-intellectual response, the discourse that provoked it reveals not only the pedant in Albert Lewin, but also the aesthete, two aspects of his character he made no attempt to subdue in Hollywood, where they were mightily out of place, revealing a third, and very interesting aspect – his perversity. Perversity, of a particular (not necessarily sexual, that is) sort, is evident in much that Lewin was and did and is built into all of his films, manifesting itself in all sorts of fascinating contradictions, paradoxes and problems. As he himself was wont to point out, Lewin's very choices of material for his films tended toward the perverse. About the choice of material for his first film, *The Moon and Sixpence*, for instance, Lewin later recalled in an interview:

> Everybody felt we'd make, at most, an artistic flop. David [Loew]'s friends tried to dissuade him, but he was steadfast. They said the story of a disagreeable character, a painter whose paintings are burned and who dies of leprosy – this is entertainment?'[22].

And in a letter to his friend, the poet Charles Reznikoff, upon completing *The Moon and Sixpence* early in 1942, Lewin remarked:

> The general impression around here seems to be that it will make a fine picture and a commercial flop. My indurated contrariness finds this very encouraging[23].

Additionally, his films often thematized a rather transgressive, indeed sadistic cruelty, and not only did several involve sexual promiscuity, deviance and manipulation, but they embodied these themes cinematically in a concertedly 'detached, studied, symbolic style'[24], which ran counter to many Hollywood conventions. Visually overloaded, yet featuring very restrained, almost anti-dynamic camera movement; aurally overloaded, too, with complex musical and dialogic counterpoints, yet dramatically circumspect, Lewin's films formally were a paradoxical, or, if you will, perverse, combination of the primitive and the baroque – and all this in an atmosphere carefully guarded by the Hays office!

Compromises to Hollywood's own self-censoring authority were made in all of Lewin's films, yet he seems to have made a point, in many cases, to figure visually, or to encode, the narrative material he was forbidden to relate. This is most graphically the case with his next film, *The Picture of Dorian Gray*, in which a strong homoerotic subtext had to be suppressed, but which nonetheless managed through metaphor, analogy and other visual tropes to figure homoerotic content[25]. By the completion

Fig. 3. *The Picture of Dorian Gray*, 1945 (Donna Reed and Hurd Hatfield). The protagonist's narcissism and homoerotic disposition are 'silently' figured variously, as here, in the mirror, in the guise of Verrocchio's sculpture of the youthful *David* (c. 1465).

of *Bel Ami*, from Guy de Maupassant's story of a bounder who advances professionally and socially through a series of sexual affairs, in 1946, Lewin's treatment of previously taboo themes had earned him the 'unrivaled reputation for bringing viciousness to the screen with the approval of the Production Code censors' and he was considered by then to have established a tradition of 'censor-proof depravity'[26].

Censor-proof, perhaps, but not critic-proof. *Bel Ami*, a film evocative, in many respects, of the artists who inspired it – not only Maupassant, but Flaubert, Manet, Degas, among others – a marvelous examination of the ethos and ambiance of the era it represents, was rather an in*succès d'estime*, as a few remarks will illustrate:

The film is elaborate and expensively produced, but for all that, is dull, dated and a rather absurdly passionate piece of celluloid, seemingly designed to shock the easily shocked and titillate the amorously curious. It's far more ridiculous, however, than wicked[27].

Really, it is incredible that a picture could be made from a Guy de Maupassant novel and be as tiresome as this ... Everybody ... acts as posily and pompously as they are compelled to talk ... the whole lot of them are as utterly artificial as the obvious paint-and-pasteboard sets[28].

As is evident from such ridicule, it was less the already problematic material that Lewin chose to bring to the screen than the purposefully complex, formally distanced and artful manner with which he did so. That manner, for which Lewin's films were so often condemned, is at odds with a prevailing idea of the American cinema. It is hard to imagine

European films that share many qualities (stylization, self-consciousness, historicism, literary allusiveness ...) with Lewin's – Michael Powell's *The Red Shoes* (1948), Alf Sjöberg's *Miss Julie* (1951), Max Ophuls' *Lola Montès* (1955), Ingmar Bergman's *The Seventh Seal* (1957), Jean-Luc Godard's *Contempt* (1963), for instance – being so readily dismissed as pretentious. These may well be better films than most of Lewin's, but not because their makers are less pretentious or more genuine men of ideas, rather because they are perhaps better, or more thoroughly, artists. Lewin was, indeed, perhaps less of an artist *because* he was more of an intellectual. His ideas often encumbered and undermined his artistry; a Lewin film can seem almost annotated, with built-in criticism – like a teaching edition of a novel. Again, this is a quirk more readily forgiven in European films, Antonioni's for instance, or Godard's, than it can ever be in their American cousins[29].

American film criticism has tended, for the most part, to cherish a fantasy of a kind of unschooled, native genius in its home-grown filmmakers (Griffith, Flaherty, Ford, Keaton and Hawks, for instance), but welcomes sophistication, erudition and artifice from abroad. As an exception to this rule, the reception of the cosmopolitan, but nonetheless very American Orson Welles is illuminating. He was not greeted with unalloyed enthusiasm in Hollywood in 1940, rather, with not a little suspicion and bemusement on the part of the 'regulars' a phenomenon captured beautifully in 'Pat Hobby and Orson Welles', one of F. Scott Fitzgerald's late stories about Hobby, the washed-up studio hack:

> 'Who's this Welles'?, Pat asked of Louie, the studio bookie. 'Every time I pick up a paper they got about this Welles'.
>
> 'You know, he's that beard', explained Louie.
>
> 'Sure, I know he's that beard, you couldn't miss that. But what credit's he got? What's he done to draw one hundred and fifty grand a picture'[30]?

And it was not only the man himself, and his signifying beard, that could alienate. According to Arthur Knight, Welles' masterpiece, *Citizen Kane*, flew equally in the face of American anti-intellectualism:

> ... at a time when the big audience in America was still the small-town, grass-roots moviegoer, *Kane* proved a chill and forbidding experience, cold, objective and intellectual. Welles had so distanced all his characters that the kind of empathy most moviegoers then expected of a picture was totally lacking. They might be impressed, but they were rarely moved[31].

The morbid and pessimistic *Weltanschauung*, the formal artifice, and almost Brechtian distancing devices that Welles brought to *Kane* are equally characteristic of most of Lewin's films – certainly the three from the 1940s, however different the particular conceits and overall approaches of the two directors may have been. Like Welles', Lewin's directorial debut, *The Moon and Sixpence* (released the following year), involved the retrospective attempt to reconstruct and understand the enigma of a great man. While Charles Foster Kane was based on William Randolph Hearst, Somerset Maugham's and Lewin's Charles Strickland was based on the French painter, Paul Gauguin. And like Kane, the character of Strickland is a man of massive contradictions: hateful and seductive, brutish but brilliant, paradoxically naive and cynical, who, in the course of the story transforms himself from a bland, witless London stockbroker and family man into a fierce misanthrope and vanguard painter. And Strickland's death, like Kane's, is inexorably central to the entire film. Lewin's solutions to the formal problems posed by Maugham's achronological, first-person narration are not as dazzling as Welles' similarly non-traditional construction, but are no less unusual.

> We bought it [rights to *The Moon and Sixpence*] from MGM for $25,000. The contract came out of the MGM legal department faster than any other contract in my experience, they were so glad to get rid of it. They thought we were screwy. But I had an angle. The reason it couldn't be adapted was that it was told in the first person and because the author at times became a participant in the action. The transposition was very, very hard to do, and the people who had tackled it never solved that problem. For this, I owe a debt of gratitude to Sacha Guitry, who made a wonderful picture called *The Story of a Cheat*, which used a

Fig. 4. *The Moon and Sixpence*, 1942. Herbert Marshall, the film's first-person narrator, observes with a cool eye the tabletop doodlings of the misanthropic Gauguin-like protagonist (George Sanders). [Richard Koszarski collection.]

narrative technique for the first time in a theatrical film. He told his story in the first person, the action carried it along, and at intervals when necessary, he talked again. I thought this was a most original and exciting thing ...[32].

Guitry's *Le Roman d'un tricheur* (1936), generally considered the French director's best film, is 'told entirely from the point of the leading character, Sacha Guitry, who describes the action in a running commentary while the characters act in pantomime'[33].

The art historian Erwin Panofsky rightly observed that *The Story of a Cheat* betrays 'a kind of nostalgia for the silent period and that devices have been worked out to combine the virtues of sound and speech with those of silent acting', in films that employ voice-over to free the picture from its narration[34]. The theme of nostalgia is central to Lewin's

The Moon and Sixpence and his borrowing of Guitry's technique reveals a similar yearning for what he felt were the greater (more imaginative, dynamic, dramatic) visual effects of the silent cinema, the loss of which he mourned until the end of his career, as is evident from this letter to the critic Dwight MacDonald:

Inspired especially by *The Cabinet of Doctor Caligari*, I started working in silent pictures because I thought the movies were an exciting new art. I was young, too, and I wanted to take part in the development of this new art. I was betrayed by the inventors. With the use of synchronized sound, the movies ceased to be an art and have never recovered. I am still at it, but without hope of finding that 'counterpoint', that non-synchronous co-ordination of visual and auditory images that Eisenstein was not permitted to experiment with. The simple truth is that an art exists *because* of its limitations, not in *spite* of them. The theorizers and critics clap their hands and jump up and down in joy whenever another limitation is removed and we take a further step in the direction of the last banality. The history of the movies has a happy ending if it is told backwards[35].

That last observation might be made of Lewin's own career, were one to judge by either criticism or profits. By the time Lewin's most 'original' film, *Pandora and the Flying Dutchman*, was released in 1951, his reputation – earned under Thalberg – as a canny producer and great judge of scripts had been overwhelmed by his newly won reputation as a rather fussy, impractical and expensive writer-director of risky, arduously ornate movies. After *Pandora*, Lewin failed to get his most cherished projects (a Goya film, an adaptation of Ibsen's *Peer Gynt*, and a Faustian fugue called *Diana at Midnight*, among others) off the ground and the two films he did manage to make were deeply flawed inherently and further weakened by second-rate acting and studio interference[36]. *Pandora*, a baroque synthesis of classical myth and Germanic legend set in Spain, circa 1930, told the story of a woman unable to love and a man unable to die, and met with mixed reviews. Few critics could deny its visual splendor (glorious Technicolor photography of Ava Gardner and the Spanish Costa Brava by Jack Cardiff), but neither could most of its English speaking critics swallow its 'confused and pretentious'[37], 'turgid'[38] script.

Many French critics, on the other hand, generally more catholic in their tastes, loved *Pandora*, not only for its sensual beauty, but also for its eccentric and literate blend of poetry and myth, tragedy and spectacle. Critics in the Surrealist circuit and those of *Cahiers du Cinéma* were most rapturous. These contrasts in the film's reception are almost as fascinating and paradoxical as the film itself. Tom Milne, an admirer, saw both the Surrealist link and the impact on the New Wave when *Pandora* was shown in England in 1985, but seemed unaware that the reception of the film had varied widely:

Made a decade or two earlier, Lewin's marvellous fantasy might at least have stood some chance of being annexed to the surrealist pan-

theon. Instead critics, surprisingly unanimously, dismissed it as an embarrassingly arty aberration, a comedy of manners that was all too unintentionally comic and much too mannered. Characters who quote as liberally as Lewin's do always seem to be a source of unease – witness reactions to Godard's early work – as though mere quotation were itself a pretension. Yet as Godard realised (and if you consider *Le Mépris* in relation to *Pandora and the Flying Dutchman*, there can be little doubt where his debt lies), allusion is a rich source of *texture*, adducing tenuous parallels, reverberating echoes and mysterious insights in support of perspectives whereby (to quote Novalis) 'The world becomes a dream and the dream becomes a world'[39].

Milne, who knew a lot about the French New Wave, must have been thinking only of Anglo-American critics; in fact, *Pandora was* annexed to Surrealist and New Wave pantheons in France, where Ava Gardner as Pandora was described in deliriously Surrealist prose under 'G' in the *Cahiers du Cinéma*'s dictionary, 'F comme femme', in its 1953 'La femme et le cinéma' special number:

Here Aurelia has the marine look and the salty tresses of Undine ... Ava Gardner's body is yet that of Pandora, the first woman, who, along with her hair, undoes the ties of all fatalities ... when the eyes of dawn open on the wet sands of an untouched beach, finally, when in the cabin mirror, Pandora reappears ... now never to leave ... cinema, once again the magic lantern of our childhood, has borne us very far and very high on the wings of dreams ...[40].

Ado Kyrou, France's most prolific late Surrealist film critic, too, adored the film, characterizing Gardner's Pandora, 'with Lya Lys (of *L'âge d'or*) the only fiercely surrealist woman in all cinema'[41].

Nor have *Pandora*'s detractors all been unaware of the film's Surrealist affiliations; some simply did not consider this a reliable endorsement. Russell Davies, for instance, also reviewing it for its London reprise in 1985, described it as having been:

... received at the time with a barrage of maledictions ('utter poverty of imagination and taste' wrote C.A. Lejeune) but it appealed, so

Fig. 5. *Pandora and the Flying Dutchman,* 1951. James Mason (the Dutchman) recites Arnold's 'Dover Beach' while Ava Gardner (Pandora) dances with an ancient god in Lewin's unparalleled attempt at box-office Surrealism that Anglo-American critics found largely ridiculous. French audiences were rapturous. [The Museum of Modern Art/Film Stills Archive.]

the re-releasers tell us, to the Surrealists ... it's the sort of mixture that commonly gets called 'high camp', but it's much too inorganic and effortful to qualify. See it, by all means, in the company of a 1950s Surrealist, but remember – with rare exceptions, they were a notoriously po-faced lot[42].

Pandora was, in fact, concertedly Surrealist, according to Lewin himself, who had become friendly with a number of Surrealist artists, including Man Ray and Max Ernst, during the Second World War and who had through them begun collecting Surrealist art.

It was natural ... that I should try to create a film with a deliberately surrealist intention. This desire took form in *Pandora and the Flying Dutchman.* The surrealist practice of juxtaposing ancient and modern images, particularly

evident in the work of de Chirico and of Paul Delvaux, especially moved me ... Among other surrealist incidents in the film I might call attention to the scene of the racing car on the beach – a modern machine being driven at great speed past the statue of a Greek goddess standing on the sands. As a matter of fact, it was this image which was the original thought that prompted me to develop the entire story and film of *Pandora*'[43].

It was not only this visually Surrealist orientation that interested many French critics, Surrealists included, in *Pandora.* More generally, French intellectuals appreciated Lewin's attempt to negotiate the perceived contradictions between the 'high' of Surrealism and the 'low' of Hollywood. Lewin, like André Breton, the father of Surrealism, loved paradoxes and sought in all of his films to resolve 'life and death, the real and the imagined, past and future, the communicable and the incommunicable'[44]. Authorially, too, he attempted to negotiate those two aspects of his character that always worked in tension with one another in his films: the critic – ironic, academic, sceptical – and the artist – sensitive, intuitive, sincere.

Pandora's reception must be seen as a gauge of the success of this attempt. And according to its reception, it was (and is) two different films, one a 'masterpiece' the other a 'supreme folly'[45]. While Lewin's film appeared a virtual travesty to many English and American critics (and, based on its revenues, audiences), in France critics and audiences saw something else. To this day, Americans persist in their discomfort with his unabashedly literary, self-conscious and stylized work, while French audiences seem to appreciate the frisson created by the exercise of such reflexivity within the studio idiom.

This disparity between the home critics and the French is not unique (but I do not want to relate it to either Jerry Lewis or Mickey Rourke). *Peter Ibbetson* (directed by Henry Hathaway), for instance, had 'a mixed reception in 1935, when some critics thought that the elaborate dream sequences failed completely, but a few years later it was discovered by the French surrealists and claimed by André Breton as "a triumph of surrealist thought", using the cinema to "turn our way of feeling upside down"[46]'.

One source of this international dispute, no doubt, is language. Lewin himself described the problem quite well in a eulogy for the silent cinema, written on the very eve of his directorial debut, 'RIP: Obituary for a Dead Art':

> ... it is probably true that since the invention of talking pictures not a single movie has been made which can be called a 'work of art' in the unique and definitive sense in which the silent Chaplin pictures, *Caligari*, *The Last Laugh* and *Potemkin* were works of art ... The only talking picture that approached being a work of art is *Maedchen in Uniform*, and it may be that I think so only because I do not understand German. Foreign pictures often seem artistic to us because we do not understand the dialogue, and consequently are still regarding them as silent pictures[47].

This is an arguable observation generally, but one with obvious relevance to *Peter Ibbetson* and *Pandora*, two of the Surrealist group's favourite Hollywood films. The often stiff, 'unnatural' quality of the dialogue of these original and oneiric fantasies cannot embarrass a foreign audience as it might a native one. The Surrealists, and French fans after them, clearly responded to the visual concreteness of the 'dream-work' of both these films, and not to the somewhat 'creaky' scripts[48].

Lewin's films are indeed characterized by a paradoxical schism between their verbose soundtracks and their highly mannered visual fields, a function of the director's technique, which, as he himself and some of his more astute critics have noted, reflects his attachment to the aesthetics of the silent film. As Sylvie Trosa remarks, 'If a very pictorial, surrealist *mise-en-scène* seems related to the silent cinema ... and has been lost, for some complex reasons, with the talkies and their realism, *Pandora* constitutes a sort of historic counterpoint, where, in a so-called "Hollywood" production, Lewin risks the visual audacities of a poetry and of an invention that the talkies seem to have made impossible or at least "silenced"[49]'.

This paradox, of a writer-director whose scripts are just about as 'talky' as they come preferring and aspiring to the qualities of the silent cinema, is not as inscrutable as might at first seem. There is a sense in which the excess of talk, especially in the form of voice-over narration, separates itself from the picture, as Richard Combs has suggested in his excellent analysis of *Dorian Gray*:

> But to look for the seed of modernism in Lewin is to find it also in the most old-fashioned qualities of his cinema, in the strong trace of silent cinema where he (most loquacious of writer-directors) began after all ... the pile-up of dialogue itself begins to suggest another dimension, perhaps even to redefine the film altogether ... towards a formal puzzle of appearances and reality, form and essence, body and soul. These are figured, as it were, in the interplay of vision and sound – or not so much an interplay, more an inconclusive confrontation. What the ceaseless epigrammatic wit of the dialogue seeks to describe, the visuals frame (like the portrait of Dorian Gray) mysteri-

ously, 'perfectly', impenetrably. *Dorian Gray* may be one of the few films that has actually weighed the value of a thousand words against that of a picture, and found the former infinitely distortable and the latter infinitely inscrutable ... The 'picture' of Albert Lewin that emerges finally from *Dorian Gray* is not of a director who was a prisoner of his high-culture pretensions, but of one with a remarkable visual sensibility that has little to do with conventional notions of style[50].

Today Lewin is, perhaps, on the verge of rehabilitation. Recent theorists have looked to the remarkable imagery of his *The Picture of Dorian Gray*, in particular, to underscore complex notions about the Classical Hollywood cinema and the 'cinematic apparatus' in general. Judith Mayne offers a particularly interesting argument about the reflexivity of the film in her recent book, *Cinema and Spectatorship*, which devotes a chapter to demonstrating the implications for spectators of *Dorian Gray's* foregrounding of portraits, mirrors and other indices of specularity[51]. Réda Bensmaïa concentrates on one stunning dissolve from *The Picture of Dorian Gray* in an essay that generalizes from this a propensity of the cinematic dissolve itself to body forth the taboo, repressed or disavowed content of narrative cinema[52].

Intelligent and persuasive as these pieces are, both betray certain familiar assumptions about the artistic agency of the film's director. Bensmaïa, with a sleight of hand all too common in structuralist theory, allows *his* ignorance of Lewin's intentions to subsume the entire problem of intentionality. A cinematic figure of great complexity is turned from a brilliant authorial conceit into a prototypical cinematic function. Mayne, more cognisant of Lewin's part, yet remains uninterested in pursuing it, betraying both the unease with auteurism and the tendency to describe many effects of the Hollywood cinema as functions of the unconscious (authorial, spectatorial or cultural) that are so common in contemporary film theory. I do not wish to argue with the psychoanalytic view of the unconscious that underlies either author's premises, or with the notion that the unconscious plays a significant role in shaping the entire cinematic experience. For me these are givens. But in examining Lewin's oeuvre, I believe,

much is potentially overlooked or misconstrued in a view that neglects his really very assertive authorial presence.

'There are unconscious artists and others who are perfectly conscious', wrote Jean Renoir about his good friend for the Cinémathèque Française's 1958 'Hommage à Albert Lewin'. 'The former are neither inferior nor superior to the latter. But the latter are indispensable in periods of transition. Albert Lewin is indispensable to our epoch ...'[53].

Notes

1. Susan Felleman, *On the Boundaries of the Hollywood Cinema: Art and the Films of Albert Lewin*. Ph.D. Dissertation, Art History (City University of New York, 1993).

2. Lewin's directorial filmography consists of: *The Moon and Sixpence* (Loew-Lewin, 1942); *The Picture of Dorian Gray* (MGM, 1945); *The Private Affairs of Bel Ami* (Loew-Lewin, 1947); *Pandora and the Flying Dutchman* (Dorkay/Romulus, 1951); *Saadia* (MGM, 1954); and *The Living Idol* (MGM, 1957).

3. 'I always tried to make pictures that would please me and some of my intelligent friends and still please the general public enough to pay off ... I did it as a kind of tight-rope walking. I was a bit of an equilibrist'. Quoted in Bernard Rosenberg and Harry Silverstein, eds. *The Real Tinsel* (New York, 1970), 123.

4. Albert Lewin, in his letter of resignation, to Eddie Mannix of MGM, 11 March 1944. Albert Lewin Papers, Cinema-Television Library and Archives of Performing Arts, University of Southern California (hereafter referred to as Lewin Papers, USC).

5. Lawrence Levine, *Highbrow/Lowbrow: The Emergence of Cultural Hierarchy in America* (Cambridge, MA, 1988), 221–222. Levine's source for the etymology of these terms is the O.E.D. Supplement.

6. *Harper's Magazine*, Vol. 198, No. 1185 (February 1949), 25.

7. Lynes, quoting Greenberg, p. 21. The passage is from Greenberg's contribution to 'The State of American Writing, 1948: A Symposium,' (*Partisan Review*, August 1948), reproduced in Clement Greenberg, *Collected Essays and Criticism, Vol. 2: Arrogant Purpose, 1945–1949* (Chicago, 1986), 257–258.

8. See, for instance, Adolf Hitler's remarks about 'de-

generate' art in his 'Speech Inaugurating the *Great Exhibition of German Art, 1937*' in Herschel B. Chipp, ed., *Theories of Modern Art* (Berkeley, 1971), 474–483.

9.   Lynes, 21.

10. Greenberg (1909–1994) became widely known, and was quite influential, especially in the field of art criticism, for the rigorous, formalist view of modernism he expounded in this and other essays for *The Partisan Review*, *The Nation* and other journals. Clement Greenberg, *Art and Culture: Critical Essays* (Boston, 1961), 3–21.

11. From a letter to Will and Ariel Durant, 14 January 1952, Lewin Papers, USC. It is perhaps ironic that this particular complaint was registered with the Durants, great popularizers and mediators of philosophy – 'middlebrow' translators of great ideas, some would say.

12. James Agee, Review of *The Picture of Dorian Gray* (10 March 1945, *The Nation*), in *Agee on Film* (New York, 1967), 147.

13. Herb Sterne, Review, *Rob Wagner's Script*, Vol. 31, No. 701 (31 March 1945), 14.

14. Lewin, who had something of an Arthurian fixation and who long wished to make a 'Knights of the Round Table' film, changed Dorian from Sibyl's 'Prince Charming,' as Wilde had it in the novel, to her 'Sir Tristan' and loaded his film with references to the fated knight.

15. From an unpublished letter quoted in Joel E. Siegel, Letter to the editors, *Velvet Light Trap*, No. 11 (Winter 1974).

16. The eloquent four-and-a-half page letter (Lewin Papers, USC), evidently never sent, defends *The Picture of Dorian Gray*, charge by charge, against Agee's criticisms.

17. Andrew Sarris, *The American Cinema* (New York, 1968), 189. Lewin's eclectic company in this category includes: Richard Brooks, John Frankenheimer, Stanley Kubrick, Richard Lester, Sidney Lumet, Tony Richardson, John Schlesinger, and Robert Wise. It should be noted that many of these 'American' directors are actually British. Compare the 'mortal sin' that damns these directors to the dubious distinction of being categorized as 'Lightly Likable', by virtue of being 'talented but uneven directors with the saving grace of unpretentiousness', 171.

18. e.g. Sarris speaks of Lewin's 'naive conception of refinement' in *Film Culture*, No. 28 (Spring 1963), 40; David Thomson writes that Lewin's 'arty aspiration showed like a teenage slip,' and 'he cultivated a garish sophistication ... and sometimes achieved real vulgarity' in *A Biographical Dictionary of Film* (New York, 1976), p. 322; and Ephraim Katz, who is more generous, still relies on such terms: 'a curious but interesting mixture of the naive and the sophisticated, the dilettantish and the fascinating, the vulgar and the refined' in *The Film Encyclopedia* (New York, 1979), 717.

19. John Russell Taylor, *Strangers in Paradise: The Hollywood Émigrés, 1933–1950* (New York, 1983), 236.

20. Richard Hofstadter, *Anti-Intellectualism in American Life* (New York, 1963), 19.

21. Arkadin [John Russell Taylor], 'Film Clips'. *Sight and Sound*, Vol. 37, No. 1 (Winter 1967–68), 47.

22. Rosenberg and Silverstein, 118.

23. Letter to Charles Reznikoff, 1/26/42, Lewin Papers, USC.

24. This is Lewin's own characterization of his style, from his unsent letter to Agee, 5.

25. See chapter 2 of my dissertation, op. cit., especially 54–62. See also Réda Bensmaïa, 'La Figure d'inconnu ou l'inconscient épinglé: *Le Portrait de Dorian Gray* d'Albert Lewin,' *Iris*, No. 14–15 (Autumn 1992), 177–186.

26. According to the *Times* as quoted in Robert Sitton, 'Albert Lewin: Director and Innovator', *Park East*, Vol. 3, no. 11 (24 March 1966), 8. On sexual themes in *Bel Ami*, see Chapter 4 of my dissertation, op. cit., especially 127–140. See also Douglas McVay, 'The Private Affairs of Bel Ami (1947)', *Movietone News*, Nos. 66–67 (13 March 1981), 62–64.

27. Jesse Zunser in *Cue*, excerpted in Irving Hoffman, "Affairs of Bel Ami' Draws Both Praise and Censure', *The Hollywood Reporter*, 18 June 1947, 8.

28. Bosley Crowther in *The New York Times*, in Hoffman.

29. As with both later directors, Lewin's previous career as a critic inflects his films with a kind of critical reflexivity, but while Godard and Antonioni tend to have been praised for the complex imbrication that often resulted, Lewin was more often excoriated.

Tom Milne, one of Lewin's admirer's, claims, in fact, that Lewin's 'style of direction, elliptically elusive and allusive, anticipates the Antonioni-Godard revolution in having actors persistently deliver lines back to the camera or in avoidance of unequivocally direct communication'. 'You are a professor, of course,' *Monthly Film Bulletin*, Vol. 52, No. 622 (November 1985), 357. Other critics, including

John Russell Taylor and several French ones, have related Lewin to these two directors, Godard in particular.

30. F. Scott Fitzgerald, 'Pat Hobby and Orson Welles,' *The Pat Hobby Stories* (New York, 1962), 41.

31. Arthur Knight, *The Liveliest Art: A Panoramic History of the Movies* (New York, 1979), 189.

32. Rosenberg and Silverstein, 118.

33. Georges Sadoul, *Dictionary of Films*, translated, edited and updated by Peter Morris (Berkeley, CA, 1972), 317.

34. Erwin Panofsky, 'Style and Medium in the Motion Pictures'. *Critique*, Vol. I, No. 3 (January-February 1947), 16.

35. Letter to Dwight MacDonald, 18 March 1958, Lewin Papers, USC.

36. Lewin meant to do *Peer Gynt*, which he had carefully researched and adapted from Ibsen's play, using Grieg's 'Suite' as a score, as a follow-up to *Pandora*, but ended up making the rather insipid *Saadia* (based on a terrible novel, *Echec au destin* by Francis d'Autheville) on the cheap in Morocco instead. He spent over a year researching and writing his Goya picture, which he intended to direct himself on location in Spain. MGM bought but scrapped his script, but did use his intended female lead, Ava Gardner, in *The Naked Maja* (Henry Koster, dir., 1958), while Lewin himself ended up with another inferior cast and cheaper location (Mexico) to make his original and bizarre *The Living Idol*. Another intended vehicle for Ava Gardner was his *Diana at Midnight*, with a Faust ballet *en-abyme*, which he was trying to get underway in 1959 when he suffered the heart attack that precipitated his retirement from films.

37. Philip T. Hartung, *Commonweal*, Vol. 55 (14 December 1951), 254.

38. Herman G. Weinberg, 'Lettre de New York (February 1952)', *Cahiers du Cinéma*, Vol. II, no. 10 (March 1952), 45.

39. Milne reviewed the film when it was shown as part of the series, 'Visual Cinema', at London's Institute of Contemporary Arts in August of 1985. *Monthly Film Bulletin*, Vol. 52, No. 619 (August 1985), 261–262.

40. François Truffaut, *et al.* 'F comme femme'. *Cahiers du Cinéma*, Vol. 5, No. 30 (Christmas 1953), 33. My translation.

41. *Amour-Érotisme et Cinéma* (Paris, 1957), 406. My translation.

42. In the London *Observer*, 4 August 1985.

43. Letter to Yves Kovacs, 1 July 1964, Lewin Papers, USC. The substantive portions of this letter, written in response to a request for a statement for a special double number ('Surréalisme et Cinéma') of *Études Cinématographiques*, appeared in French translation in the journal's second volume on this subject, Nos. 40–42 (1965), 167–169.

44. André Breton, 'Second Manifesto of Surrealism', *Manifestoes of Surrealism*, Richard Seaver and Helen R. Lane, trans. (Ann Arbor, MI, 1972), 123.

45. In the 'masterpiece' camp, one finds: François Truffaut, *et al.* (1953), Ado Kyrou (1957), Jean-Paul Török (1980), Vincent Amiel (1982), Raphaël Bassan (1982), Jacqueline Nacache (1982), and Tom Milne (1985), among others. The harshest members of the opposing camp include: C.A. Lejeune (1951), Richard Winnington (1951), Russell Davies (1985) and John Coleman (1985), who deemed *Pandora* a 'supreme folly'. For complete citations, see the bibliography in my dissertation, *op. cit.*

46. Kingsley Canham, 'Henry Hathaway,' in *World Film Directors*, Vol. I, 1890–1945, John Wakeman, ed. (New York, 1987), 442–43.

47. Unpublished, unfinished, undated typescript, c. 1941, Lewin Papers, USC.

48. *The New York Times* 'Television' section in its capsule review of *Peter Ibbetson* (2–8 May 1993, 29) describes it as a 'heavy, musty antique. It creaked even then'. The *Times*'s TV section is often an education in arch transmission of received opinions. One I have never been able to forget: 'sick, sick, sick, but fascinating', about Joseph Mankiewicz's adaptation of Tennessee Williams's *Suddenly, Last Summer* (1959).

49. Sylvie Trosa, 'Pandora: Albert Lewin'. *Cinématographe*, Vol. 73 (December 1981), 59. My translation.

50. Combs, 355–356.

51. Judith Mayne. *Cinema and Spectatorship* (London, 1993), 105–122.

52. 'La Figure d'inconnu ou l'inconscient épinglé: *Le Portrait de Dorian Gray* d'Albert Lewin,' *Iris*, No. 14–15 (Autumn 1992), 177–86.

53. Statement in: Cinémathèque Française, *Hommage à Albert Lewin* (Paris, c. 1958). My translation.

Film History, Volume 7, pp. 401–425, 1995. Copyright © John Libbey & Company
ISSN: 0892-2160. Printed in Great Britain

Romaine Fielding: The West's touring auteur

Linda Kowall Woal

Vivid – dynamic – compelling – thus has Romaine Fielding been described. Prodigally gifted, in him are found the perceptions of the artist, the acumen of the man in business, and the powers of execution dowered only to one created to command. His thorough training had fitted him to assume any character, however complex ... He writes his own stories, plays the principal roles, directs his productions, and manages his own company. Fielding's offerings are today called classics[1].

These words of effusive praise for Romaine Fielding were written in 1914 by veteran theatrical producer and critic Robert Grau. Found among the hundreds of cameo descriptions of forgotten motion picture artists in Grau's *The Theatre of Science*, one of the first attempts at a comprehensive survey of the motion picture industry, they raise tantalizing questions about the unchronicled career of a figure once recognized as one of the early film industry's most popular filmmakers and, although the label was yet to be coined, one of its first acknowledged *auteurs*. As testimony to his prominence, by 1913 he was voted second place in the *New York Morning Telegraph*'s popularity poll and awarded first place in the *Motion Picture Story Magazine*'s Most Popular Player Contest, to which Fielding fans across the United States and Europe mailed in over 750,000 vote cards, giving him a total that exceeded the combined total for Broncho Billy, Francis X. Bushman, Mary Pickford, Blanche Sweet, Pearl White, Arthur Johnson and Carlyle Blackwell[2].

Remembering Fielding nearly a decade later,

his former colleague and Lubin Film Company scenario writer, Norbert Lusk reminisced, 'He was unique. Repellent, yet fascinating; uncanny – often tender, appealing. His plays, if you saw him at his best, transpired in the open. They were "Westerns", but unconventional ones. Mostly of his own devising, they usually pivoted around a mental condition such as fear, revenge or thought transference. Indeed, he was the first to attempt the psychological film'. Continuing his brief sketch, Lusk drew a portrait made all the more intriguing by questions it, too, left unanswered: 'According to romantic myth, he was born in Corsica ... [He was] the ugliest man I had ever seen, and one of the most gracious and generous. Swarthy, each feature a contradiction, his age was as doubtful as his birthplace, but he oozed personality ... From Arizona he brought his motorcar, nearly as big as the ark, embellished with a dozen innovations of his own design and lights so huge and piercing that they had to be diminished to conform to city conventions ...[3].

Who was Romaine Fielding and what is now known of the Fielding offerings that were once called 'classics'? A search for the answers involves plunging into a veritable garden of forking paths.

The man who called himself Romaine Fielding remains a mystery. 'He is a rather difficult subject

Linda Kowall Woal was co-curator of the 1984 Peddler of Dreams exhibit on Siegmund Lubin. She has been researching the Lubin Film Company for the last 15 years and is currently nearing completion of a book on Lubin director, Romaine Fielding. Correspondence c/o Navajo Lodge, HC 32-Box 1, Continental Divide, New Mexico 87312, USA.

for an interviewer. His answers could all be described by the adjective laconic. His personality is like his acting – thoughtful, reserved, forceful', was how *Motion Picture Magazine*'s interviewer, and dozens of others, described this enigmatic figure[4]. Reporter after reporter invariably fastened on 'that mysterious smile of his and those haunting eyes with their searching gaze'[5]. 'Official' biographies stated that he was born in Corsica of mixed Spanish, Italian and French ancestry. After losing his inheritance and coming to America, they continue, he attended Shattuck Military Academy, the University of Minnesota and, later, Columbia's College of Physicians and Surgeons before entering the theatre and, after a number of years, motion pictures[6]. The truth, pieced together years later by his son, the late Romaine Fielding, Jr., is far more colourful. Born William Grant Blandin in May 1868 in Riceville, Iowa, Fielding was the unwanted offspring of a shotgun marriage. His early birth so embarrassed his father's family that Romaine's teenage parents were forced to leave. Abandoned by his young mother, Romaine was raised by his grandparents who changed his name to Royal Blandin and altered his birth records to obscure his illegitimate birth. Shuffled between Minnesota and Iowa, he was raised alternately by his father and grandparents. Leaving the University of Minnesota after his grandmother's death, Fielding bounced between an assortment of odd jobs ranging from assistant manager of the Sioux City Engine Works and travel agent (1899–1901) to prospecting for Klondike gold (1901–06), where he established a friendship with Jack London, and opening a doctor's office as Romanzo A. Blondin in Kansas City, Missouri (1907)[7].

After several years as a barnstorming actor in legitimate theatre, Fielding entered motion pictures in 1911 as an actor for the Solax Company before moving on later that year to Siegmund Lubin's Philadelphia-based Lubin Film Company. Within a few months, as the leading man of a new Lubin traveling film 'stock company' under the direction of the equally obscure Captain Wilbert Melville, Fielding boarded the troupe's specially-appointed Pullman car and headed West[8]. This departure in January of 1912 marked the beginning of a remarkable four-year filmmaking odyssey through the American Southwest that would take Fielding to Texas, the

Colorado Rockies and New Mexico, throughout Arizona and along the Mexican border.

Sadly, of the 106 films Fielding is known to have written, produced, directed or starred in – and sometimes all four – while on location for the Lubin Company, fragments of only eight are currently known to survive[9]. Today, documentation of Fielding's filmmaking adventure falls largely to the scores of yellowing trade publication and newspaper clippings collected in the Free Library of Philadelphia's *Lubin Scrapbook Folios*. Datelined 1912–15 from El Paso and Galveston, Texas, the Garden of the Gods and Colorado Springs, Colorado, Silver City and Las Vegas, New Mexico, throughout the new state of Arizona from Tucson, Phoenix and the Grand Canyon, to the bordertowns of Douglas and Nogales, old ghost towns and military forts at Jerome and Camp Verde, and dozens of locations in between, they provide a rare behind-the-scenes glimpse at production of many of the first films shot on location in the real West – as opposed to the eastern 'wilds' of Philadelphia, upstate New York and New Jersey – and at the breathless film-making-on-the-run production methods of the flamboyant Fielding. As the starting point for reconstructing the lost films and forgotten career of Romaine Fielding, they also provide a unique opportunity for examining the uncertainties of artistic attribution and questions of authorship from 1909–16, during the film industry's transitional years of movement towards artistic specialization.

The Lubin Western film crew's first stop, in El Paso, Texas, and across the border in Juarez, Mexico, quickly served as Fielding's baptism of fire into the adventure-filled rigours of filming on location. Taking advantage of the opportunity to film an actual bullfight in Juarez, a scenario was hastily developed for *A Mexican Courtship*, set in Juarez and featuring Fielding as 'the most famous matador in Mexico'[10]. Romance abruptly gave way to reality, however, when, underestimating the tensions along the border during the early years of the Mexican Revolution, Fielding and the entire Lubin film crew were arrested after the mock battle they staged with 300–400 local extras for *The Revolutionist* (in which he played a doctor who reluctantly becomes a Mexican revolutionary leader) was mistaken for the real thing[11].

Escorted out of El Paso, after manager Melville

Fig. 1. Fielding and his crew taking a break from intensive filming along the Mexican border near Silver City, New Mexico, 1913. [New Mexico State Records Center and Archives.]

escaped and wired Lubin for the funds to bail every-one out, the crew hastened to accept the gracious invitation extended by Douglas' Secretary of the Chamber of Commerce to come film in Douglas, Arizona. Only one week before their arrival, Arizona, the last of America's western territories, had officially become a state. Within a few days, the crew had already established its headquarters at Douglas' luxurious Gadsden Hotel, rented the Open Airdome Theater as a make-shift studio, begun building an outdoor stage there, and pre-pared to start filming their first picture, while Melville took an automobile tour to scout for interesting locations[12].

'In anticipation of probable trouble along the border, two troops of cavalry, in command of Captain King, are ordered to Douglas, Arizona, a little town along the Mexican border and a port of entry into Mexico', reads the published plot summary of *Captain King's Rescue*.[13] One of the crew's first Douglas productions, it suggests not only the atmos-phere that greeted them there, but the extent to which the crew's scenarios were already being col-oured by actual experience.

Hardly the old West as romanticized in dime novels and the popular Wild West shows of Buffalo Bill and his imitators, Douglas embodied the incon-gruities of the new West the Lubin crew encountered and increasingly came to reflect in their films. Estab-lished in 1901 and formally laid out according to a modern 'model city' plan, by February 1912, Douglas was the fourth largest city in Arizona. Nonetheless, guests of its elegant Gadsden Hotel were assaulted by the smells of smoke and manure that pervaded this city dominated by the Copper Queen Smelter. US Cavalry troops massing at Camp Douglas had to deal with frightened refugees seeking sanctuary from the hostilities in Mexico, arms and ammunition being smuggled across the border, and bandits taking advantage of the chaos. Against this background, and a smallpox epidemic which caused the city's theatres to be shut down as a precaution, the crew filmed at the smelter, at Camp Douglas, at nearby ranches and at the Gads-den Hotel. They completed their unfinished El Paso productions and made four additional one-reel films during their six week stay in Douglas: *Captain King's Rescue*, *The Salted Mine*, *The Thief*, and *The*

Fig. 2. Filming an interior for *The Man From the West* on an outdoor set in Silver City, New Mexico, one of the more than a dozen outdoor stages he built in locations scattered throughout the American Southwest. [Silver City Museum.]

Ingrate, which, as a farewell gesture of thanks to their host city, concluded with a cafe scene featuring city officials and twenty-five local couples filmed at the Gadsden Hotel[14].

Then, loading the two special railway cars that transported their scenery and effects, wardrobe to equip 40 men as soldiers, cowboys, Mexicans or Indians, costumes for 25 women, firearms, and saddles and bridles for 15 horses, the Lubin troupe of 30 actors and actresses, cameramen and technical personnel, boarded the train and headed for Tucson, Arizona[15].

Arriving in Tucson on 29 March, the crew worked under Melville with little fanfare until mid-May, when he was sent West to open a Lubin studio in Los Angeles and Fielding was promoted to head Lubin's Southwestern Company[16].

After a year of working in virtual anonymity, a year in which one fanciful interviewer credited him with 'having already taken more than 300 parts and written many successful photoplays', Fielding had become a veteran screen actor[17]. Judging from Edward Sloman and Henry King's later accounts of working under producer Melville's assembly-line style of 'studio efficiency', Fielding's practical ex-

perience already included a considerable amount of directing as well[18]. Made in an era when the then dominant Patents Company producers were still loathe to credit, let alone publicize, individual actors for fear they'd demand higher salaries, and writers and directors were being given even less recognition, aside from evidence to be gleaned from filmstills and occasional credits given in trade magazine reviews, the exact nature of Fielding's artistic contributions to the productions from his first year of filmmaking will never be known. With his promotion to head of Lubin's Southwestern Company, Fielding, whose energy and imagination were matched only by his flair for self-promotion, quickly inaugurated a change.

Within little more than a month of taking over the company, Fielding had completed five one-reel pictures: *A Romance of the Border*, *The New Ranch Foreman*, *The Ranger's Reward*, *A Western Courtship*, and *The Sandstorm*. While the source for their scenarios is unknown, it's worth noting that two of these films, *A Romance of the Border* and *The New Ranch Foreman*, featured Mexican heros, setting the tone for later films in which Fielding went against prevailing stereotypes to present hispanic characters not as bandits and 'greasers', but in a favourable light[19]. *The Sandstorm*, a grim little film that represented nature as a malevolent force mocking human endeavour, presented another theme – the Westerner's psychological relationship to the landscape – which was to become an obsessive thread running through many of Fielding's most remarkable productions[20].

Fielding had much greater ambitions, however. Little more than a month after assuming his new position, he began writing the scenario for *The Sleeper*, a film that boldly asserted his skill in drawing dramatic inspiration from his locations, and the magnetic personality that enabled him to fully exploit the civic boosterism of his host cities to greatly enhance the production values of his films.

In 1912, Tucson's modern commercial centre co-existed side-by-side with the adobe buildings and narrow sidestreets of the city's Old Town district which remained virtually unchanged after nearly 200 years. As Fielding told a local reporter, 'If I want to get pictures of the old town in its famous frontier days, all I have to do is go down on Meyer Street. If I want something modern, all I have to do is take the machine and company in the newer residence sections or the business sections'[21]. Struck by the sense of growth and change suggested by this juxtaposition, Fielding sought to capture it on film in *The Sleeper* by writing a western variation of *Rip Van Winkle* around the passing of an era in frontier history.

Although no footage is known to survive, as reconstructed from contemporary plot synopses, reviews and local newspaper articles detailing its production, the film's narrative focused on Dave Ryland, an old prospector living in Tucson with his wife and grandson. Flashing back over a generation, it told of how Ryland, sleeping in the hills one day, became the object of a practical joke by some drunken cowboys who erected a miner's monument near his head with a tag reading 'The Sleeper'. Upon awakening, Dave discovers a rich nugget nearby and touches off a goldrush. Separated from his wife and children in the ensuing chaos, Dave's efforts to be reunited with his family occupy the second part of the film. Paralleling Ryland's long search with the story of Tucson's growth triggered by Dave's discovery, and with the coming of age of a new generation of Tucsonians represented by

the old prospector's grandson, Fielding concluded *The Sleeper* with a gala twentieth anniversary celebration of Dave's discovery, in which accounts of the historical events were related by flashbacks. Whether by intent or felicitous accident, the result was to construct a film that presented the sense of a continuous present through visual juxtapositions of the present co-existing with its past which were then a reflection of modern Tucson itself and, indeed, the entire American Southwest.

As Fielding conceived them, *The Sleeper*'s two central scenes – the goldrush and its gala twentieth anniversary celebration – required considerable cooperation from the citizens of Tucson to provide extras, animals, props and even railroad cars to depict an immigrant train of prospectors. Putting out a call for help in the *Arizona Daily Star*, Fielding told an interviewer, 'I would like to have everyone in Tucson come out and help on the picture'[22]. A born charmer, he wooed the citizens with assurances that, 'It will be one of the best things for the town that Tucson has had happen for some time. It will go all over the country and all those wishing to boost for the city will have an excellent chance here'[23]. Adding his own endorsement, a spokesperson for the newly established Tucson Chamber of Commerce called the production, 'The greatest boost for Tucson that could be imagined'[24]. In a series of feature articles and interviews from 20 June – 14 July 1912 excitedly detailing the film's preparations and production, the *Daily Star* reported on the town's response. 'Everybody entered into the spirit of it gaily and enthusiastically. Everybody went'[25]. The Southern Pacific Railway contributed the use of a train, and 300–400 extras, including a few real oldtime prospectors, reported for filming in rough clothes, carrying bedrolls and mining tools as props. To make it 'look more like the real thing', Fielding also hired 75–100 of the town's Mexican-American residents to ride burros. Drawing, perhaps, on his own memories of goldrush days in the Yukon, Fielding led this impressive entourage on a veritable expedition to Tucson's Sentinel Peak to film scenes receating an old miners' camp. Even Tucson's *Daily Star* took part in the production, lending its offices for a scene of the paper making up the 'Extra' edition, headlined 'Big Gold Strike', that touches off the goldrush[26].

This production, which publicly announced

Fielding's presence as a filmmaker, was praised by the *New York Dramatic Mirror* for 'not only being possessed of good scenes and photography but of a plot and development which is both intense and interesting'[27]. A passing of an era film, *The Sleeper* established a precedent for what were soon to become widely recognized as trademarks of Fielding's best films – intense, unconventional and increasingly strange Westerns, set not in the nineteenth century time frame of already traditional Westerns, but in the contemporary West as Fielding found it, or in another West of his own imagining, somewhere out of time.

The Sleeper established a precedent for Fielding's mode of operation as well. Having won the hearts and minds of Tucson's citizenry in the course of the film's production, and fed local boosters' dreams of the advantages of establishing a permanent studio 'from a financial as well as an advertising standpoint', Fielding packed up his troupe and moved on, with promises to return he would never keep[28].

Heading 200 miles north, he now set about the conquest of a new location, Prescott, Arizona. Site of the gold strike that led to the annexation of Arizona to help the Union finance the American Civil War, by the time of Fielding's arrival in mid-July 1912, Prescott had weathered some dramatic changes in its history as a major mining centre, territorial capital and, finally, as a mountain retreat for tuberculosis sufferers. The ambitious filmmaker found a willing and influential ally in Prescott's Chamber of Commerce secretary, Malcolm Fraser. As chairman of the Arizona Good Roads Association, Fraser, who was leading the move to build and map passable roads to connect the newest state's major cities and scenic areas, was also quick to recognize the motion picture's potential as an incomparable marketing tool in the promotion of tourism to the American Southwest.

Arriving in the Mile High City after an exhausting trip from Tucson, Fielding who, 'with his inscrutable smile and low pitched voice seems to marshall and command his cohorts without the least apparent effort', wasted no time in inviting the town to participate in the making of motion pictures and in suggesting stories 'with true local colour'[29]. After renting a house to serve as production headquarters, and beginning to set up the troupe's outdoor

stage with cantilevered diffusers, the indefatigable director set out with Malcolm Fraser to scout locations and began writing scripts. During the company's four-month stay in Prescott, Fielding produced, directed, and frequently wrote and starred in an astonishing 15 films, or roughly one one-reel production per week.

It was during his sojourn in Prescott that Fielding himself actually took to the road. His purchase of a big Buick enabled him and ten members of his troupe to cover formerly unheard-of distances in pursuit of novel stories and settings. A formidable adventure only to be undertaken by the strong of heart or, in Fielding's case, youthful experience as a mechanic, it is difficult to fathom now what automobile travel circa 1912 in the American Southwest entailed. Most of the rocky, rutted and dusty or mud hole strewn main arteries between railroad towns could hardly be called 'roads', and the first roadmaps were still on the drawing boards. Automobile machinery was temperamental, tyres were fragile, and a team of draft animals was often needed to pull even moderately steep grades. Undaunted, Fielding and his seasoned crew traveled to the scenic Granite Dells outside town, south of Prescott to the famous American Ranch, north to Skull Valley, into the forests of Spruce Mountain, further north to the ghost town of Jerome, and southeast to Camp Verde and the Verde Valley, writing scenarios and filming as they went.

At the original site of the Burnt Creek Indian Uprising, the crew filmed *The Uprising* based on local accounts of the event, with a survivor of the incident appearing in the film and serving as technical advisor[30]. Their trip to Spruce Mountain to capture footage of an actual forest fire inspired Fielding to write *The Forest Ranger*, an adventure depicting the workings of the forestry service that offered a new variation on the traditional Western cowboy hero[31]. Attending a major Indian pow-wow in the Verde Valley, which gathered together an estimated 500 Apaches and representatives of the 35 surviving members of the massacred Yavapai tribe, Fielding was inspired to make *Chief White Eagle* and *Who Is the Savage?*, two Indian films that left critics confused or downright angry. Although no footage of either film survives, a few filmstills, plot summaries and reviews suggest *Chief White Eagle* to have been a psychologically com-

Fig. 3. Romaine Fielding s *The Cringer*, filmed outside Prescott, Arizona, 1912. [Theatre Collection, Free Library of Philadelphia.]

plex exploration of the red man caught between two cultures theme, with Fielding himself donning a long-haired wig, slouch hat and frock coat to play the film's ambiguously drawn Native American anti-hero, who exacts brutal revenge for racial injustices and then, ironically, sacrifices himself to the white man's justice. Dismissed as 'senseless', *Chief White Eagle*'s reception was tame compared to the scorn that greeted *Who Is the Savage?* a gallows humour turnabout on the white-baby-kidnapped-by-savage-Indians plot, about which the *New York Dramatic Mirror*'s bewildered reviewer wrote, 'the spectator, right up to the close, does not know how to take it'[32]. Describing it as 'on the order of a travesty or serious farce', it, too, was dismissed as 'more like a nightmare than a photoplay'.[33] Although his subject matter and treatment sometimes left critics in a daze – as evidenced by the reception of *Chief White Eagle* and *Who Is the Savage?* – Fielding was developing a reputation both for his acting and for the production of films that were

beginning to have a recognizable directorial signature. Opening its review of *A Soldier's Furlough* by announcing that Romaine Fielding had just completed 'one of his favourite type of pictures', *Moving Picture World* described the film as being 'pregnant with the Indian atmosphere and the types true to the wild Southwest'[34]. Although its plot synopsis suggests a seemingly ordinary melodrama involving a soldier, Indians and a squaw man, the fact that Fielding shot *A Soldier's Furlough* partly on location at Fort Whipple, an historic frontier cavalry fort, was undoubtedly the kind of detail that enabled him to provide even a potboiler with memorable images and atmosphere.[35]

Meanwhile, Fielding's acting was being described as 'characterized by quiet forcefulness, poise and dignity'[36]. Asked by a *Motion Picture Story* interviewer about his interests, he replied, simply but revealingly, 'Character study is my favourite hobby'[37]. With *The Cringer*, Fielding brought together with particularly striking effect the combination of Western atmosphere and intense character study that was already coming to be recognized as the hallmark of a Romaine Fielding Lubin production.

Fielding drew his initial inspiration for *The Cringer* from his knowledge of the caste system that existed in Prescott – and throughout the West – between cattlemen and sheep and goat ranchers, and from images drawn from his visit to a famous angora goat ranch nearby whose herd was large enough to justify being described as spectacular.[38] As in *The Sleeper*, Fielding appears to have used contrasting settings to provide both atmosphere and visualization of his narrative tension. Film stills showing the sunlit open spaces of the goat ranch, with its ocean of soft, white animals flowing across the landscape towards the horizon, contrast with other stills from *The Cringer* focused on the visual confines of the cowboy 'civilization' beyond, and tight – literally 'in your face' – shots depicting personal confrontations. Corresponding to this visual contrast in settings, Fielding's scenario focused on issues of defining manhood that emerged through the conflict between the film's peace-loving young goat herder (played by himself) and the brutal cowboys who cruelly taunted their sensitive neighbour. To this conflict, which would soon become central to Prescott author Harold Bell Wright's bestselling novel, *When a Man's a Man*, and to such classic Western films as *Shane*, Fielding offered a uniquely intense, dare one say psychotic, psychological twist. A synopsis of *The Cringer*, reconstructed from its film release bulletin and contemporary trade magazine descriptions, offers what is probably a pale shadow of an idea: taunted for his unmanly sensitivity and brutally bullied into believing he's a coward, the film's peace-loving hero is finally driven to frenzied acts of irrational violence. Stealing a horse, he rides into town, starts setting fires, and holds up a bank. Pursued by a posse, he takes refuge in a log hut where he is gunned down. His dying words are, 'I wasn't afraid'[39].

This was hardly the image of the Western hero moviegoers of 1912 had already been conditioned to expect and, understandably, reaction to *The Cringer* was quite mixed. Highly impressed by the film's power, a leading critic cautioned nontheless that it was 'not a subject that proves exactly pleasant when brought to your close contemplation', adding that 'had it been made by a less able hand it would be utterly repulsive ... however it commands attention'[40]. Prescott citizens' response, as reflected in the film's cryptic local newspaper ad, could best be described as ambiguous. It read, simply, 'Some picture. Ask your friends'[41].

Increasingly plagued by rain in Prescott, Fielding folded his tent in mid-November and sent his crew ahead by train to their next destination, the bordertown of Nogales, Arizona, while he made the nearly 300 mile trip by car.

As in the time of Fielding's stay, the two Nogales – the sister cities of Nogales, Arizona and Nogales, Mexico – remain a study in contradictions. Today, the citizens proudly share the long and rich heritage of Hispanic-American cross-cultural cooperation that has bound the two cities together and enriched them both, while in the underground storm drains that physically connect them, orphaned 'tunnel rats', high on glue, prey on the hundreds of illegal immigrants monthly who pour into the American side from Mexico via the underground drains, or through a gaping hole in the wire fence a few hundred feet from the border marker where, eighty years earlier, Fielding and his crew took time out from the serious business of filming to mug for a few photographic souvenirs. 'Here', in the words of Mexican historian Alberto Suarez Bar-

nett, 'one resides geographically as well as mentally, culturally as well as racially, at the end of one dimension and the beginning of another'[42]. Here in Nogales, Fielding productions would come even more strongly to reflect a new kind of geography, a physical and psychological landscape where one dimension ends and another begins.

In an interview given soon after his arrival in Nogales, Fielding indicated one of the added dimensions he hoped to bring to his work by expressing his desire to focus on Mexican characters, and to produce films with pro-Mexican themes. 'Whereas the Mexican has usually been made the scapegoat in pictures heretofore', Fielding said, he now intended to 'make him a hero as well'[43]. *The Unknown*, among the first of his Nogales films, and produced from a sympathetic Mexican scenario, seems to have indeed reflected a combination of the new racial, psychological and visual dimensions that were becoming an identifiable feature of his work, as acknowledged in the *New York Dramatic Mirror*'s enthusiastic review:

> Mr. Fielding has proven his ability in the past to give us pictures that are DIFFERENT yet artistic and highly dramatic in every sense of the word. In the present case we have Mr. Fielding in the role of a foreign emigrant who makes his way to Northern Mexico to meet tragedy of a pitiful sort. The make-up is only part of the fine work this actor does to make the character powerfully real and appealing. The photography and settings are superior in every way to the usual standard: one scene in particular which draws our attention is the coming of the soldiers over the mountains. For miles we can see the single file of horses racing like a snake over the hills and down the pass. Through an act of bravery, Julio, the Unknown, is taken into the private family of Juanita's father. Juanita he afterward learns to love, though Juanita is not for his kind. He lives on at the place until hope is finally extinct and then leaves to roam out alone in the hills ...[44].

The occasional racially stereotyped potboiler still inexplicably escaped under Fielding's direction but films like *A Perilous Ride*, whose villain, attempted rapist, kidnapper and bandit, Senor Gazanga, embodied every unsavory Mexican image

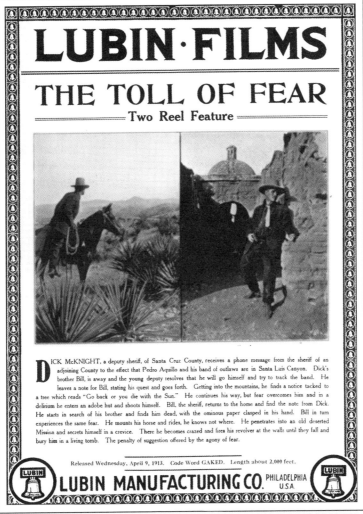

Fig. 4. Lubin release bulletin for *The Toll of Fear*, Fielding's celebrated 'one man picture' which he wrote, produced, directed and played both of the films's only two characters. One of the screen's earliest psychological Westerns, it firmly established the writer-producer-director-actor as one of the film industry's leading artists and first *auteurs*.
[Theatre Collection, Free Library of Philadelphia.]

in film history's unhappy canon, were an aberration in a succession of productions otherwise remarkable for their sensitive depiction of hispanic characters and culture[45].

Set against a background of Mexican and American troops massing along both sides of the border, *An Adventure on the Mexican Border* presented a progressive twist to the eternal triangle in which an American trooper's stormy advances on a 'bright-eyed Senorita' are rejected in favour of a Mexican army officer (Fielding) who 'wins the maid by his quiet love and kindness'[46]. A publicity photo circulated with the film suggests that, revolving on the notion that all's fair in love and war, *An Adventure on the Mexican Border* probably ended with a scene showing the two rival army men shaking hands at the international border marker and then returning to their opposing sides[47].

In addition to its romanticized scenario in which a Mexican named Ramon (played by Fielding) helps an Anglo woman from the East to regain her health and reunite with her lover, *In the Land of the Cactus*, filmed in what is now the Saguaro National Monument between Nogales and Tucson, was another of the director's 'different' films. Possibly influenced by local Papago Indian legends about the saguaro, Fielding attributed mystical healing powers to the desert through his presentation of the landscape as an otherworldly garden inhabited by these grotesque, quasi-human shaped giant cacti[48]. An appreciation for the film's strange beauty and power were perhaps best suggested by the *New York Dramatic Mirror*'s reviewer who wrote, 'Because of the theme and rare treatment it receives, this picture, acted and directed by Romaine Fielding, is of positive success among those who care for a picture of depth and originality. The camerawork is beautiful with settings that create a true atmosphere'[49].

Not even the power and strangeness of *In the Land of the Cactus* and his previous work offered any preparation for one of Fielding's next and most celebrated films, *The Toll of Fear*, an intense and disturbing psychological Western he shot outside Nogales, in and around the ruins of the abandoned 17th century Tumacacori Mission. The mission's crumbling walls, surrounded by empty landscape and a scattering of graves marked with weather-beaten wooden crosses, paid mute testimony to the hostile landscape's victory over repeated attempts to civilize it. This no-man's-land inspired Fielding to write a scenario as pitiless as the setting. The resulting film offered a view of the West as audiences had never experienced it before.

In addition to his choice of location, Fielding quickly established a brooding tone of isolation and danger in *The Toll of Fear* by peopling its landscape with only two characters, deputy sheriff Dick McKnight and his brother, Sheriff Bill. To underscore this, Fielding played both roles. The film opened in the sheriff's office with Dick McKnight taking a telephone message alerting him to a marauding band of outlaws. Resolving to track the bandits himself in his brother's absence, Dick leaves a note for Bill and heads out alone. From the moment Dick enters the landscape, the film's tone becomes increasingly strange:

Getting into the mountains, he finds a note tacked to a tree which reads, 'Go back or you die with the Sun'. He continues his way, but fear overcomes him and in a delirium he enters an adobe hut and shoots himself. Bill returns ... starts in search of his brother and finds him dead, with the ominous paper clasped in his hand. Bill in turn experiences the same fear. He mounts his horse and rides, he knows not where. He penetrates into an old deserted Mission and secrets himself in a crevice. There he becomes crazed and fires his revolver at the walls until they fall and bury him in a living tomb: the penalty of suggestion offered by the agony of fear[50].

Written, produced, directed by and starring Fielding in both roles, *The Toll of Fear* was hailed throughout the industry as 'the one man picture'[51]. It caused a sensation for its bizarre scenario and characterizations, and as an audacious technical *tour de force*. With no dialogue after the story's opening phone message, and probably no more than a few titles to convey interior monologues, this extraordinary two-reel feature relied entirely on the strength of Fielding's acting and the suggestive images offered up by his choice of setting, which Fielding self-consciously used to transform this unique Western into a brooding meditation on the psychological power of the western landscape. Duly impressed, the *New York Dramatic Mirror*'s critic wrote, 'Truly it was a daring undertaking that Mr. Fielding mapped out when he sought to utilize an abstract principle in a one man picture and drive that principle home'[52]. A 'one man picture' about the power of isolation, a silent film about the power of silence, *The Toll of Fear* was called 'a monument to the talent of Romaine Fielding'[53], who had now been clearly recognized not merely as a lowly filmmaker, but as an artist.

In discussing Fielding's stay in Nogales, mention must be made of his own adventures on the Mexican border during the Battle of Nogales. A brief skirmish in the long and bloody Mexican Revolution, the battle erupted on 13 March 1913. Seeking permission to go behind the lines from Col. Emilio Kosterlitzky, leader of the federalist troops defending the city from being taken by insurgents, Fielding was denied. Undaunted, he festooned his

Fig. 5. In addition to providing some exciting on-screen action, beginning production in Silver City, New Mexico with the filming of a barroom brawl in the city's business district also served to advertise the Fielding troupe's arrival and pique local interest in the company's upcoming productions. [Silver City Museum.]

auto with the Geneva Cross and drove behind the lines. Although it's still unknown whether Fielding ever actually attended the Columbia College of Physicians and Surgeons or was merely a true believer in his own publicity, he was reported to have made numerous trips across the border to transport the wounded from both sides and, working closely with pioneer physician and diplomat Dr. Albert Gustetter, was listed as one of the four Red Cross surgeons who treated the casualties. In the company of revolutionary leaders Juan Cabral and General Alvaro Obregon, he also shot a reported 12 hours of documentary footage while he and his cameraman dodged bullets and their camera took a number of hits[54]. Of this footage, only a reel of *Mexican War Pictures* survives, a compilation of fragmentary moving vignettes which, despite their incompleteness, provide valuable historical footage of the battle from both sides, the leaders featuring Obregon who would become the first President of Mexico, and the Red Cross surgeons, including Drs. Gustetter and Fielding, treating the wounded[55]. Changing light conditions indicate that the footage was shot over an extended period of time and a mystery remains as to the fate of the other footage and why, at least by Lubin, it was never released. Did Siegmund Lubin's pacifist sentiments prevent him from releasing it, as they later prevented him from showing some of the earliest documentary footage of the first World War shot by his cameraman in Belgium? Were excerpts passed off, ironically, as staged battle footage and cut into some of Fielding's dramatic productions about the Revolution? We may never know. One thing that is known is the profound effect the Battle of Nogales experience had on Fielding's personal view of war, a view that was about to be reflected in a searing picture entitled *The Clod*, filmed a few months later in Silver City, New Mexico, and in two five-reel features, the deadly serious *The Horrors of War* and the sardonically humorous *The Battle of Gettysgoat*, both filmed the following year during the troupe's brief stay in Galveston, Texas.

At the urging of his half-brother, Robert, a mining engineer for the Chino Copper Company in Santa Rita, New Mexico, Fielding moved his company from Nogales to the former hometown of Billy the Kid, Silver City, New Mexico. After a grueling trip in which his two Buicks kept breaking down, leaving most of the company's equipment stranded in the desert, the inexhaustable director immediately set to work producing four one-reelers and four two-reelers during their six week stay between late May and early July.

As much to elicit the townspeople's excitement and future cooperation by showing them a movie crew at work as to capture authentic looking footage, Fielding took the crew down to one of the city's main streets, transformed a local business into the Red Onion Saloon, and proceeded to stage a rousing bar room brawl for a film he was envisioning as a 'romance'[56]. Footage showing the awe-inspiring giant steam shovels and other aspects of the working's of the Chino Mine, one of the world's first industrialized open pit copper mines (and the future site of the labour strike by Mexican-American mine workers that inspired the blacklisted film *Salt of the Earth*), was also taken for this curious romance[57]. To this, Fielding injected elements of stylization that would become increasingly important to his later work. The film's story is an obvious romantic fairy-tale in which a mysterious stranger with noble intentions and deadly aim comes to the rescue of a modern-day princess, the mining company president's daughter. Vaguely sensing Fielding's attempt to present a figure who self-consciously embodied all the qualities of the quintessential

Western hero, the *Moving Picture World*'s reviewer described *The Man From the West*, the two-reel film that resulted, as 'one of Romaine Fielding's strange stories, picturing one of those virile characters of which Fielding is a prototype'[58]. Although *The Man From the West* no longer survives, the self-consciousness of Fielding's approach is suggested not only by the film's title, but most obviously by Fielding's creation of a courtly hero with no name, known only as 'The Gentleman', and by the half-fairytale, half-biblical, 'once upon a time' tone of his descriptive text for the film's release bulletin: 'A strange man came out of the East and settled in New Mexico. No one knew his history but he was respected by all. He was a dead shot and a law unto himself...'[59]

Perhaps the most striking of all Fielding's Silver City productions, however, was *The Clod*, described in its release bulletin with uncharacteristic understatement as 'A Strong Two-Reel Feature'[60].

Local newspaper accounts of *The Clod*'s production focused on the frighteningly convincing battle scenes Fielding was staging on Chihuahua Hill with 200 extras costumed as *insurrectos* and *federales*, and on the old adobe Fielding consigned to the flames in his relentless quest for realism[61]. Coming off his experiences treating the wounded at Nogales, however, Fielding now had much more to say about war than could be told with gunpowder and smoke. A description of *The Clod* taken from its release bulletin suggests that this feature's real power lay not in its spectacle, but in its finely detailed and impassioned depiction of the toll war takes on the innocent, as shown through the personal tragedy it wreaks on Pedro Mendez, a simple-minded Mexican peasant caught up in a revolution he cannot understand. Recruited by the revolutionists, Mendez (played by Fielding), unable to understand what it's all about, returns to his home instead. War soon finds him, however, as passing soldiers confiscate his horses and intimidate him into submission. The next day brings rebels who raid his farm and carry off his chickens and cattle. Another wave of troops takes over his house, making it into a barricade. His house is shot to pieces and his wife is killed in the crossfire. Carrying his invalid mother outside, he returns for the body of his dead wife, only to find upon reaching his mother again that she is now dead, too. 'His dormant passion and strength is aroused, his wife and mother dead, his farm in

Fig. 6. Romaine Fielding on horseback, with his crew and cast of local extras on location along the Mexican border at Chihuahua Hill outside Silver City, New Mexico, 1913, filming *The Clod*, 'perhaps the most vivid impression of the Mexican Revolution that could be shown'.
[Library of Congress; Motion Picture, Broadcasting & Recorded Sound Division.]

ashes, he wrenches a gun from a dead soldier and plunges into the fight ... attacks anyone, not knowing which side he is fightng. At last he is shot and staggering to the place where his mother lies, rolls over on his face dead'[62].

'The photoplay is fearfully and wonderfully made and cannot fail to leave a strong impression', wrote a *Moving Picture World* reviewer so impressed by *The Clod*'s realism as to believe it was, indeed, filmed on Mexican soil, with hundreds of Mexican federals and guerillas to assist the Lubin players[63]. In a review headlined '"The Clod" Will Long Be a Classic', it was an anonymous newspaper critic, however, who came closest to finding words for what Fielding had expressed so eloquently through motion pictures. Attempting to convey why *The Clod* was 'perhaps the most vivid impression of the Mexican Revolution that could be shown', the reviewer captured Fielding's intent with a simple description of how, just before death, the Clod realizes 'that war is merely a succession of events in which the physical power of one man or

men over others in stealing and destroying is employed to the blotting out of happiness of innocent men'[64]. A future wartime generation of writers and philosophers would coin a term for this vision of the abyss; they'd call it the Absurd.

Fielding's next stay, in Las Vegas, New Mexico, a former stop along the Santa Fe Trail, nestled between high desert to the south and the photogenic cliffs and pine forests of Gallinas Canyon just outside of town, provided the inspiration for a collection of particularly odd or overtly symbolic films, including *The Harmless One* and *The Rattlesnake*, two of his most audacious productions.

One of only two New Mexico cities with electric streetcars in 1913, Las Vegas, with its extensive trolley system, presented Fielding with the opportunity to film a unique and extraordinarily harrowing chase scene. Around this dangerous chase, he wove a scenario featuring an insane young man (Fielding) whose infatuation with a streetcar motorman's fiance brings him to kidnap her by hijacking the trolley[65]. A social message picture in the guise

Fig. 7. Noted for their strangeness, Fielding Westerns often ventured into the uncharted frontiers where alien settings and psychological aberration converge. *The Rattlesnake – A Phychical Species*, filmed on location in Las Vegas, New Mexico, was one of his most bizarre as well as successful efforts at combining these elements. [Theatre Collection, Free Library of Philadelphia.]

of a thriller, *The Harmless One* attracted much attention. Reporting that the film was honoured by being chosen by the Orpheum Theaters throughout the country for showing to all their 'exclusive vaudeville patrons', and that many newspapers were according Fielding as much stature as the live headlining acts, the *New York Dramatic Mirror* concluded by calling *The Harmless One* 'a great moral and educational subject, showing in a dramatic manner the fallacy of letting "harmlessly" insane people roam at large'[66].

The Rattlesnake – A Psychical Species, a bizarre Western whose Mexican setting introduced an added note of exoticism, also centred around Fielding's vivid depiction of an aberrant psychological state. 'Mr. Fielding writes his plays from the scenic material surrounding his locations', wrote a local reporter attempting to describe the mysterious symbiosis of landscape and psychology that inspired *The Rattlesnake*. 'While making a trip over the country ... he noticed a location that would naturally be adaptable for the habitation of a rattlesnake. Having in mind other connecting thoughts, he finally selected those pieces which would be necessary for the production and wrote the scenario'[67]. The resulting two-reel feature, one of the director's eight known surviving films, is at once a striking study of psychological obsession and a fascinating example of Fielding's symbolic use of the landscape.

As the film opens, 'happy Tony', a carefree vaquero (played by Fielding) is in love with Inez. Scenes of the couple's romantic idyll are set against a verdant landscape in which the lovers are usually shown framed by the hollyhocks in Inez's garden. A jealous suitor tries to kill Tony, but is struck down by a rattlesnake. Out of gratitude for saving his life, Tony adopts the snake as a pet and soon begins to absorb the reptile's characteristics. Repulsed by the changes in Tony, Inez rejects him. The setting now moves to the desert where years are shown to pass imperceptibly as Tony, banished from the garden, lives with and becomes possessed by the snake, exiled from love and human society. Juxtaposing long shots of the rocky wasteland with extreme close-ups of Tony and the snake, Fielding reinforces the correspondence between the barren landscape and Tony's mental and physical desolation. Inez, meanwhile, has married an American surveyor and raised a young daughter. Jealous of her husband, Tony moves to poison him with the snake, but kills the rattlesnake instead when it threatens to strike the couple's child. In killing the snake, his reason returns. The film concludes with a scene showing Tony, restored to sanity and now a beloved family friend, being warmly greeted by the little family in the couple's garden; a scene once more framed by Inez's hollyhocks.

Set at a place in the physical and mental landscape where the natural and supernatural intersect, *The Rattlesnake*, like so much of Fielding's other work, was applauded for its realism. In its review headlined, '*The Rattlesnake* Realistic', the *New York Dramatic Mirror* praised the originality in conception and development Fielding applied to a story based on 'the venom of jealousy', as well as the director's 'hand of a careful worker, a master of technique in the development of the atmosphere to the last essence'[68]. Defending some of the film's more grotesque scenes, which 'half-offended some as being raw', an anonymous critic who considered them worthy of high praise speculated, 'It is not, for some reason, a pleasant thing to look squarely at life and ... since all our art is cooked, true realism always seems raw. At his best Mr. Fielding is head and shoulders above nearly all other producers we know'[69].

Fielding concluded his stay in Las Vegas with *The Golden God*, a film whose making was a dramatic illustration of his charismatic leadership, in combination with the enthusiastic cooperation of local movers and shakers, in the service of motion picture production as both art and civic promotion.

Weeks of almost daily feature stories in the *Daily Optic* on the making of *The Golden God* present a seemingly incredible behind-the-scenes account of Fielding's recruitment of thousands of extras, and ultimately, the participation of the state constabulary and the National Guard in mob and battle scenes for what was to be a five-reel futuristic epic (set in 1950), loosely based on his friend Jack London's novel *The Iron Heel*, that envisioned a coming holocaust brought on by the clashing forces of labour and capital. An airplane, the first ever seen in the state of New Mexico, was brought in from Texas to depict warfare of the future – aerial reconnaissance and bombardment – in all its horror. Southwestern dignitaries and busloads of extras and spectators came from across the entire state via special excursions arranged by the Las Vegas Commercial Club[70]. Despite the picture's probably inflated budget estimates – a reported $50,000 – *The Golden God* was nonetheless one of the most expensive productions of its time[71]. Although the Lubin Company spared no expense in shipping a trainload of costumes, props and ammunition to its most celebrated director, a film on the scale of *The Golden God* could never have been undertaken on location without the enormous local support of townspeople and important allies like Ludwig Ilfield, heir to the largest dry goods supply business in the Southwest, who was virtually able to put the town's and state's resources at Fielding's disposal.

Judged too 'inflammable' by the censors, *The Golden God* was never released[72]. Before some of its footage could be recycled into other films, it joined the thousands of films lost in the 13 June 1914 Philadelphia film vault explosion that destroyed the master negatives of every Lubin Company film produced up to that time.

Meanwhile, Fielding and his crew wintered in Galveston, Texas where they made two more ill-fated five-reel productions, the Mexican Revolution-inspired drama *The Horrors of War* and *The Battle of Gettysgoat*, an extended satire on the revolution, which featured 1000 soldiers from Fort Crockett assisting in a scenario that revolved around two 300-pound revolutionaries, with Fielding as Colonel Furiosa, 'the Interchangeable Spy'[73]. Following a get-together with his old buddies Jack London and Rex Beach, and a brief excursion to Mexico, Fielding left to set up yet another new location in the Colorado Rockies at Colorado Springs[74]. There in the strange and extraordinarily beautiful 'Garden of the Gods', he settled in what he came to call his 'Castle of Dreams'[75], the 60-room Glen Eyrie Castle of Colorado Springs founder General William Palmer. Fielding set to work writing a series of short comedies showcasing a recent addition to the troupe, celebrated vaudeville comedian Eddie Sedgwick, and started production on five multiple-reel features at the same time[76].

Most notable of these Colorado Springs productions was *The Eagle's Nest*, a venerable stage-play adapted for the screen by Fielding and Harry Chandlee, co-starring Fielding and the play's author, Edwin Arden. In addition to the expense of purchasing the rights to the play and Arden's services, Lubin added to its heavy investment in the project by sending 220 players from Philadelphia and footing Fielding's bill for hiring local stuntriders and extras who swelled the cast to 500[77]. Local accounts of the film's production marveled at Fielding's unsparing quest for realism, ranging from his extensive search for authentic costumes and properties to the effort and danger involved in lowering Arden over a precipice, with two cameramen suspended immediately below him, to shoot one scene alongside an actual eagle's nest[78]. Glowing reviews suggest that these production values were not in vain. 'This famous film has probably had the longest and most successful run of any motion picture thrown on the screen and has been shown oftener to the same audiences than any other set of reels made ... ', wrote an anonymous newspaper critic. 'It combines a fascinating love story, an abundance of wild, exciting western realism, and the most beautiful scenery that has ever been worked into a motion picture'[79]. Headlined 'Romaine Field-

ing's Art Displayed in Lubin's *Eagle's Nest* ...', the *New York Dramatic Mirror*'s review ranked the film 'among the biggest and most impressive of Western photoplay spectacles'. Praising the film's power and Fielding's mastery of switchback editing and cut-ins to build dramatic tension, the critic singled out scenes depicting the massacre of an emigrant wagon train. 'Alternating with panoramas showing the approach of Indians along the mountain defiles, and the pitiable inadequacy of the pioneers' defences in the centre of the great plain, are close-ups to emphasize significant personal incidents in the tragedy'[80].

Suddenly called to Philadelphia by Lubin for what was to be an assignment to Europe to film documentary footage of the first World War, Fielding reluctantly left Colorado Springs promising, as he had in Nogales and Silver City and Las Vegas, that he'd return. He never did. During his brief stay at Lubin headquarters, the versatile Fielding demonstrated his surprising technical expertise in helping Lubin engineer Edward Simons create the special dramatic effects for one of early cinema's most spectacular locomotive crashes. Using two additional locomotives as pushers to increase the velocity of the crash, Fielding spotted twelve cameramen behind protective shields to capture the colliding locomotives as they collapsed in on each other in a steaming wreckage of twisted iron. The stunning footage was edited into four Lubin productions, including two of Fielding's Colorado Springs features – *The Valley of Lost Hope* and *In the Hour of Disaster* – as well as *A Partner to Progress*, the only surviving episode of actor-director Arthur Johnson's *Beloved Adventurer* serial[81].

Instead of sending him to Europe, Lubin charged Fielding with two imposing assignments. The first, development of a portable lighting generator, was to be field-tested by Fielding in filming Lubin's next Western spectacle, *The Great Divide*, at the Grand Canyon. Fielding's other assignment was to design the collapsible studio he would use in his projected travels as the head of Lubin's new 'Round the World Company'. Fielding accepted the challenge. Within a month, reports of his successful development of the collapsible studio appeared from Phoenix, the opening stop on his Round the World Company's projected two-year tour. Completely portable and able to fit in a sixty-foot bag-

Fig. 8. Not content to typecast himself as the same character in film after film in the manner of his better known Western colleagues Broncho Billy Anderson, Tom Mix and William S. Hart, the cameo portraits bordering this *New York Dramatic Mirror* advertisement suggest how the restless Fielding reveled in portraying an unending variety of characters ranging from the heroic to the cowering, cringing and insane. [The Author.]

gage car, it was capable of being erected in six hours and struck in three[82]. Meanwhile, 'In the twilight bed of the Grand Canyon, in caves that man's eye has never explored, the new portable electric plant devised by Romaine Fielding will give the necessary light for scenes which otherwise would be denied the world'[83]. Developed from one of his high-powered Mitchell cars, Fielding's portable electric plant boasted equipment for running wires and the capability of powering a 12-inch naval searchlight with the capacity to generate 4,500,000 candlepower[84]. Announced soon after the 1915 opening of Carl Laemmle's Universal City,

the appearance of these technical developments that promised to revolutionize location film production coincided, ironically, with the trend towards moving film production indoors into the studio, and with consolidation of the motion picture industry in Hollywood. These trends and the ongoing anti-trust suit against the Motion Picture Patents Company, of which Lubin was a member, were mere stormclouds on the horizon, however, as Fielding spent the summer and early autumn of 1915 travelling throughout Arizona filming what were to be the last of his unique on-location Westerns.

Working in the over 100 degrees Fahrenheit

Fig. 9. Writer, Producer, Director, Leading Man and Character Actor, Romaine Fielding, 1914.
[Wisconsin Center for Film and Theater Research.]

summer temperatures around Phoenix and the Salt River Valley most likely inspired the harsher image of the desert that emerged from such Phoenix-based productions as *The Great Lone Land* and *When Souls Are Tried* that presented the desert as the crucible in which love and the human will are subjected to the ultimate test[85]. *A Desert Honeymoon*, a Western perhaps unequaled in its time for its passion and erotic intensity, would later be reminiscent of King Vidor and David O. Selznick's frenzied *Duel in the Sun* in its presentation of the desert as a tempestuous physical landscape reflecting the stormy psychological landscape of its inhabitants. 'Answering the call of the desert waste', the film's upstanding Eastern hero becomes intoxicated with tequila and his lust for a Mexican dancing girl. In a drunken rage, he kills his best friend over the girl and is condemned to death. The girl refuses to leave him and they determine to die together. *A Desert Honeymoon* closes as 'they enter the trackless desert and the screen darkens on the two lovers half buried by the windswept sand'[86]. As was now typical with new Fielding releases, critics struggled for words to describe this Wagnerian love-death in the sand. 'In dramatic intensity, character portrayal and power,' wrote Lynde Denig, 'this three-part drama so far excels the average Western subject that there are few points of comparison'[87]. The stay in Phoenix inspired other utterly unique productions. 'Night photography and unusual camera effects are responsible for a feeling of a strange story in a strange land', wrote a *New York Dramatic Mirror* critic trying to evoke the oddity of Fielding's *A Species of Mexican Man*, an action-adventure romance featuring a Mexican revolutionary hero destined to become the President of Mexico[88]. As in *The Man From the West*, Fielding made his hero a man with no name, a messianic deliverer, in a film whose mythic overtones were suggested by his text for its release bulletin – possibly echoed in its opening titles – which read: 'A "Man" born of woman in a republic of darkness, walked straight and true, preaching the doctrine of light, intelligence and progressiveness, and thereby developed a strength and manhood that the people respected ...'[89].

The Great Divide, Fielding's six-reel feature filmed on location at the Grand Canyon and one of his most ambitious undertakings, was also his last Lubin Western and his last significant film shot on location in the Southwest. Adapted from Anthony P. Kelly's famous stage play, the film starred House Peters and Ethel Clayton in a story whose western setting was symbolic of 'the great divide' separating East and West, culture, class and gender. Although missing an entire reel plus other sections of missing or badly decomposed footage, the surviving film still presents House Peters and Ethel Clayton giving understated and highly believable, 'realistic' performances, evocative western settings, and several nighttime scenes taken with the aid of Fielding's portable generator, that convey a suggestion of the film's original grandeur.

On 15 September 1915, Siegmund Lubin received word of the federal court's decision to dissolve the Motion Picture Patents Company. With most of the company's cash tied up in expensive feature films under production, and studios not only in Philadelphia but spread across the country, Lubin struggled to recover financial equilibrium. Consolidating operations in Philadelphia, he called his regional studio directors – including Fielding – in from the field. It was a difficult choice for the filmmaker who had become a public figure in the Southwest with the stature to star Governor George Hunt, the first governor of Arizona, in one of his features and to be called upon to offer the opening benediction for the giant Roosevelt Dam, the nation's first federal water reclamation project[90]. A homeless man in search of an identity, Fielding had finally found both in the open spaces of the Southwest. In a full-page feature article headlined, 'Phoenix Always My Home Says Romaine Fielding, Arizona's Movie Pioneer', Lubin's premier filmmaker announced his decision to leave Lubin rather than leave his beloved West[91]. *The Great Divide* was nearly completed; Fielding returned the footage to Lubin's Philadelphia headquarters where it was finished and ultimately credited to Edgar Lewis. Unknowingly, his decision to leave the Lubin Company marked the end of Fielding's career as one of the motion picture industry's first acknowledged artists. Finding short-term assignments as a hack director until 1923, he kicked around the country doing an assortment of odd jobs before ending his days in Hollywood as a character actor. He died in 1927, leaving behind a wife, two known sons, an unknown number of illegitimate children, and an estate of $8.00.

Since Andrew Sarris first coined the term, critics have debated the qualifications that entitle a filmmaker to be designated an 'auteur'. By uneasy consensus, there is general agreement that an auteur must have a high degree of creative control and have created a body of works identifiable by their recurrent themes, images and technique. Judging by these criteria, Fielding would easily have qualified. Except for limitations imposed by the industry's (self) censorship board – which censored his *The Golden God* – during his four years with Lubin, Fielding was one of the motion picture industry's rare filmmakers working with complete artistic control and a practically unlimited expense account. At a time when the emphasis was starting to shift away from jack-of-all-trades production personnel towards the studio system of job specialization and departmentalization, Fielding's mobility and geographic distance from the Lubin Company's home studio necessarily gave him the responsibility – and the extraordinary freedom – to control every creative aspect of his films, from production to scenario writing and selection, directing, casting and performance. In addition, working under the umbrella of Lubin, one of the world's largest and most eccentrically managed film companies, offered Fielding a virtually unprecedented carte blanche for the lavish expenses necessary to actualize the fruits of his fertile imagination. Needing only to ask for trainloads of costumes, props and ammunition, an aeroplane, and money to hire the entire town of Las Vegas, New Mexico and busloads of additional extras for *The Golden God*, $1000 per month to rent Glen Eyrie Castle, the enormous expenses involved in filming *The Eagle's Nest* ... he told an astonished reporter, 'Expense is nothing to the Lubin Company, so long as the company gets results'[92].

In public talks and interviews given throughout his Lubin years, Fielding offered occasional clues to the impetus driving, as *Photoplay* described it, 'the fiery intensity and consuming ambition with which he works toward still higher goals of artistic achievement'[93]. Indicating a rare consciousness of his position as a pioneer in an emerging, and paradoxically technological art form, he told *New York Telegraph* film correspondent Carolyn Lowrey, 'After the mechanical end has been fully mastered, there will come a greater consideration for the highest form of directorship'[94]. Revealing the

unusually high regard in which he held his audience, a regard which he manifested in productions that required an exceptional level of maturity from his spectators, he continued, 'The public is an exacting mistress. The director who ignores or overlooks this fact makes a great mistake'[95]. In an interview headlined 'Says Limit of Photoplay Development Has Not Yet Been Reached', he said, 'Nobody appreciates more than myself the moral responsibility resting on the shoulders of a director of motion pictures. It is a pretty high calling for any man. Editors and newspapermen are called molders of public opinion. I think the motion picture director is in the same class'[96]. Catching him during production of *The Golden God* in Las Vegas, correspondent Gertrude Price concluded her particularly perceptive report with the observation, 'Romaine Fielding's idea in writing and producing pictures is to teach, elevate or inspire his audiences ... And in most of the subjects there seems to be either a poetic theme or a mystical vein'[97].

In many ways, the body of work Fielding produced during his four-year filmmaking odyssey for Lubin can be seen as a kind of metafilm in which recurring themes, images and styles of presentation were woven together in an extended meditation on the West as both a mental and geographical frontier. The journey through newly settled territories outside the old bounds of American society offered him opportunities to explore progressive social issues ranging from capital punishment in *A Western Governor's Humanity*, to Capital's exploitation of Labor in *The Golden God*; from *The Harmless One*'s depiction of potential dangers posed by the supposedly 'harmless' insane persons idly wandering the streets, to war's victimization of the world's ordinary 'clods' who ask nothing more from life than peace and happiness. Harbouring considerable respect and a romantic fascination for Hispanic culture, Fielding's continual return to Mexican settings, the portrayal of Mexican heros, and his penchant for costuming himself in the striking black and silver outfit of old fashioned Mexican vaqueros, injected an element of exoticism into his Westerns and, most importantly, marked a major rehabilitation of the Mexican screen image.

Rarely reflecting an interest in the ordinary, Fielding films continually demonstrated his preoccupation with extremes. In films exploring questions

The Higher Ideals of
The Silent Drama—

—Attained

Romaine Fielding

The Realist

Current Releases—
Hiawanda's Cross
The Harmless One
(Selected for all the Orpheum Vaudeville
Theatres)
When Mountain and Valley Meet
The Penance of Blind Power

Managing Director
LUBIN NEW MEXICO CC.
LAS VEGAS, N. M.

Fig. 10. Advertisement from the *New York Dramatic Mirror*, December 1913. Fielding's intense psychological characterizations, his use of authentic Western locations, and his relentless attention to detail earned him a reputation as 'the man who put the "real" in realism'. [The Author.]

of masculine identity, his heros were invariably at the fringes, either society's victims and social outcasts like the Clod and the Cringer, or supermen like Myton Power, respected and hated as the 'Golden God', the mysterious 'Gentleman' from *The Man From the West*, and the nameless deliverer in *A Species of Mexican Man*. Time and time again, the word most often applied to his films was 'strange'. Writing about *A Species of Mexican Man*, the *New York Dramatic Mirror*'s reviewer offered a strong sense of what set them apart:

> Romaine Fielding pictures are different because he makes of his lead – usually played by himself – a unique figure. It is a figure that looks different and thinks in superlative terms ... Add to such a figure a country as bizarre as the man himself, a land of stone and cacti, cacti that

grow in strength and weird shapes in a land that photographs beautifully because of the clear atmosphere and we have an almost ideal character and topographical combination...'[98]

With *The Toll of Fear, In the Land of the Cactus, The Rattlesnake*, and dozens of his other works, Fielding was quite possibly the only filmmaker of his time to repeatedly attribute overtly symbolic qualities to the Western landscape. With his nineteenth century Romantic's approach to mood and setting (a sometimes gothic approach that mixed equal parts of the English Lake Poets with Edgar Allan Poe), he drew inspiration from the natural landscape, and especially the everchanging desert, in his quest for physical correspondences to the mysterious landscape of the human psyche. An avowed Christian Scientist, Fielding's fascination with the power of human thought resulted in making a number of his most celebrated films – most notably *The Rattlesnake* and *The Toll of Fear* – into explorations of uncharted realms of obsession and the final frontiers of the human mind.

The first serious recognition of motion picture directors as artists seems to have started in 1913 with the push towards legitimization of film as an art form that began in earnest with the advent of imported foreign feature films, independent production of American-made features, and the opening of the first of the great motion picture palaces catering to a middle and high-class audience. The filmmakers leading the charge were D.W. Griffith, perhaps film history's most widely recognized and studied auteur, and Romaine Fielding, one of its most obscure.

Two exceptionally versatile and ambitious men in search of recognition as artists, both Fielding and Griffith, like most of the industry's early pioneers, entered motion pictures in the modest hopes of merely finding a steady job. Among the first to recognize motion pictures' enormous potential for development, however, they soon wholeheartedly hitched their professional and personal destinies to its future. 1913 marked a turning point in both their careers, signaled by Griffith's resignation from Biograph in search of greater artistic freedom, and the release of *The Toll of Fear*, Fielding's celebrated one man picture. As Fielding neared completion of his mammoth spectacle, *The Golden God*, Griffith was making preparations to film his epic feature of the South, *The Clansman*, that would change motion picture history when it was released as *The Birth of a Nation*. Both filmmakers' quests for professional recognition culminated at the end of the year with a flurry of trade magazine ads giving star treatment to the director. On 29 November, *Moving Picture World* carried an ad announcing, 'Romaine Fielding's following is distinct, individual and faithful – people who appreciate the finer things in the screen drama. 'The Belasco of the Photoplay' Writes his own plays –, Plays the leads –, Directs his own productions –, Manages his own company'[99]. Taking out his now famous full-page ad in 13 December's *New York Dramatic Mirror* headlined 'Producer of all Great Biograph Successes', Griffith credited himself with 'revolutionizing Motion Pic-

ture Drama and founding the modern technique of the art'[100]. A Fielding *Dramatic Mirror* ad quickly followed that week announcing, 'The Highest Ideals of the Silent Drama Attained – Romaine Fielding, the Realist'[101]. Albeit self-proclaimed, the age of the Great Director had dawned.

In an art form so dependent on the skills of a small army of artists and craftspeople, credit for the finished work has always been a difficult question, a question compounded by time that has now taken its toll on the films themselves, surviving paper records, and on living memory. With an intriguing feature article he wrote for the *New York Dramatic Mirror* entitled 'Who Gets the Credit'?, Romaine Fielding became one of the first American filmmakers to formally address this prickly question of motion picture authorship[102]. Looking back over his own career as writer, director and player to offer a thoughtful and 'Surprisingly Frank Article on the Relative Importance of Author, Director, Player – and Press Agent – By "One Who Knows" and Who is Not Afraid to Speak', he offered a fascinating self-critique of his own work as well. Acknowledging that '… my observation assures me that the director, in the majority of cases, is more largely responsible for the quality of a film play than any other one person having a hand in its production and … closely defined, is like the finisher in a suit factory: he does the rounding up, builds up here and takes in there, putting on the final touches, making of the garment a perfect product', Fielding continued his examination of the equally valuable contributions often made by a film's writer or actors with illustrations from his own work in all these capacities. Venturing that 'the photoplaywright, in my candid opinion, has been the goat of the film industry', in citing his own work as writer of *The Toll of Fear* as deserving of the real credit for that film's success, he wrote, 'Now, the great problem in this play lay with the author … A director who is purely a director, has little time to take an abstract idea and drive it through; the scenario writer must furnish the plot, the incident, the situation. It would never do for him to furnish the idea alone'. Turning to acting, he continued, 'On the other hand, take *The Clod* … it was the finest piece of acting I have done during my career. I directed the picture and I had a hand in the development of the plot – but I should have, perhaps, accomplished quite as much with any other director at the helm. The plot was minor – the character was the thing.' Referring to *A Dash for Liberty* as an example of a film whose mediocre scenario and sketchy characterization were redeemed by good direction, Fielding quoted the critic who observed, '"It shows Romaine Fielding at his best as a producer, but as a writer, though very clever, not in his most human vein". He was right. The play was all direction with the incidental business, the little effects which only the director can furnish … I played one of the lead roles … besides writing and directing it, but knew, as did my friend the reviewer, that it was the direction which counted'. Citing *The Weaker Mind* as an ideal film in which the levels of acting, scripting and directing were all in balance, the filmmaker renowned for his excesses concluded, 'It is striking the happy medium … It's that total impression which is more to be sought than all else: and once achieved, there should be no question of where to give credit. It would be director, actor, author, camera man, and so on down the line through the factory'.

In his final words on the subject of Who Gets the Credit?, referring to publicity, 'the magic wand which helps to sell ability and soap', Fielding referenced earlier comments about the power of publicity to make and break careers when he added,'But I still maintain that we must not forget that there are kings and, what is more, the MAKERS OF KINGS'. With less than a year left to enjoy his virtually unprecedented creative autonomy made possible by the enormous Lubin Company resources at his command, he could not have known how prophetic these words were to be. Without the financial backing and able publicity department of his Philadelphia-based 'Maker of Kings', Romaine Fielding, one of the motion picture industry's first auteurs, returned to the obscurity from which, only four years earlier, he originally emerged.✪

Acknowledgements. I would like to thank the virtually hundreds of film and local historians, ranging over an expanse of time and geography, who have made this article possible. Of special note are Geraldine Duclow, curator of the Lubin materials at the Free Library of Philadelphia; Robert Anderson whose unpublished master's thesis on Fielding scouted the terrain; and Arizona film historian John LaDue, who generously shared research and his knowledge of the Southwest. Special thank yous must also go to Emily and William Armstrong Jr., Siegmund Lubin's granddaughter and great grandson, whose donation and preservation of the Lubin Scrapbooks has at last made this irreplaceable material available to scholars; to the late Romaine Fielding, Jr., who provided valuable background on his father; to Kaaren Fielding Boothroyd, Fielding's granddaughter, who has generously loaned me his scrapbook and family history and given me her own thoughtful perspective; and most importantly to Dr Mike Woal, my most insightful critic and enthusiastic companion in thousands of miles of travel to the locations used over 80 years ago by Romaine Fielding.

Notes

1. Robert Grau, *The Theatre of Science* (Broadway Publishing Co., 1914), 486–487.

2. *New York Morning Telegraph*, 13 November 1913, n.p.; *Motion Picture Story Magazine*, September and October 1913.

3. Norbert Lusk, 'Memories On My Own Screen', *Picture Play*, November 1922, 98.

4. *Motion Picture Magazine*, June 1912, 130.

5. Henry Russell Wray, 'Artist, Author, Director, Painter', *Motion Picture*, November 1914, 101

6. 'Romaine Fielding, of the Lubin Company', *Motion Picture*, June 1912, 130.

7. Romaine Fielding, Jr., telephone interview with the author, 16 April 1980 and subsequent telephone interviews.

8. 'A Dozen Lubin Favorites', *NYDM*. 31 January 1912: 55.

9. This number of films in which Fielding had any kind of creative involvement, ranging from acting to writing, producing and/or directing, was derived from a study of illustrations and sometimes production credits in Lubin Film release bulletins, contemporary trade magazine reviews and production notes, and from contemporary newspaper accounts of Fielding at work.

10. *NYDM*, 6 March 1912: 28.

11. *NYDM*, 28 February 1912:29; 27 March 1912: 28.

12. *Douglas Daily International*, 24 February 1912.

13. Unid. Clipping, 20 April 1912, *Lubin Scrapbook Folios*.

14. *Douglas Daily International*, 7 March 1912; 26 March 1912; *Douglas Daily Dispatch*, 26 March 1912.

15. *Douglas Daily International*, 24 February 1912.

16. *NYDM*, 17 July 1912: 33.

17. 'Romaine Fielding, of the Lubin Company,' *Motion Picture*, June 1912:130.

18. Kevin Brownlow, *The Parade's Gone By* (Alfred A. Knopf, 1978), 159–161; Henry King, telephone interview with the author, 12 August 1980.

19. *NYDM*, 5 June 1912: 31; *MPW*, 3 August 1912: 28.

20. Unid. clipping (plot synopsis), 1912 *Lubin Scrapbook Folios*.

21. *Arizona Daily Star*, 30 June 1912.

22. *Arizona Daily Star*, 20 June 1912: 8.

23. *Arizona Daily Star*, 20 June 1912: 8.

24. *Arizona Daily Star*, 28 June 1912: 6.

25. *Arizona Daily Star*, 14 July 1912.

26. *Arizona Daily Star*, 7 July 1912: 6.

27. *NYDM*, 25 July 1912: 26.

28. *Arizona Daily Star*, 11 July 1912: 6.

29. *Prescott Journal-Miner*, 14 July 1912: 4.

30. *Prescott Journal-Miner*, 2 August 1912.

31. *Prescott Journal-Miner*, 6 August 1912: 4; *Lubin Bulletin*, 26 October 1912.

32. *NYDM*, 27 November 1912; 29 January 1913: 33.

33. *NYDM*, 29 January 1913: 33.

34. *MPW*, 30 November 1912: 885.

35. *MPW*, 30 November 1912: 885.

36. 'Romaine Fielding, of the Lubin Company,' *Motion Picture Magazine*, June 1912:130.

37. *Motion Picture Magazine*, June 1912: 130.

38. Lubin Archive, Free Library of Philadelphia, filmstills and 1912 *Lubin Scrapbook Folio* clippings; *Lubin Bulletin*, 12 October 1912, author's collection.

39. *Lubin Bulletin*, 12 October 1912; *NYDM*, 23 October 1912: back cover.

40. *NYDM*, 23 October 1912: 30.

41. *Prescott Journal-Miner*, 24 October 1912: 8.

42. Alberto Suarez Barnett, *Voices From the Pimeria Alta*, (Nogales: Pimeria Alta Historical Society, 1991):173.

43. 'Lubin Company is Now in Nogales,' *Arizona Daily Star*, 15 November 1912: 3.

44. *NYDM*, 5 March 1913: 4.

45. *Lubin Bulletin*, 22 May 1913.

46. *Motography*, 1 March 1913: 174–175.

47. *Lubin Scrapbook Folios*, 'An Adventure on the Mexican Border,' unidentified newspaper clipping and illustration, March 1913.

48. *Lubin Bulletin*, 29 March 1913; film stills in the Margaret Herrick Library, and in the private collection of Robert S. Birchard.

49. *NYDM*, 19 April 1913: 29.

50. *Lubin Bulletin*, 9 April 1913.

51. *Lubin Scrapbook Folios*, Vol. 2, March-May 1913, various clippings of trade publication reviews, articles, illustrations and ads.

52. *NYDM*, 26 March 1913: 35.

53. Unidentified review quoted in Carolyn Lowrey, 'Photoplays and Players,' *New York Telegraph*, 1 November 1914: n.p.

54. *Lubin Scrapbook Folios*, Vol. 2, March 1913, 'Fielding on Job in Mexican Troubles' and other various newspaper and trade magazine clippings; *Nogales Vidette*, 14 March 1913; 'Fielding Decidedly Busy', *Motography*, 3 May 1913: 306; Carolyn Lowrey, 'Photoplays and Players', *New York Telegraph*, 1 November 1914: n.p.

55. The master is in the collection of the British Film Institute; the Museum of Modern Art holds a print.

56. *Silver City Independent*, 3 June 1913.

57. *Silver City Independent*, 22 April 1913; production stills in the collection of Robert S. Birchard.

58. *MPW*, 24 January 1914: 422.

59. *Lubin Bulletin*, 12 November 1914.

60. *Lubin Bulletin*, 18 September 1913.

61. *Silver City Independent*, 8 July 1913; *Silver City Enterprise*, 11 July 1913.

62. *Lubin Bulletin*, 18 September 1913.

63. *Moving Picture World*, 20 September 1913.

64. Unidentified newspaper review, probably New Mexican, given to the author by former Las Vegas, New Mexico historian, Elmo Baca.

65. 'This One Surely Will Be Real Thriller', *Las Vegas Daily Optic*, 6 September 1913.

66. 'Gossip of the Studios', *NYDM*, 17 December 1913: 31.

67. *Las Vegas Daily Optic*, 16 August 1913.

68. *NYDM*, 12 November 1913: 32.

69. *Lubin Scrapbook Folios*, unidentified clipping, c. November 1913.

70. *Las Vegas Daily Optic*, 1–22 November 1913.

71. *Las Vegas Daily Optic*, 15 November 1913; *Lubin Bulletin*, December 1913.

72. *Arizona Republican*, 10 March 1915: 5.

73. *MPW*, 8 April 1914.

74. K.W. Baker, 'Romaine Fielding: A Man of the Mountains', *Photoplay*, March 1915: 34.

75. *New York Telegraph*, 21 September 1914, n.p.; reference to a lunch with Fielding on 23 April 1914 in Charmaine London's diary reported to the author by London Archivist Russ Kingman, Glen Ellen, Ca., 1988.

76. 'Glen Eyrie Castle Leased by Romaine Fielding as Setting for Lubin Movies', *Colorado Springs Gazette*, 14 May 1914, p. 1; 'Produces 5 Features At Same Time,' *MPW*, 12 December 1914: 1541.

77. 'Big Company Will Act in Six-Reel Feature', *Colorado Springs Gazette*, 24 June 1914: 5; '500 People Are Now at Work on Eagle's Nest', *Colorado Springs Gazette*, 5 July 1914: 8.

78. '500 People Are Now at Work on Eagle's Nest'.

79. '"The Eagle's Nest" Comes to the Orpheum', *Lubin Scrapbook Folios*, unid. clipping, c. December 1914.

80. *NYDM*, 30 December 1914: 26.

81. *Altoona Record*, 8 September 1914; Photo with caption 'What Happened When Romaine Fielding Wrecked Two Trains for a Picture', *NYDM* 23 September 1914, n.p.

82. *MPW*, 6 February 1915: 840.

83. 'Light Travels Fast', *Photoplay*, November 1915: 118.

84. 'Lubin's New Nocturnal Picture Power Plant', *Camden Telegram*, 4 September 1915.

85. *Lubin Bulletin*, 9 August 1915; 20 August 1915.

86. *MPW*, 2 October 1915.

87. Ibid.

88. *NYDM*, 1 September 1915: 37.

89. *Lubin Bulletin*, 25 August 1915.

90. *Arizona Republican*, 16 April 1915.

91. *Arizona Republican*, 28 September 1915: 7.

92. '500 People Are Now At Work on Eagle's Nest', *Colorado Springs Gazette*, 5 July 1914: 8.

93. *Photoplay*, March 1915: 35.

94. Carolyn Lowrey, 'Photoplays and Players', *New York Morning Telegraph*, 1 November 1914, n.p.

95. Ibid.

96. *Colorado Springs Gazette*, 19 July 1914: 8.

97. Gertrude M. Price, 'This Movie Star is Never Tired By Work', *Toledo News Bee*, 25 February 1913. (Robinson Locke Collection, New York Public Library at Lincoln Center).

98. *NYDM*, 1 September 1915.

99. *MPW*, 29 November 1913: 1085.

100. *NYDM*, 3 December 1913: 36.

101. *NYDM*, 17 December 1913: 36.

102. *NYDM*, 27 January 1915: 41, 46, 60.

Film History, Volume 7, pp. 426–449, 1995. Copyright © John Libbey & Company
ISSN: 0892-2160. Printed in Great Britain

The misreading and rereading of African American filmmaker Oscar Micheaux

a critical review of Micheaux scholarship

Charlene Regester

Oscar Micheaux, an African American – pioneer, writer and filmmaker – made his mark in the first half of the 20th century. The question to address as we near the 21st century is: Should we preserve Micheaux's mark, and if so, how shall we read that mark?

J. Ronald Green asserted that critics 'have repeatedly derided Micheaux for being "white", "bourgeois", "fatuous" and "middle class" ... Micheaux has been judged by the standards of classical cinema, when in fact his films, like other race movies, are as different from classical cinema as the race music of the same period is from classically based music'[1]. Green's assessment of how Oscar Micheaux has been portrayed by scholars and researchers may present a clue to the seemingly harsh criticism Micheaux received in both the field of cinema and literature prior to the 1960s.

The assessment of Micheaux that follows implies that he has been misread and misinterpreted. Second, this assessment will suggest that criticism of Micheaux is even now evolving, with the verdict still being out on Micheaux. As more of Micheaux's films surface, scholars and researchers are being forced to re-think their position on Micheaux and

his works. Third, this assessment takes into account the difficulty of examining African American filmmakers by the same standards as those used for criticizing white filmmakers without taking into consideration the unique obstacles that complicated African American filmmaking efforts. The question arises of whether or not an equitable comparison can be made at all. African American filmmakers were, in the pre-Civil Rights era, operating under a completely different set of circumstances and were part of a complex set of dynamics over which they had little or no control. Ultimately this had to affect the films they produced. Such variables disproportionately affected African American filmmakers, for while similar conditions may have had some effect on white filmmakers they certainly did not have the same impact in terms of impeding their growth,

Charlene Regester is co-editor of the *Oscar Micheaux Society Newsletter* and a visiting assistant professor at the University of North Carolina. She wrote on Stepin Fetchit for *Film History*. Correspondence c/o African and Afro-American Studies, CB #3395, 401 Alumni Bldg, UNC, Chapel Hill, North Carolina 27599-3395, USA.

Fig. 1. Oscar Micheaux, as he appeared in his novel *The Conquest*. [Lincoln, Nebraska: Woodruff Press, 1913.]

development, progress and success. African American motion picture producers had to contend with limited theatres catering to black audiences, minimal capital for producing pictures, inadequate resources, lack of filmmaking training and skill, poorly trained scriptwriters, producers, directors and actors, and distribution practices that were severely limited in comparison to those employed by the major motion picture studios.

Despite such seemingly insurmountable obstacles, African American filmmakers such as Micheaux did in fact survive and provided a portrayal of African American life on the motion picture screen never portrayed fairly by white Hollywood. This capsule of black life preserved by Micheaux's films makes an important comment about the fabric of American life and how blacks figured into the complex social, economic, political and racial cli-

mate of American culture. Its contribution to cinema history is beyond measure.

Micheaux has been referred to as an auteur filmmaker because he was involved in almost every aspect of the filmmaking process, from writing the script to producing, directing, and even distributing his own motion pictures. In fact, according to Andrew Sarris' interpretation of auteur theory, classifying a director as such is contingent upon a director's technical competence as a filmmaker, the personality that emerges in his work and, finally, the tension between the director's personality and his body of work[2]. Regardless of what position is taken in the debate surrounding auteur theory, Micheaux would be classified as such. Having classified Micheaux as an auteur filmmaker affords the opportunity for obtaining a much better understanding of Micheaux, himself, and his ideological views. Until this understanding has been developed, the extent to which Micheaux operated as an auteur filmmaker remains purely conjectural. Because of the circumstances that complicated his filmmaking efforts, it is difficult to determine how much of his films reflected his artistic talent and how much reflected deliberate attempts to cut costs or to delude film censors. The difficulty in constructing a profile of Micheaux as an auteur filmmaker may be lessened if his portrayals of some of the characters in his works are viewed as carbon copies of himself – reflecting his ideals. As a filmmaker, Micheaux seemed to convey messages to both his black and white audiences. As a person, Micheaux was distrusting of ministers; as a filmmaker Micheaux projected his distrust. Micheaux also provided the first black protest films and as a filmmaker even took a somewhat progressive stance in terms of his treatment of women and women's issues[3]. This emerging profile of Micheaux, however, has to be constructed cautiously based on the divergent criticism he received.

The focus of this examination is to investigate how the critical profile of Micheaux has been constructed by scholars and researchers, how this critical profile has changed over time, and how this critical profile continues to evolve. It seems that scholarship on Micheaux the person, as novelist and filmmaker, should be viewed as several waves – from the period before the 1970s to the criticisms that have surfaced over the last twenty-plus years. In conducting this examination, the critics' profile of Micheaux will be investigated by providing a historical overview of research on Micheaux before the 1970s, exploring his reception among researchers and scholars in the decade of the 1970s, examining his critical profile in the 1980s, and analysing his critical profile in the decade of the 1990s.

Several limitations hamper this investigation. First, because the works of Micheaux are constantly being discovered, Micheaux's critical reception is likely to change as more of his works become available and accessible to scholars and researchers. Second, subjective views will influence this discussion in terms of assessing how scholars have critiqued Micheaux and his works. Third, the works mentioned in this discussion may not include all works that have been compiled on Micheaux and,

therefore, may not be exhaustive. Within these limitations, however, this investigation is determined to construct an extensively researched and objective critical profile of Oscar Micheaux, an African American auteur filmmaker.

Historical overview of Micheaux scholarship before the 1970s

The first wave of Micheaux scholarship focused in large part on acknowledging Micheaux's existence as a black filmmaker who was among the leaders of race movies and who made the transition from the silent to the sound era of filmmaking, a feat in and of itself. Scholars and researchers in the period before the 1970s focused on including Micheaux in early cinema history by recognizing and identifying his contributions to black film history, as a filmmaker. Micheaux was often presented as a 'shoddy' filmmaker, a capitalist who was more concerned with making money than making films, and as a haphazard filmmaker who dedicated little time or attention to the artistic aspect of filmmaking. This perception of Micheaux was influenced by his portrayal in the African American press during the second period of his filmmaking career (1930–48) when he was declining as a filmmaker and had to rely on financial support provided by whites if he was to continue cultivating his filmmaking craft. In addition, this impression is believed to have surfaced when critics' viewing was limited, because many of his films in existence at the time were those produced in the second period of filmmaking, the declining period. *Body and Soul* (1924), for example, is possibly the only silent film that Micheaux produced which was known to exist at the time, and still remained virtually inaccessible to scholars and researchers. If only films from his second period of filmmaking provided the basis upon which scholars formulated their views, it becomes easy to understand their 'premature' and negative conclusions.

If critics were depending on reviews of the African American press, particularly in this second period of filmmaking, it becomes readily apparent why Micheaux was dismissed as a serious filmmaker. For example, in a review of *Ten Minutes to Live* (1932) the *Chicago Defender* reported unkindly:

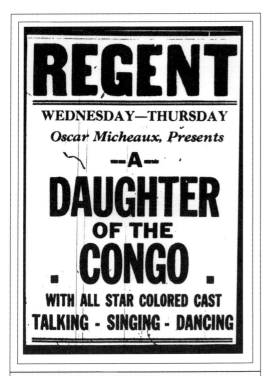

Fig. 2. Advertisement for Micheaux's *A Daughter of the Congo*, from the Baltimore *Afro-American,* 23 August 1930. [This, and other advertising cuts in this article, reproduced by permission of the *Afro-American*.]

Although *Ten Minutes to Live* created no particular stir in movie circles during its recent run at the Metropolitan theatre, the film was admitted to be an improvement over *Veiled Aristocrats,* another one done by Oscar Micheaux. Lack of funds with which to carry out his plans is working against Oscar in all his attempt to crash the talkie field[4].

Micheaux's harshest criticism came from Theophilus Lewis of the *New York Amsterdam News* who criticized his *A Daughter of the Congo* (1930) for its 'persistent vaunting of intraracial color fetichism', for portraying Native Africans who act like 'half-wits', and for its poor acting as well as directing[5]. Lewis declared, 'As a matter of fact, the picture is thoroughly bad from every point of analysis, from the continuity which is unintelligible, to the caption writing, which is a crime'[6]. With the release of *The Betrayal* (1948), a film that signalled the end of Micheaux's filmmaking career, he was again

harshly criticized by the African American press. The *Chicago Defender,* after providing reviews of the film that had appeared in other papers that described it as boring, unprofessional and devoid of plot, concluded 'All of which goes to say that from the viewpoint of competent critics, *The Betrayal* is a betrayal and is pretty awful'[7].

Despite such reviews in the African American press, during this period Micheaux was still regarded as one of the leading filmmakers of African American films. *Who's Who in Colored America* (1930–31–32), attested to his contributions to black filmmaking, reporting that 'Out of a total of forty Negro photoplays produced in the United States, twenty-five of them have been directed and produced by [Micheaux]'[8].

Academic journals seeking to provide a much more inclusive study of African American contributions to various fields of study (e.g. literature, history, sociology) also began to include Micheaux in their works. In this phase of criticism scholars largely concentrated on Micheaux's literary works and only occasionally made reference to the motion pictures he produced.

In fact, in this period Micheaux was more often noted for his literary works than for his contributions as a filmmaker. In the 1950s, Carl Milton Hughes included Micheaux in his discussion of black American novelists from 1940 to 1950. Hughes stated: Micheaux 'attempts to be a serious writer, but he hardly has creative imagination and misses the reality of things by his theatrical posturing'[9]. Five years later, Robert Bone, in his examination of black novelists, referred to Micheaux as one among several writers who 'treat the colorline as nonexistent or unimportant'[10]. Bone contends of Micheaux and other novelists, 'The sudden appearance of these assimilationist authors, who have lost all contact with Negro life and culture, is symptomatic of a broader crisis in the development of the Negro novel'[11].

Micheaux's lukewarm reception as a literary figure similarly pervaded his filmmaking career, when some ten years later critiques of his filmmaking efforts began to surface in the literature. For example, in 1969, Thomas Cripps, in a review of black film history, referred to Micheaux as one of the most famous and best black silent filmmakers[12]. However, such critiques were often qualified, as

Cripps did in reviewing Micheaux's *The Exile* (1931), when he stated that the film, 'revealed both the virtues and the needs of black filmmaking. Even though no white man appeared on the screen, the plot still moved on white terms'[13].

Before the 1970s, Micheaux, although commended for undertaking the task of making films and writing novels, was thought to be compromising his own identity to construct and create his works. Bone refers to him as an assimilationist, while Cripps suggests that he was emulating white values and lifestyles in the development of his story lines, a criticism that would be challenged in later years by a new generation of scholars.

Micheaux's critical profile in the decade of the 1970s

Upon the advent of the Civil Rights movement, the way African Americans were portrayed on the screen began to undergo a significant change, and the 'black exploitation' era commenced. African American filmmakers began to gain a considerable amount of attention and visibility as scholars and researchers reflected upon those who paved the way for this new generation of filmmakers. Micheaux's contributions to literature and filmmaking began to be subjected to renewed critical review.

For example, Janis Hebert critiqued Micheaux's first two novels, *The Conquest* (1913) and *The Homesteader* (1917) on the basis of their historical validity and Micheaux's perception of himself as a black man homesteading in the Midwest. Hebert contends that Micheaux 'does give a reasonably accurate account of the area's development'[14], but as for his perception of himself, he provides an ambiguous portrayal. According to Hebert, Micheaux on the one hand views himself as being different from or 'better' than other blacks, while on the other hand he castigates the whites for impeding the progress of all African Americans[15]. Hebert's critique of Micheaux's literary works points to the importance of including his literary work in the canon of writings on the Midwest, since Micheaux was providing the perspective of a black homesteader.

Arlene Elder acknowledged the importance of Micheaux's contributions as a writer who provided his own perspective of the Midwest. Elder was es-

Fig. 3. From the Baltimore *Afro-American*, 29 January 1927.

pecially concerned with the profile that Micheaux created of himself as an African American who had migrated westward in pursuit of the American dream. In review of Micheaux's literary works, Elder concludes:

> The paradoxes of the personal and racial tensions in Micheaux's books render them fascinating testaments to the Black identity struggle at the beginning of the twentieth century as well as illuminations of the Afro-American experience in a section of the country seldom examined in this regard, the rural and urban Midwest. The Black pioneer's perception of his visibility among European immigrants in the Wilderness and his invisibility among his own people on Chicago's South Side results in our literature's most revealing views of the Black's dual role as 'America's metaphor' and her scapegoat[16].

Hebert's and Elder's review of Micheaux demonstrate that by the 1970s he was respected and appreciated as a literary figure for providing a unique portrayal of the Midwest, if for nothing else.

A similar reception of Micheaux would also begin to surface in reviews of his film career. Even the sheer increase in the number of reports on Micheaux's career attests to the fact that he was beginning to become better respected as a filmmaker by the 1970s; he was transformed from being virtually excluded in film histories to being included in nearly every report on black film history. Such reports, however, did not omit the adverse criticism that seemed to attach to Micheaux.

Scholars and researchers, during the decade of the 1970s, began to situate Micheaux within black film history. Reports appeared in reference works, film histories, and critical journals, in addition to magazines. Among the reference works, the *Dictionary of American Biography* provided a profile of Micheaux and elucidated his literary and filmmaking career. Dwight W. Hoover reflected upon Micheaux's philosophical position by stating that Micheaux 'believed in the efficacy of initiative as a solution to poverty and attacked blacks for their alleged criminality, lack of education, and especially for their lack of incentive'[17]. Such 1970s views of Micheaux, however, would be challenged in later years.

Edward Mapp referred to Micheaux as the 'Dean of Black Filmmakers' in his *Directory of Blacks in the Performing Arts*, where he also provided a rather incomplete list of Micheaux films, some of which were without dates, reflecting upon the difficulty of establishing an exact date of release or production for many of his films. Mapp reported that Micheaux published some five novels, when he actually published as many as seven. Finally, Mapp incorrectly wrote that Micheaux died on 1 April 1951, a date that appears in several sources and is believed to have been taken from an incorrect report that appeared in the African American press. Mapp's work perhaps best reflects the lack of adequate resources available to these early scholars who were attempting to construct profiles of Oscar Micheaux[18]. It is noteworthy that Mapp would correct many of these errors in a revised edition of his work.

Film histories written and published in the decade of the 1970s that chronicled black film history

began to piece together Micheaux's filmmaking career from scanty sources, while sharing their own views on his filmmaking style and technique. In 1973 Donald Bogle referred to Micheaux as a 'fiendishly aggressive young entrepreneur' who modeled his stars after white Hollywood personalities, shot scenes in one take to save film footage, shot without adequate lighting, seldom allowed retakes, used light complexioned actors in primary roles, and was not above using amateur actors in his films[19]. Bogle contends:

> That [Micheaux's] films reflected the interests and outlooks of the black bourgeoisie will no doubt always be held against him. His films never centred on the ghetto; they seldom dealt with racial misery or decay. Instead they concentrated on the problems of 'passing' or the difficulties facing 'professional people'. But to appreciate Micheaux's films one must understand that he was moving as far as possible away from Hollywood's jesters and servants. He wanted to give his audience something 'to further the race, not hinder it' ... He created a fantasy world where blacks were just as affluent, just as educated, just as 'cultured,' just as well-mannered – in short, just as white – as white America[20].

Eileen Landay similarly referred to Micheaux and asserted that 'there was little "ethnic truth" to these films ... he perpetuated many white stereotypes ...'[21]. There remains a question of how many of Micheaux's films Landay, as well as other critics, had actually seen. Landay continued:

> While some of [Micheaux's] films dealt with the problems of being black, this was never from the point of view of the ghetto dweller or sharecropper; his subjects were the black bourgeoisie. By presenting them, Micheaux hoped to instill race pride in all who saw them. His attitude was not unlike the Belafonte–Poitier integrationists who followed him, though his energy in seeking out 'his audience' and his total control over the financing of his films was much like that of Melvin Van Peebles[22].

While these scholars and researchers noted Micheaux's contributions as a filmmaker, they did not do so without including and commenting on the criticism he received for his poor production techniques, portrayal of black middle-class lifestyles, and failure to avoid providing many of the same stereotypes that had popularized Hollywood motion pictures. This critical profile of Micheaux, continued by other scholars and researchers, became the 1970s norm.

Gary Null, in commenting on Micheaux's technique as a filmmaker in his *Black Hollywood* (1975) stated that:

> He used every exploitationary gimmick he could muster to grab the audience; for example, displaying large photos of rape scenes and semi-nude figures. He would insert sequences quite unrelated to the story into his films. Once he even inserted a scene of a Harlem dance troupe into a Western movie. The audiences loved the nudity and voiced their approval to the theatre managers. However, films attempting to deal with racial injustices were not being made by independent producers, black or white[23].

Null's blanket assessment lost its validity in subsequent decades upon the re-emergence of several of Micheaux's 'lost films'. But in the 1970s, Micheaux's inability to achieve artistic excellence, while setting his sights on achieving box-office receipts, was an unchallenged profile.

During the same year, Daniel Leab published his *From Sambo to Superspade* (1975) in which he described Micheaux's films as being complex, often with controversial plots and containing 'stalwart heroes undaunted by adversity, heroines faced with extraordinary dangers'[24]. Leab, like other film critics of the period, emphasized Micheaux's technical failures as a filmmaker, his deteriorating relationship with the African American press, and his use of light-complexioned actors in his films. Leab concludes:

> Oscar Micheaux's silent motion picture works cannot be considered outstanding. He is significant, however, because he was one of the first independent black producers making popular and for a time profitable movies with black actors and actresses for ghetto audiences. Despite his public utterances, Micheaux's films were not designed to uplift or to enlighten. They

THURSDAY—FRIDAY—SATURDAY

Oscar Mischeaux

PRESENTS HIS

Latest and Greatest Achievement in Colored Films

'The Conjure Woman'

Featuring The Most Beautiful and Talented Actress On The Screen

EVELYN PREER

And An All-Star Cast

Fig. 4. From the Baltimore *Afro-American*, 19 March 1927.

were meant to entertain, to appeal to his concept of black popular taste, and to make money[25].

Leab may actually have drawn such a conclusion from research, perhaps, without having seen some of Micheaux's more recently uncovered silent films.

Switching away from the nebulous attribute of artistic quality, many of the 1970s critics concentrated on Micheaux's philosophical positioning and his entrepreneurship. In 1977, Henry Sampson referred to Micheaux and his company mentioning that Micheaux had received little attention from historians but acknowledging that among his contemporaries, Micheaux was regarded as 'a skilled entrepreneur, an astute businessman and a man who was sensitive to the needs of the black film audience'[26]. Sampson added that Micheaux seemed to have felt the need to depict accurately the social, political, and economic climate of blacks in American society. 'Although perhaps not intended as such, some of his films can be considered as protest films'[27]. Sampson's review of Micheaux focuses less on Micheaux's skill as a filmmaker and more on the provocative and controversial themes and issues addressed in his films. Sampson provided a new interpretation of Micheaux by referring to his films as protest films.

Thomas Cripps situated Micheaux within the larger context of the independent filmmaking movement of 'race' movies that worked outside of Hollywood cinema and referred to Micheaux as the 'black analogue to a white independent like Sam Goldwyn'[28]. While other critics paralleled Micheaux with Booker T. Washington (a logical comparison since he dedicated his first novel, *The Conquest*, to Washington, and refers to him in his work) Cripps parallels Micheaux to W.E.B. DuBois, though not without recognizing their differences. Cripps conjectures that they were similar in that 'both men, standing on the frontier of race, looked with fine acuity into the hidden crannies of racial mores'[29]. In review of Micheaux, Cripps commented on Micheaux's business practices, referring to them as 'brassy,' commended the unique promotion and distribution strategies whereby Micheaux traveled the country distributing his own films in any way and in any place he could, and noted his haphazard editing techniques as well as faulty shooting style. However, Cripps differed from other scholars, much in the same manner as did Sampson, in that he began to focus more critically on Micheaux's message, themes, plots and portrayal of black life in his pictures[30].

For example, of *Body and Soul*, Cripps acknowledges that this picture:

... reached beyond the capacity of Hollywood. Either the picture was an exposé of a social condition deep within, and relevant to, only Negro circles; or it used the medium of the dream-flashback to sketch an allegorical black figure alternately dominated by his two sides, the prim role of bourgeois aspiration according to the rules of the game and the arcane black hustler for whom the game has been a fraud. It seemed to say that the survival drive of Afro-Americans living under oppressive conditions may almost casually choose either route as an escape[31].

Cripps' impression of this film is a testament

that Micheaux was beginning to be regarded as a filmmaker who provided a sophisticated portrayal of black life. Because now it was not just blacks who were witnessing the diversity of black life provided by Micheaux's films; whites were now beginning to gain exposure to a black lifestyle that was not one-dimensional, a life that previously many whites had not been aware of.

This newer critical review showing Micheaux as a filmmaker and portrayer of multi-faceted black lifestyles on the screen continued to surface in journal articles published in the 1970s. In 1975, Daniel Leab, in another examination of all-black cast films during this period, again turned his attention to Micheaux's filmmaking effort. Leab reported that Micheaux's first sound picture, *The Exile* (1931) 'was crude, old-fashioned, and not very interesting'[32]. Leab claimed that the film was so poor in quality that Harlem audiences laughed in the wrong places, while Micheaux was subjected to harsh criticism from the African American press. According to Leab, *God's Stepchildren* (1937) was also protested by blacks affiliated with various communist groups[33]. He concluded that Micheaux's 'sound films especially reflected the limitations of his technique, capital and concepts'[34]. (The word 'capital' probably referred to Micheaux's having to seek white financial assistance during this period.) However, according to Leab, 'Micheaux is important because he represents an energetic attempt by a Black to break through the barriers erected by White society, but it was a failed attempt that ultimately resulted in a parroting of the industry's demeaning image of the Black'[35]. Such views would be countered in later years. Interestingly, Leab, though so involved with Micheaux's story, like others erroneously reported Micheaux's death date and noted that Micheaux's death created little stir[36].

James Hoberman of the *Village Voice* referred to Micheaux as a filmmaker who was a faulty technician and who ignored production values. Hoberman stated, 'To call Micheaux's work problematic is to say the least. His films were made on a shoestring and are characterized by a surreal degree of corner-cutting. He seemed to be oblivious to the laws of cinematic continuity'[37]. Hoberman described Micheaux's *Ten Minutes to Live* (1932) as being so disjointed that 'it demands to be seen as a Marienbad-like attempt at 'pure' narrative

Fig. 5. From the Baltimore *Afro-American*, 21 April 1928.

cinema'[38]. Micheaux's use of cabaret scenes and 'inadequately trained' actors could also not escape criticism. Hoberman contended that Micheaux's films both 'amused and embarrassed' black audiences. 'It was not so much Micheaux's ipso facto avant-gardism as his severe racial ambivalence that infuriated his critics'[39].

Hoberman then focused on the ideology that managed to surface in Micheaux's films, and that Hoberman found disconcerting. He noted that Micheaux often reflected lifestyles of the black bourgeoisie in his films, focused on the colour divisions that existed in the African American community, and promoted his own views regarding self-sufficiency, while in the words of Hoberman, he blamed the 'victims of a racist society for the injustices perpetrated upon them'[40]. Undoubtedly, Hoberman's views, many of which would be contested by a later generation of scholars, exerted a major impact on the critical profile of Micheaux in the decade of the 1970s.

In 1976, Penelope Gilliatt in a *New Yorker* magazine article covering the Whitney Museum's tribute to black independent filmmaking, provided a brief discussion of Micheaux and his works. She acknowledged the obstacles that black filmmakers faced during this period and provided justification for why filmmakers like Micheaux attempted to explore controversial themes in their works. Gilliatt wrote:

It is not only that the blacks who made the films were barred from knowing anything about film technique and distribution, and were dependent on tenth-rate white personnel who took no trouble except to make a fast buck, and were forced to haul prints around in the backs of old cars to be shown in churches or schools or revival-meeting halls. It is also that the rules of social strata were usually held to be binding and immutable, and that ignominy at the hands of other breeds led to the dealing out of disrepute to your own. The black women in the films have to be bashed about to get them to show proper respect: 'To make a woman love you, knock her down' says an advertisement for Oscar Micheaux's *The Brute* (1920)[41].

Despite the conflicting perceptions of Micheaux, these reviews all had one thing in common, and that was that Micheaux was commended for his effort at bringing black life to the screen, regardless of distortions. One such source provided one of the most comprehensive filmographies and bibliographies of Micheaux's oeuvre. This was Bernard L. Peterson's article in *The Crisis* in 1979. Peterson contended that he compiled this annotated, chronological filmography of Micheaux to rekindle interest in his works[42]. To date, Peterson's work, especially his updated filmography in the following decade, remains unparalleled. Peterson asserted that Micheaux was 'one of the great black geniuses of his age, whose accomplishments must be regarded as phenomenal when one considers the limitations imposed by his lack of formal education and training, the lack of financial backing and large studio support, the inadequacy of equipment, facilities, personnel and resources, the denial of wide distribution and booking, and the general restrictions imposed by the racial climate of the period'[43].

A filmography of Micheaux's works was similarly provided in this period by Phyllis Klotman's *Frame by Frame*. Klotman provided one of the most comprehensive filmographies of Micheaux's films to date; her listing has been updated in later years[44].

By the end of the 1970s Micheaux's critical profile as a novelist and filmmaker was mixed. As a novelist, Micheaux's works were regarded as significant partly because they provided a portrayal of the Midwest from the unique perspective of an African American homesteader. Critiquing Micheaux as a filmmaker, on the other hand, most writers acknowledged that he was to be commended for his very survival, let alone his charting of a course few black filmmakers would have dared to follow. He was often portrayed as an aggressive filmmaker who despite overwhelming odds made and produced an extensive number of films, and succeeded in exhibiting these films through his unique promotion and distribution strategies. On the other hand, Micheaux was portrayed as a filmmaker whose films lacked fully developed plots, who conveyed middle-class values and lifestyles in his films, to the exclusion of other aspects of black life, ignored the technical aspects of filmmaking, and hired actors without regard for talent. Micheaux was further accused of injecting into his films his personal oppression angst that manifested itself in the creation of characters who were victims of self-hate. Micheaux's critical profile at the end of this decade was one of a filmmaker who was both respected and disrespected. This dichotomous portrayal was transferred to the next decade, the 1980s, where it underwent re-examination.

Micheaux's critical profile in the decade of the 1980s

In the decade of the 1980s, as specialized studies in cinema, and African American cinema in particular, began to move from the margins toward the centre of academic studies, Micheaux again emerged as one of the most significant figures in African American cinema history. Micheaux, it seems, was beginning to take his rightful place in American cinema as a filmmaker. Although working outside of Hollywood and operating as an independent filmmaker, particularly in his first period of filmmaking, Micheaux was finally acknowledged to have contributed as much to cinema as many of the leading white filmmakers of his time. In fact, some argue that had Micheaux been a product

of Hollywood he would have rivaled the successes of such leading filmmakers of his day as Samuel Goldwyn. In the 1980s, film scholars and researchers finally began to re-examine Micheaux's filmmaking. A number of researchers began to reconstruct the film history of African Americans by searching for and locating several of Micheaux's lost motion pictures, while others attempted to unravel facts about his life.

Since 1980, Micheaux scholarship has surfaced in reference works, journal articles and film histories. In 1982 Micheaux appeared in the *Dictionary of American Negro Biography*, where both his novels and films were reviewed and treated critically – albeit not always favourably. Kenneth Wiggins Porter in review of Micheaux's literary works, asserted 'While the style of *The Conquest*, which Micheaux had [had] revised by semiprofessionals, is dull and pedestrian, *The Homesteader* is a literary disaster, with an unbelievably complicated plot, long-winded, pretentiously awkward writing, stilted conversations, and the grotesque misuse of words'[45]. As for his films, Porter seems to have based his critique on the opinion of his 1970s colleagues. Porter referred to Micheaux's films as 'quickies' and 'cheapies' made on a shoestring budget, shot on location as opposed to studios, hindered by the absence of re-takes when actors flubbed a line, and suffering from inadequate lighting or editing techniques. Porter, however, acknowledged Micheaux's contribution to cinema, pointing out that despite the fact that he may have created a fantasy world modeled after the black bourgeoisie, he moved away from the traditional stereotypes that plagued the African American screen image. Porter was another critic who erroneously reported Micheaux's death date[46].

In the 1980s many more reference works began to include African American filmmakers in their American cinema history. Unfortunately, these sources often contained inaccuracies. For example, *World Film Directors* inaccurately reported that black American cinema began as a direct response to D.W. Griffith's, *The Birth of a Nation* and that the first black film was *The Birth of a Race*. Apparently, the writer was unaware of the works of William Foster who made motion pictures in Chicago prior to *The Birth of a Nation*.

But *World Film Directors* provided one of the

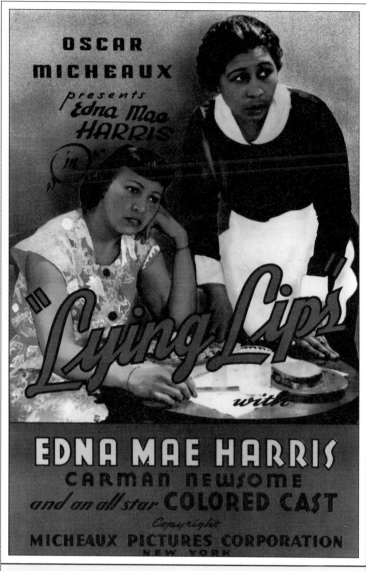

Fig. 6. Poster for *Lying Lips* (Micheaux Pictures Corp., 1939).

most extensive examinations of Micheaux to appear in a reference book. As for Micheaux's filmmaking entrepreneurship, this source commented on his unparalleled promotion and distribution techniques. It was noted that Micheaux engaged in poor filmmaking techniques for economic reasons and not aesthetic reasons as some critics wanted to assume. This critique similarly noted Micheaux's featuring of cabaret scenes in his films with scantily clothed chorus girls, mixing professional actors with amateurs, featuring light complexioned actors in his

films, and billing his actors as the 'black Valentino' or 'sepia Mae West'[48]. However, Micheaux was commended for addressing topics 'that no other black filmmaker of his day dared touch,' such as lynching, hypocritical black leaders, the Ku Klux Klan, interracial prejudice, intraracial prejudice, prostitution, criminality, etc[49]. This source examined Micheaux's film plots. Unfortunately, much of the information was taken from film reviews and even some of these were incorrectly reported. In comparing reviews of Micheaux's works, for example, *World Film Directors* juxtaposed James Hoberman's critique of *Body and Soul* with Thomas Cripps's interpretation of the film. This source did allude to Micheaux's censorship difficulties as well as the protests he evoked from black film audiences who were offended by his themes. Despite a fairly extensive examination by their writers, however, once again Micheaux's death date was incorrectly reported[50].

Biographical reviews of Micheaux appeared much more frequently in reference works in the 1980s. It seems that there was beginning to be a conscious attempt to comment on his strengths as well as his weaknesses, his successes along with his failures. Reports were even beginning to focus on the divergent criticism of Micheaux, and explanations for his behaviour as a 'careless' filmmaker were beginning to surface. Clearly, however, much of the criticism that emerged in the 1970s still influenced and shaped that which evolved in the 1980s.

Among other sources to examine Micheaux in this decade were several journal articles. As a literary figure Micheaux was included in a collection of essays on the Great Plains[51]. Chester Fontenot introduced a critique of Micheaux by asserting that as a novelist and filmmaker, '[Micheaux] believed that one solution to the problems that plagued black urbanites was for them to abandon the cities and to look to the Great Plains as a place where they could build an alternative society'[52]. Fontenot noted that Micheaux was the first black writer to portray a leading character in the role of a pioneer and although he faulted Micheaux for portraying black middle-class lifestyle, he praised him for providing characters in his motion pictures that countered those provided by white Hollywood. Fontenot contended that Micheaux's characters in his novels 'moved black people from the category of sub-human creatures incapable of carrying out the most ordinary human functions to one of a dignified people whose problems are much like those of white Americans'[53]. In Fontenot's critique of Micheaux's literary works, he noted that while Micheaux is often portrayed as an ardent supporter of Booker T. Washington, he diverges from Washington's philosophy that the South is the ideal place for African Americans and instead argues that the 'Great Northwest' is a much more suitable milieu. Fontenot

applauds Micheaux's philosophical views in both his novels and films, crediting Micheaux because he believed that African Americans could rid themselves of their weaknesses if they avoided interracial marriages, accepted moral responsibility, and embraced education. Fontenot then shifted to a discussion of Micheaux's film criticisms and how Micheaux responded to such critics. Fontenot contended that critics of Micheaux have often ignored his conscious intent. 'It was through the creation of the black pioneer as an individual able to collapse the distinction between race and class that Micheaux made his most lasting contribution to black literature and films'[54]. Fontenot contributed heavily to a more positive image of Micheaux.

Journal articles less concerned with his literary contributions, and more concerned with his films, were provided by a number of scholars, critics and researchers in the 1980s. James Hoberman, in a review of bad movies – movies referred to as 'inconsequential trash', movies based on mistakes, and movies chided as failures – included Oscar Micheaux's motion pictures. Hoberman found Micheaux 'another filmmaker whose anti-masterpieces are so profoundly troubling and whose *weltanschauung* is so devastating that neither the Medveds nor the World's Worst Film Festival are equipped to deal with him. In fact, five decades after their release, his films still have no place in the history of cinema'[55]. Such an assumption would be refuted in the following decade by scholars and researchers and may even have provided the impetus for the increased attention that Micheaux received in the 1990s, as many defended him and came forward to provide a re-examination of Micheaux and his works. To substantiate his assertion, Hoberman cited several Micheaux films that demonstrated that he indeed was a 'bad' filmmaker, such as *The Betrayal*, a film that was harshly criticized for inadequate acting, directing and scriptwriting. Hoberman further conjectured that Micheaux's alienation even among some black film historians or critics was due to 'the painful ambivalence of Micheaux's racial attitudes' that pervaded his films (e.g. 'Colored men will sell out anyone for fifty cents' or 'only one Negro in a thousand tries to think')[56]. Hoberman contended that Micheaux internalized racism and then projected it on to his own people. Also, according to Hoberman, Micheaux's films

Fig. 7. From the Baltimore *Afro-American*,
3 August 1929.

were technical failures. Hoberman stated of
Micheaux:

> His camera ground relentlessly on while the key
> light wandered, traffic noise obliterated the
> dialogue, or a soundman's arm intruded upon
> the frame. Actors blew their cues, recovered,
> and continued. Wasting nothing, he re-used
> footage with impunity, carried the post-dub-
> bing of his soundtracks to the outer limits of
> possibility, saved up his out-takes and fa-
> shioned them into second films[57].

Hoberman cynically concluded 'It's been said
that Micheaux deliberately left mistakes in his finished films "to give the audience a laugh" ... The
longer Micheaux made films, the badder they got.
I'm haunted by these facts because they suggest that
Micheaux knew what he was doing. And if Oscar
Micheaux was a fully conscious artist, he was the
greatest genius the cinema ever produced'[58].
Hoberman's view of Micheaux as a 'bad' filmmaker
was to some extent influenced by the profile that
had emerged in previous decades. It is speculative

that Hoberman utilized the term 'bad' to mean
'good'. His commentary was very significant, however, because he provided considerable detail in
his critical examination of Micheaux's filmmaking
style and technique. His critique was nonetheless a
personal view and would be challenged in the following decade.

Providing a more positive assessment of Micheaux, in 1982 Pearl Bowser applauded Micheaux's portrayal of African American women.
While many filmmakers either excluded African
American women, distorted their image, or relegated them to minimal roles Micheaux provided
more diverse portrayals of African American
women and allowed them to assume roles of importance in his films. Bowser asserted that 'His female
characters were easy prey for hustlers in the big city
including the jackleg preacher whose terrain was
both urban and rural'[59].

Some two years, later in 1984, the Whitney
Museum of American Art paid tribute to Micheaux
by exhibiting his motion pictures, and this exhibit
was covered by James Hoberman of the *Village
Voice*, who again portrayed Micheaux as a filmmaker who was confused and ambivalent in his
representation of race. He further contended that
Micheaux's technical failings became his trademark as a filmmaker. More specifically, Hoberman
rationalized that 'The slap-in-the-face irrationality
of many Micheaux fade-outs seem to me indicative
of his profound pessimism and understandable mis-
trust of American justice'[60]. Of Micheaux's pictures,
God's Stepchildren in particular, Hoberman continued his philosophizing: 'This nightmarish account
of self-directed racism and misplaced mother love
is the director's anti-masterpiece, as profound and
powerful an embodiment of American racial patho-
logy as D.W. Griffith's *The Birth of a Nation* or John
Ford's *The Searchers* ...'. This critique of Micheaux
may bring into question Hoberman's judgement on
the sociopolitical climate of the period in which
Micheaux operated and Hoberman's self-assured,
from-on-high explanation as to why Micheaux conveyed such ambivalence in his films.

Donald Bogle, agreeing with Hoberman's position that Micheaux's pictures were technically inferior when compared to Hollywood productions,
argued that despite these weaknesses, Micheaux
'Intertwined in all his films ... the consciousness of

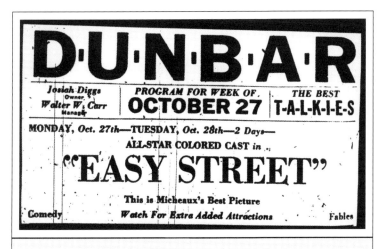

Fig. 8. From the Baltimore *Afro-American*, 25 October 1930.

necessarily result in increased proceeds at the box office. Grupenhoff stated, 'Oscar Micheaux was the quintessential self-taught grass roots filmmaker, and that fact is perhaps partly responsible for his naive approach to cinema technology and for his rather parochial sense of visualization and *mise-en-scène*'[65]. As for Micheaux's portrayals in his films, Grupenhoff suggests that Micheaux rarely portrayed blacks negatively, even though they exhibited negative behaviour. Grupenhoff, as opposed to previous critics and researchers, was at least beginning to allow for practical alternative reasons why Micheaux engaged in certain practices. Grupenhoff further pointed out the difficulty of conducting research on Micheaux in view of the scant resources available and stressed the importance of relying on primary research such as interviews with former actors and documents such as letters supplied by relatives.

how race is a force in black life. Just as Negro newspapers and magazines took major news stories and reported them from a black angle, Micheaux took the typical Hollywood script and gave it a black slant'[62]. Bogle confronted critics who objected to Micheaux's portraying middle-class lifestyles. Bogle saw this as an anti-Hollywood response to their portrayal of blacks as jesters and servants. Furthermore, says Bogle, Micheaux's pictures remain 'a fascinating comment on black social and political aspirations of the past'[63].

Richard Grupenhoff provided a somewhat different examination of Micheaux. Grupenhoff noted that in 1987 Micheaux was awarded a star on Hollywood Boulevard by the Directors Guild of America, in addition to being named the recipient of the Golden Jubilee Special Directorial Award. If Micheaux was receiving such accolades, Grupenhoff posed, how was it that Micheaux's achievements had gone virtually unrecognized? In his critique of Micheaux, while chronicling his early years reconstructed from his novels, however, Grupenhoff conceded that 'Micheaux gave little consideration to the formal conventions of film art that had recently been developed by his contemporaries Porter and Griffith. Micheaux was not a film artist, nor was he a meticulous craftsman; at best, he was a novelist working as a filmmaker'[64]. In an interview between Grupenhoff and Lorenzo Tucker, a former Micheaux actor, Tucker declared that Micheaux deliberately avoided heightening the aesthetic quality of his films because it did not

Grupenhoff's critique, however, did not go unchallenged. J. Ronald Green and Horace Neal, Jr. responded to Grupenhoff's assertion that negative stereotypes held up to ridicule were minimal in Micheaux's pictures. Green and Neal argued that numerous reports in the African American press attacking Micheaux's images provided evidence that 'negative criticism has been integral to the long history of the reception of Micheaux's films'[66]. Green and Neal pointed to numerous characters in Micheaux's films who are indeed stereotypical of African Americans and who delivered racial slurs. Green and Neal concluded, 'His racial slurs are expressly intended for the improvement of the race; maybe his intentions justified his means, but the means retain their character as racial slurs. Micheaux's unabated righteous indignation toward what he considered flaws in his race is one of the central themes of his vision. His frankness may be disturbing to some, but he considered frankness essential to progress'[67]. However, Green and Neal argued, Micheaux's tendency to favour light complexioned actors was not consistent throughout his films. Green and Neal's critique demonstrated that Micheaux was being misread and misinterpreted. Their critique pointed to the need for a greater variety of competing explanations to surface to provide a much broader view of Micheaux.

Film scholar Mark Reid, pointing to the importance of Micheaux's films as precursors to the later black action films that would evolve in the 1970s, stated, 'The 'colored man with bricks' who defeats the Klan in *Symbol [of the Unconquered]* can be considered a superhero. Similar actions became quintessential requirements for Black action-film heroes (or heroines), in which physical acts of racism, Black-on-white violence, tend to expiate the white-on-Black violence with which the film began'[68]. Reid also concludes that because Micheaux had to rely on capital backing provided by whites in the later period of his filmmaking career, it is inappropriate for him to be referred to as an independent filmmaker during this period[69].

In addition to journal articles on Micheaux, in the decade of the 1980s, there were also film histories (or books) that included him. For example, Donald Bogle updated his discussion of Micheaux in his profile of the filmmaker in *Blacks in American Films and Television*. Bogle reflected on Micheaux's reception among black audiences:

> ... when some of his works were screened at festivals or conferences, many film enthusiasts were openly disappointed: his movies were technically crude (sometimes downright atrocious) and artistically misshapen. Consequently, by the 1980s, some were ready to dismiss Micheaux altogether. Actually, Micheaux was neither a supreme artist nor simply an inept dud. Instead he made movies that were, yes, frankly, sometimes terrible but which captured some of the spirit of his times and also heralded a new idea: that black movies could be entertainment vehicles for the mass black audience, that indeed a black star system could also exist[70].

Richard Grupenhoff, in his book *The Black Valentino*, seems to have broadened his research a little more than many of the critics, by actually interviewing an actor who appeared in Micheaux's films – for example, Lorenzo Tucker[71].

During this decade one of the most comprehensive examinations of Micheaux's literary works surfaced in Joseph Young's work, *Black Novelist as White Racist*. Young examined Micheaux's leanings toward Booker T. Washington's accommodationist philosophy, a highly controversial view at the time, and one Young suggested Micheaux used to gain financial wealth and marginal acceptance. Nonetheless, Young also accused Micheaux of being what today's language might term a 'closet-racist'. Young seemed to believe that Micheaux camouflaged his personal racist views by projecting them on to his characters. Young pointed to Micheaux's novels and provided examples of characters in the novels who espouse such views. Young stated that Micheaux 'condemned blacks to perpetual third-class citizenship, [by] holding them responsible for their condition. And he used the pseudoscience craniology to dismiss the majority of Blacks as genetically inferior'[72]. Such strong assertions are unfounded when Micheaux is explored in his entirety and this assertion, more importantly, reflects upon the extent to which Micheaux is continually misread or misinterpreted by scholars and researchers.

Although Young argued well in presenting his case, his work remains controversial. Once again, it seems that the Micheaux-interpretation has been a selective one, a pick-and-choose sampling of source material.

Richard Dyer wrote one of the most critical reviews Micheaux had ever received. *Body and Soul* (1924), according to Dyer, was a film in which Micheaux 'a black filmmaker, torn apart by the contradictions posed for black culture and politics by the image of an active black male sexuality, registers the problem of handling the image'[73]. Dyer was referring to Micheaux's casting of Paul Robeson in dual roles – one representing the abstract 'good' and the other representing the 'bad,' within a story about African Americans. In fact, Micheaux's reason for assigning duality of opposing roles to one actor – particularly the famous and sensational Paul Robeson – was much more complex than Dyer seems to have understood, and might easily be the subject of an entire paper in and of itself.

An overview of the critical works on Micheaux in the decade of the 1980s results in a profile of

Micheaux as a filmmaker who gave little time and attention to the technical aspects of filmmaking but who deserves to be commended for the portrayals of black life that he provided on the screen. The 1980s writers seemed to have dug deeper into Micheaux's background than those of the

Fig. 9. From the Baltimore *Afro-American*, 14 November 1931.

1960s and the 1970s. As a result, the 1980s writers gained a slightly better understanding of his motives, his ambiguities, and his actions. Still, these critics lacked ready access to resources and a well enough informed cultural historical view to correctly evaluate Micheaux's strengths and weaknesses. Such an evaluation did not emerge until the decade of the 1990s.

Micheaux's critical profile in the decade of the 1990s

In the 1990s journal articles and film histories dealing with Micheaux continued to evolve. Micheaux was now included in reference works such as the *International Dictionary of Films and Filmmakers*, where he was described as the most famous and prolific of black filmmakers. This source noted that assembling a complete list of his works was still under investigation by scholars and researchers and that Micheaux's provocative themes invited censorship difficulties[74].

In addition to inclusion in biographical dictionaries, Micheaux was the focus of several journal articles. For example, in 1991, Micheaux was featured in *American Film* in an article entitled 'One Man Show' where he was described as the original auteur of African American film[75]. Richard Gehr referred to Micheaux as 'A combination of Samuel Goldwyn and Samuel Glick who embraced the self-determination philosophies of W.E.B. DuBois, Booker T. Washington, and Marcus Garvey ...'[76]. In an uncomplimentary vein, Gehr contended that many of Micheaux's films give the impression that you are seeing the same story in every film. 'Micheaux appears to have only one story to tell – his own – and he tells it repeatedly'[77].

And although Gehr provided an insightful review of Micheaux, he, like other critics before him, continued to comment on Micheaux's inadequacy as a technician. Gehr stated, 'Micheaux's incompetence always entailed a naive, almost folkloric beauty, even if that might be at least partially credited to his use of second-rate post-production facilities'[78].

Gehr took note of the fact that Micheaux received criticism from both white and black critics. According to Gehr, black critics were disturbed by the fact that Micheaux reflected the colour divisions that existed in the African American community. In comparison, white critics, in particular film censors, were disturbed by his provocative themes. Gehr argued that 'Micheaux's was a world full of dichotomies; black/white, light/dark, rural/urban, rich/poor, even productive/shiftless'[79]. He contended that despite such criticisms, Micheaux still remained to be fully explained because while he exposed vices that permeated African American life, he also celebrated black achievements. Gehr believed that the decade of the 1990s would represent the beginning of a much more exhaustive critical review of Micheaux, as scholars and researchers attempted to further explain his motivations.

Two years later in 1993, *Black Film Review* dedicated an entire issue to early black filmmaking. In the article 'New Finds/Old Films', Pearl Bowser and Jane Gaines began to challenge the perception of Micheaux as an inept filmmaker and argued that this was 'an evaluation that doesn't hold up when one looks at an exceptionally well-preserved sound title such as *Swing* (1936) or Micheaux's more recently discovered silent films'[80]. Following the recent emergence of *Within Our Gates* (1919) and

A LICHTMAN THEATRE

BROADWAY

1515 Seventh Street, N. W.

GALA HOLIDAY PROGRAM

SUNDAY-MONDAY-TUESDAY
-WEDNESDAY
MAY 30—JUNE 2

—4 BIG DAYS—

Oscar Micheaux's
All-Colored Cast
in

'UNDERWORLD'

Starring

OSCAR POLK
BEE FREEMAN
SOL JOHNSON

Fig. 10. From the Baltimore *Afro-American*,
29 May 1937.

Symbol of the Unconquered (1920), films previously believed to have been lost, Micheaux is being reconsidered by film scholars and critics. In this same issue of *Black Film Review*, Alex Albright alluded to Micheaux's technique of recruiting former black vaudeville or stage entertainers such as Evelyn Preer, Sandy Burns, J. Homer Tutt, and Salem Tutt Whitney to appear in his films[81]. Gloria Gibson-Hudson in her examination of the Norman Film Manufacturing Company unveiled letters of correspondence between Micheaux and Richard Norman concerning Micheaux's impression of his competitors. This information is considered vital in reconstructing Micheaux's profile and in attempting to assess his level of expertise in the filmmaking business itself. In one letter, Norman referred to Micheaux as a genius who had fallen victim to exploitation because he had to operate with limited financial resources[82]. Clyde Taylor, in review of the changing black cinema and its audiences in the 1930s and 1940s, referred to audiences and re-

viewers' protests that erupted in response to Micheaux's insulting comments made in *God's Stepchildren*. Taylor stated 'That kind of message was too much for this new breed of young militants. It opened up a gulf between what looked to them as Tomism and the 'progressive and enlightened' kind of movies they wanted to encourage him to make'[83].

J. Ronald Green challenged the prevailing view of previous decades that Micheaux was an inadequate filmmaker, contending that 'Micheaux's style might be understood better as a retention of early film traits, from before the advent of glossy illusionism, than as a failed imitation of white movies. It is, in fact, a non-assimilative style that glosses a living struggle with an implicit "twoness", the double-consciousness of the African American experience'[84]. Green concluded that Micheaux's films combined high stylistic values with lower production values. 'Though he would like to assimilate into American cinema, he illustrates assimilation as a dangerous attraction'[85].

In 1994, two articles appeared that added to this growing body of literature on Micheaux. In *Popular Culture Review* I focused on Micheaux's most controversial films and argued that it was Micheaux's ability to create dispute, disagreement and discussion that in part explained his success and longevity as a filmmaker. I divided Micheaux's filmmaking career into two distinct periods – 1918–29 (a period in which he received positive reviews in the African American press, made many pictures, and produced films of relatively finer quality) and 1930–48 (a period in which he received more unfavourable criticism in the African American press, made fewer films, produced a number of re-releases or re-makes, and made more poor quality films). The article revealed that Micheaux was married twice and that he had named some of his unsympathetic film characters after identifiable family members and in-laws, inviting – nay virtually guaranteeing – protests and censorship difficulties, as in his first film, *The Homesteader* (1918). Because Micheaux patterned a hypocritical minister in the film after his father in-law he invited protest from African American ministers in Chicago who contended that the film was based on a minister of this city and thus petitioned Chicago film censors to halt its exhibition. Micheaux's fascination with lynching, the Ku Klux Klan, interracial relationships, and passing, are among the many themes he used to generate attention and create box-office appeal for his films[86].

In the second article mentioned above, James Hoberman explored the theme of passing and skin-colour bias as treated by Micheaux's films. Hoberman suggested that in *Veiled Aristocrats*, Micheaux improves upon Chesnutt's novel, *The House Behind the Cedars*, by having light-skinned Rena, the protagonist, marry a poor but honest dark-skinned black man. Hoberman stated, 'Playing to the audience, the eavesdropping trio deduces that her desire is sexual: "Once you've had a black man, you never go back". Whether or not you take this as Micheaux's comment on the poisonous irrationality of America's racial illness, it's safe to say that once you've seen a Micheaux movie, Hollywood 'perfection' will never seem the same'[87].

As journal articles began to provide more coverage of the works of Micheaux, scholars were taking a closer look at his seemingly ambivalent messages and at what were previously regarded as technically 'bad' movies. In the 1990s, Micheaux's critical profile was undergoing a change.

Bernard L. Peterson updated his previous Micheaux filmography in a chapter in *Celluloid Power*[88]. Peterson provided a more complete discussion of Micheaux's novels, film synopses and censorship difficulties. His work also identified and discussed actors who appeared in many of Micheaux's films. Peterson's work is very useful in ferreting out fact from fiction regarding Micheaux's work. For instance, Peterson suggested, 'Just how [Micheaux] went about learning the craft of movie-making is still not known. Since Leonard Galezio is listed as cameraman for *The Gunsaulus Mystery* ... it is conjectured that Micheaux originally learned the techniques by observation, trial and error'.

During the same year Bell Hooks examined Micheaux in her book *Black Looks: Race and Representation*[90]. Hooks asserted that:

Oscar Micheaux worked doggedly to create screen images that would disrupt and challenge conventional racist representations of blackness. ... Though Micheaux aimed to produce a counter-hegemonic art that would challenge white supremacist representations of 'blackness', he was not concerned with the simple reduction of black representation to a 'positive' image. In the spirit of oppositional creativity, he worked to produce images that would convey complexity of experience and feeling ...[91]

Bell Hooks provides one of the best explanations offered that fully explores Micheaux's ambivalent and duplicitous characters. She further stated, 'Though a race man, eager to work for the uplift of black people, he refused to accept the notion that black cultural production should simply be a response to white representations of blackness and, thereby, only portray blackness in a positive light. Insisting on diversity and complexity of image, his films set an example'[92]. In addition to journal articles, Micheaux critiques also surfaced in books or lengthier works such as conference proceedings. For example, papers presented on the works of Micheaux at a conference sponsored by the Black Film Center Archive at Indiana University in 1992 were published in 1994 by Phyllis Klotman and Gloria Gibson-Hudson. Among the papers included in these proceedings were J. Ronald Green's discussion of Micheaux's *Darktown Revue* and class conflict that existed within the African American community as reflected in this film. Green contended that criticism stating that Micheaux was preoccupied with portraying middle-class lifestyles in his films was unfounded. Green asserted 'While it is true that his narrative strategies often revolve around an idea of class, and that at times valorizes the middle class, Micheaux is not simply capitulating to whiteness. Rather he is seeking some middle ground, a vantage from which to explore the agonistic strength of class conflict, and from which to fight both fronts of the class war – the oppression from above and the degradation from below'[93].

Micheaux's critical profile as a filmmaker was examined in my article entitled 'Oscar Micheaux's *Body and Soul*: A Film of Conflicting Themes', in which I argued that Micheaux explored a variety of tensions that existed in the African American community in his films in order to expose such issues and to heighten audience awareness. For example, in *Body and Soul*, Micheaux explored the theme of good *vs* evil, using light-complexioned actors *vs* dark-complexioned actors, 'standard' English vs.

Fig. 11. From the Baltimore *Afro-American*, 1 October 1938.

dialect, and women vs. men. Micheaux, it can be argued was attempting to expose such dichotomies while using them in stereotypical techniques, as opposed to reinforcing negative images or portrayals of African Americans. Thus, Micheaux can no longer be viewed as providing insulting portrayals *per se*, because in this film, although he provided a portrayal of a hypocritical minister, played by Paul Robeson, he similarly provided a foil to this character, the minister's brother, also played by Robeson. 'By doing so, he leads the viewer to see affinities between these two characters, to "connect" the two images of goodness and evil and see the relationship both figuratively and literally'[94]. In concluding, I argued that the film is significant in black film history because it represented the joining of forces of two of the most controversial as well as outstanding African Americans in their respective fields, Robeson and Micheaux.

Other works, more specifically a collection of

essays that provided a much more critical examination of Micheaux's works than existed before the 1990s, included Manthia Diawara's *Black American Cinema*, in which J. Ron Green, Jane Gaines and Thomas Cripps shared their views. Green, in his examination, argued that Micheaux's style was a reflection of the cultural identity referred to by W.E.B. DuBois as 'twoness'. However, Green challenged Cripps's views that the twoness dilemma was resolved by opting for assimilation. Green stated: 'Cripps has described the pervasive, typical "mistakes" in Micheaux's style, and has shown that the Micheaux company was aware of them but unable to correct them because of the prohibitive expense of higher shooting ratios, retakes, master shots and professional editing. The apparatus of Cripps' own critical assessment, however, is founded on the unresolved contradiction of twoness'[95]. Green added that perhaps 'mistakes' should be characterized as such based on the criteria established by the culture from which they emanated (African American culture) as opposed to judging them by Hollywood standards. As for Micheaux's style, Green concluded 'My case is not that Micheaux intended every aspect of his style, but that the style is appropriate to and worthy of his situation and his issues, and that, therefore, his accomplishment was greater than has been recognized. Micheaux's style has served important themes and has provided a complex but worthy answer to the twoness dilemma. Micheaux has represented both the hope for and dangers of assimilation'[96].

Jane Gaines in her critique of Micheaux argued that his *Within Our Gates* (1919) was a response to D.W. Griffith's inflammatory *The Birth of a Nation* (1915). While Griffith emasculated African Americans with his despicable portrayals, Micheaux challenged and reversed Griffith's portrayals by featuring a lynching, race riot and attempted rape of a black woman by a white man – a man later discovered to have been her father. Gaines, comparing the reactions to the two films stated, 'While Griffith's "masterpiece" was enshrined, Micheaux's answer to it was "run out of town", so to speak'[97]. She added that 'Micheaux's film counters the White supremacist ideology of *The Birth of a Nation* in its images of the White lynch mob and White patriarch's assault on a Black

Fig. 12. American Museum of the Moving Image, 'Quarterly Guide to Exhibitions and Programs', January/March, 1994.

woman'[98]. In her discussion she too focused on Micheaux's style and stated that 'recent considerations of Micheaux do suggest that his maverick style confounds complacent assumptions about the connection between race, class, and aesthetic form'[99]. She further challenged pre-existing views that Micheaux was a technical amateur and created unflattering portrayals of African Americans. Gaines asserted that 'we could treat this style as more of an ingenious solution to the impossible demands of the conventions of classical Hollywood style, shortcuts produced by the exigencies of economics, certainly, but also modifications produced by an independent who had nothing at stake in strict adherence to Hollywood grammar'[100]. In response to his class position and unflattering portrayals of African Americans, Gaines, like Green, suggested that W.E.B. DuBois' school of thought regarding the 'double-consciousness' with which African Americans view themselves within the context of American society is an appropriate way to explain Micheaux. Gaines stated, 'It is really no wonder that the cultural products of an aspiring Black intellectual in this period gave us black men as scoundrels, religious hypocrites, gamblers and sluggards, and black women as madames, seductresses, and cheats. For he was seeing this black culture through the eyes of the White culture, for which this vision of an irredeemable Black underclass was flattering and entirely functional'[101].

Cripps, in review of Micheaux, concentrates his examination on the limitations imposed on the first generation of scholars to explore black film history; these scholars faced disinterested publishers and a lack of film indexes, filmographies or indexes of African American newspapers, among other resources, thus limiting their capacity to adequately reconstruct Micheaux. Cripps stated, 'Under these conditions, merely getting the story as straight as possible was a lofty ambition'[102]. Cripps, however, suggested that new scholars must be forced to address new questions surrounding Micheaux. He stated 'Particularly, we must insist on reaching beyond merely finding Micheaux a giant intellect who managed to make silk purses out of the sow's ear of poverty that he was given to work with. In what specific ways did he deviate from Hollywood practice, other than casting and rough edges? To what extent was this conscious? What do his surviving letters say that allow us to find him ...'[103]? Cripps concluded, 'Now we need to get on with it, neither raising more monuments nor living him down, but instead understanding him across the years in all his ambivalence and ambiguity'[104].

Perhaps all of the above comments must be taken into consideration to guide the scholarship on Micheaux in the decade of the 1990s. While much of it, to some extent, seems to have been inspired by an overwhelming desire to respond to and correct the early research on Micheaux (research that contained errors and misrepresentations, based on a paucity of material), contemporary scholars who have greater access to valid data certainly need to channel their energies into further exploring both the known and unknown about Micheaux. It is true that many scholars are in agreement on many aspects of Micheaux; still, much remains uncertain

about this filmmaker and therefore is deserving of further study. Several questions remain that will need to be explored in charting the course for conducting future research on Micheaux[105].

However, as for Micheaux's critical profile in the decade of the 1990s: he has been reinterpreted as a black filmmaker who elevated African Americans as opposed to denigrating them; he has begun to be thought of as a political activist because of his public display of lynchings and race riots; he is no longer regarded as a 'technically bad' filmmaker, but rather one whose technical failings could be excused because of excruciating work conditions; and his seeming ambivalence could be interpreted as a reflection of the twoness with which he viewed himself as an African American residing in American society and culture. It should be noted, however, that this profile is not an attempt to explain away his shortcomings but is an attempt to situate Micheaux in his appropriate historical context and bestow upon him the credit he deserves without making him either a 'hero' or 'villain'. As Micheaux's critical profile continues to evolve, scholars and critics who attempt to characterize this auteur filmmaker will be both criticized and applauded. He undoubtedly was, at the very least, in the words of Bell Hooks, always 'celebrating blackness'. Micheaux will remain a significant figure in American film history.

As Micheaux continues to be explored, several archives and museums are attempting to preserve his works or pay tribute to Micheaux. The Smithsonian Institution, American Museum of the Moving Image, Museum of Modern Art, International Museum of Photography at George Eastman House, Schomburg Collection, and the Library of Congress have attempted to either restore or celebrate Micheaux films. More recently, an *Oscar Micheaux Society Newsletter* has been created as an organ or vehicle by which to promote dialogue and advance the state of research on Micheaux. The American Museum of the Moving Image in 1994 presented a retrospective on Micheaux and his works and Yale University in January of 1995 held a conference on Micheaux. Additional film studies conferences have also paid tribute to Micheaux. Collectively, these efforts have been made to expand the scholarship and research on Micheaux as he continues to be explored as an auteur African

American filmmaker who remains one of the most significant filmmakers in American cinema history.

The 1990s have become the decade to assure the permanence of a historic position for Oscar Micheaux in the story of American cinema. Micheaux's mark is indeed worthy of preserving, and we are well on the way to knowing how to read that mark.○

Notes

1. J. Ronald Green, 'Oscar Micheaux's Darktown Revue: Caricature and Class Conflict' in *In Touch With the Spirit: Black Religious and Musical Expression in American Cinema, Conference Proceedings*, July 1992, Phyllis Klotman and Gloria Gibson-Hudson, eds. (Bloomington: Indiana University, Black Film Center/Archive, 1994), 73.

2. Andrew Sarris, *The American Cinema: Directors and Directions 1929–1968* (New York: E. P. Dutton & Co., 1968), 25–37 and Edward Murray, *Nine American Film Critics: A Study of Theory and Practice* (New York: Frederick Ungar Publishing Co., 1975), 38–66.

3. Mark Reid, *Redefining Black Film* (Berkeley and Los Angeles: University of California Press, 1993), 11–14.

4. 'Going Backstage with the Scribe,' *Chicago Defender*, 18 June 1932, 8.

5. Theophilus Lewis, 'The Harlem Sketch Book', *New York Amsterdam News*, 16 April 1930, 10.

6. Ibid.

7. 'Betrayal, Severely Criticized, A Bore', *Chicago Defender*, 10 July 1948, 28.

8. Thomas Yenser ed., *Who's Who in Colored America: A Biographical Dictionary of Notable Living Persons of African Descent in America*, Third Ed. (New York: Who's Who In Colored America Corp, 1933), 302.

9. Carl Milton Hughes, *The Negro Novelist: A Discussion of the Writings of American Negro Novelists 1940–1950* (New York: The Citadel Press, 1953), 130.

10. Robert A. Bone, *The Negro Novel in America* (New Haven: Yale University Press, 1958), 49.

11. Ibid.

12. Thomas Cripps, 'Black Films and Film Makers: Movies in the Ghetto, B.P. (Before Poitier),' *Negro Digest* (February 1969): 25.

13. Ibid., 27.

14. Janis Hebert, 'Oscar Micheaux: A Black Pioneer', *South Dakota Review* 11, No. 4 (Winter, 1973–74), 62–69.

15. Ibid., 68–69.

16. Arlene Elder, 'Oscar Micheaux: The Melting Post on the Plains', *The Old Northwest* 2, No. 3 (September 1976), 306.

17. Dwight W. Hoover, 'Oscar Micheaux' in *Dictionary of American Biography*, Supplement Five (1951–1955), John Garraty ed. (New York: Charles Scribner's Sons, 1977), 490.

18. Edward Mapp, *Directory of Blacks in the Performing Arts* (Metuchen: Scarecrow, 1978), 251–252. According to Oscar Micheaux's death certificate provided by the North Carolina State Board of Health, Bureau of Vital Statistics, Micheaux died 27 March 1951 in Charlotte, N.C.

19. Donald Bogle, *Toms, Coons, Mulattoes, Mammies, and Bucks: An Interpretative History of Blacks in American Films* (New York: Continuum Press, 1989 [1973]), 109–115.

20. Ibid., 115–116.

21. Eileen Landay, *Black Film Stars* (New York: Drake Publishers, 1973), 45.

22. Ibid., 45–46.

23. Gary Null, *Black Hollywood: The Negro in Motion Pictures* (New York: The Citadel Press, 1975), 11.

24. Daniel Leab, *From Sambo to Superspade: The Black Experience in Motion Pictures* (Boston: Houghton Mifflin, 1975), 76.

25. Ibid., 81.

26. Henry Sampson, *Blacks In Black and White: A Source Book on Blacks in Films* (Metuchen: Scarecrow Press, 1977), 42.

27. Ibid.

28. Thomas Cripps, *Slow Fade to Black: The Negro in American Film, 1900–1942* (New York: Oxford University Press, 1993 [1977]), 183.

29. Ibid.

30. Ibid.

31. Ibid., 193.

32. Daniel J. Leab, 'A Pale Black Imitation: All-Colored Films 1930–60', *Journal of Popular Film* 4, No. 1 (1975): 72. This same article appeared as a chapter in Leab's *From Sambo to Superspade*.

33. Ibid., 73.

34. Ibid., 74.

35. Ibid.

36. Ibid.

37. James Hoberman, 'A Forgotten Black Cinema Surfaces', *Village Voice* 20 (17 November 1975): 86.

38. Ibid., 88.

39. Ibid.

40. Ibid.

41. Penelope Gilliatt, 'The Current Cinema: Retorts To *The Birth of a Nation*', *New Yorker* 52, No. 6 (29 March 1976), 88.

42. Bernard L. Peterson, Jr.,'The Films of Oscar Micheaux: America's First Fabulous Black Filmmaker,' *The Crisis* 84, No. 4 (April 1979): 136.

43. Ibid., 141.

44. Phyllis Klotman, *Frame by Frame – A Black Filmography* (Bloomington: Indiana University Press, 1979). An updated version of this work is in press.

45. Kenneth Wiggins Porter, 'Oscar Micheaux', in *Dictionary of American Negro Biography*, Rayford Logan and Michael R. Winston, eds. (New York: W.W. Norton & Co., 1982), 433.

46. Ibid., 433–434.

47. John Wakeman, ed., *World Film Directors Vol. I 1890–1945* (New York: H.W. Wilson, Co., 1987), 766.

48. Ibid., 767.

49. Ibid., 767–770.

50. Ibid.

51. Chester Fontenot, Jr. 'Oscar Micheaux, Black Novelist and Film Maker', in *Vision and Refuge: Essays on the Literature of the Great Plains*, Virginia Faulkner and Frederick C. Luebke, eds. (Lincoln: University of Nebraska Press, 1982), 109–125.

52. Ibid., 109.

53. Ibid., 110.

54. Ibid., 123.

55. James Hoberman, 'Bad Movies', *Film Comment* 16 no. 4 (July-August 1980): 11.

56. Ibid., 11–12.

57. Ibid., 12.

58. Ibid.

59. Pearl Bowser, 'Sexual Imagery and the Black Woman in American Cinema', in *Black Cinema Aesthetics: Issues In Independent Black Filmmaking*, Gladstone Yearwood, ed. (Athens: Ohio University Center for Afro-American Studies, 1982), 47.

60. James Hoberman, 'Film: American Fairy Tales', *Village Voice* (12 June 1984), 48.

61. Ibid.

62. Donald Bogle, 'No Business Like Micheaux Business "B" ... for Black', *Film Comment* 21, No. 5 (September-October 1985), 32.

63. Ibid., 33.

64. Richard Grupenhoff, 'The Rediscovery of Oscar Micheaux, Black Film Pioneer', *Journal of Film and Video* 40, No. 1 (Winter 1988): 40–48.

65. Ibid., 46.

66. J. Ronald Green and Horace Neal, Jr., 'Oscar Micheaux and Racial Slur: A Response to "The Rediscovery of Oscar Micheaux"', *Journal of Film and Video* 40, No. 4 (Fall 1988): 67.

67. Ibid., 70.

68. Mark Reid, 'Pioneer Black Filmmaker: The Achievement of Oscar Micheaux', *Black Film Review* 4, No. 2 (Spring 1988): 6.

69. Ibid., 7.

70. Donald Bogle, Blacks in *American Films and Television: An Illustrated Encyclopedia* (New York: Fireside-Simon & Schuster, 1988), 422.

71. Richard Grupenhoff, *The Black Valentino: The Stage and Screen Career of Lorenzo Tucker* (Metuchen: Scarecrow Press, 1988).

72. Joseph A. Young, *Black Novelist As White Racist: The Myth of Black Inferiority in the Novels of Oscar Micheaux* (Westport: Greenwood Press, 1989), xi.

73. Richard Dyer, *Heavenly Bodies: Film Stars and Society* (New York: St. Martin's Press,1986), 115.

74. Rob Edelman, 'Oscar Micheaux' in *International Dictionary of Films and Filmmakers – 2 Directors*, Second Edition, Nicholas Thomas, ed. (Chicago: St. James Press, 1991), 576–577.

75. Richard Gehr, 'One Man Show', *American Film* (May 1991): 34.

76. Ibid.

77. Ibid., 36.

78. Ibid., 38.

79. Ibid., 39.

80. Pearl Bowser and Jane Gaines, 'New Finds/Old Films', *Black Film Review* 7, No. 4. (1992): 2.

81. Alex Albright, 'Micheaux, Vaudeville, and Black Cast Film', *Black Film Review* 7, No. 4 (1992): 7+.

82. Gloria Gibson-Hudson, 'The Norman Film Manufacturing Company', *Black Film Review* 7, No. 4 (1992): 20.

83. Clyde Taylor, 'Crossed Over and Can't Get Black', *Black Film Review* 7, No. 4 (1992): 25.

84. J. Ronald Green, 'The Micheaux Style', *Black Film Review* 7, No. 4 (1992): 32–33.

85. Ibid., 34.

86. Charlene Regester, 'Lynched, Assaulted, Intimidated: Oscar Micheaux's Most Controversial Films,' *Popular Culture Review* 5, no. 1 (February 1994).

87. James Hoberman, 'Race to Race Movies', *Village Voice*, (22 February 1994).

88. Bernard L. Peterson, Jr., 'A Filmography of Oscar Micheaux: America's Legendary Black Filmmaker', in *Celluloid Power: Social Film Criticism from* The Birth of a Nation *to* Judgment at Nuremberg, David Platt, ed. (Metuchen: Scarecrow Press, 1992), 113–141.

89. Ibid., 117.

90. Bell Hooks, *Black Looks: Race and Representation*, (Boston: South End Press, 1992). Hooks' chapter entitled 'Micheaux: Celebrating Blackness' was first printed in the *Black American Literature Forum* 25, No. 2 (Summer 1991).

91. Ibid., 351.

92. Ibid., 354.

93. J. Ronald Green, 'Oscar Micheaux's *Darktown Revue*: Caricature and Class Conflict', In *Touch With the Spirit: Black Religious and Musical Expression in American Cinema Conference Proceedings*, July 1992, Phyllis Klotman and Gloria J. Gibson-Hudson, eds. (Bloomington: Indiana University. Black Film Center/Archive, Department of Afro-American Studies, 1994), 73.

94. Charlene Regester, 'Oscar Micheaux's *Body and Soul*: A Film of Conflicting Themes', in *In Touch With the Spirit: Black Religious and Musical Expression in American Cinema Conference Proceedings*, July 1992, Phyllis Klotman and Gloria J. Gibson-Hudson, eds. (Bloomington: Indiana University, Black Film Center/Archive, Department of Afro-American Studies, 1994), 64–65.

95. J. Ronald Green, '"Twoness" in the Style of Oscar Micheaux', in *Black American Cinema*, Manthia Diawara, ed. (New York: Routledge, 1993), 31.

96. Ibid., 45.

97. Jane Gaines, 'Fire and Desire: Race, Melodrama, and Oscar Micheaux', in *Black American Cinema* Manthia Diawara, ed. (New York: Routledge, 1993), 50–51.

98. Ibid., 61.

99. Ibid., 62–63.

100. Ibid., 64.

101. Ibid., 66.

102. Thomas Cripps, 'Oscar Micheaux: The Story Continues', in *Black American Cinema*, Manthia Diawara, ed. (New York: Routledge, 1993), 75.

103. Ibid., 77–78.

104. Ibid., 78.

105. J. Ronald Green has developed a set of guiding questions to direct the course of research on Micheaux in an unpublished manuscript.

Film History, Volume 7, pp. 450–455, 1995. Copyright © John Libbey & Company
ISSN: 0892-2160. Printed in Great Britain

Edward D. Wood, Jr. - Some notes on a subject for further research

Robert S. Birchard

I n an odd sense Edward D. Wood, Jr. has become the latter-day equivalent of Erich von Stroheim – the 'Hollywood Scapegoat' in this age of devolution. That Wood has been elected 'The Worst Director of All Time' by those curmudgeonly arbiters of the worst in filmmaking, Harry and Michael Medved, adds to the critical aura that currently surrounds Wood and his work, while Rudolph Grey's oral history/biography *Ed Wood – Nightmare of Ecstasy* and Tim Burton's 1994 *Ed Wood* biopic have created a highly romanticized fable that prints legend with just enough verisimilitude to suggest that it's all true. In these works Ed Wood emerges as a schizophrenic character, at once a victim of capitalist oppression, denied access to the means of production and distribution by the dark forces of commercialism, while at the same time strangely able to express his (admittedly alternative) psyche in a highly personal autobiographical cinema.

The current misplaced nostalgia for Ed Wood ignores a number of historical realities that ought to be considered before the filmmaker's career can be put into perspective. I will attempt to explore some of these issues to provide a jumping off point for future film historians and critics.

Ed Wood was not unique

For those unfamiliar with the low-end fringes of Hollywood filmmaking before the age of video it is easy to assume that Ed Wood was an original, but in fact he was simply one of many toiling in rather fruitless fields. Without straining my brain I can think of a handful of filmmakers whose work was every bit as demented as that of Ed Wood.

Victor Adamson (professionally known as Denver Dixon) used to turn out feature Westerns in the early 1930s for $2,500.00 The economies involved in these efforts included purchasing food for the location shoots at the damaged canned goods store in east Los Angeles. In Dixon's cinema every cut was a mismatch, every actor an amateur, and every plot incomprehensible. In an effort to avoid making opticals, Dixon was known to lower a piece of black cardboard over the lens to simulate a wipe.

Dwain Esper created such demented masterworks as *Maniac* (1935), which concedes nothing to Ed Wood's *Plan 9 From Outer Space* in its mind-numbing awfulness. Esper and his producer Dan Sonney carved out financially successful careers in the movie business by offering investors a hundred thousand dollar picture for a fifty thousand dollar investment. The pictures were produced for eight to ten thousand. Esper and Sonney pocketed the difference, leaving the investors holding the bag when the films failed to perform at the box-office.

Robert Birchard wrote on Jack London and the Movies for the first issue of *Film History*. His most recent book is *King Cowboy: Tom Mix and the Movies*. Correspondence c/o 3207 Brookhill Street, La Crescenta, California 91214, USA.

Kroger Babb (pronounced like Roger, with 'K' in front, Bobb) became a legend among exploitation filmmakers with his 'educational' *Mom and Dad*, a hodgepodge of graphic medical footage of a woman giving birth, and soft-core pornography with a modicum of tacked-on redeeming social value.

Joe Robertson, who had an Ed Wood screenplay and performance for *The Photographer* (1969), certainly didn't need Wood to create *The Slime People* or *The First Nudie Western* (ca 1975).

Ted V. Mikels brought *The Corpse Grinders* (1973), *The Worm Eaters* (1975), *Ten Violent Women* (1982) and others to the screen with labour from unwitting volunteer film students who are still waiting for their profit participation checks to come through.

Gene Bicknel, middle-aged owner of a chain of Pizza Huts with a bad hair-weave and a shoe polish dye-job cast himself as the dashing romantic hero in *The Gypsy Angels* – notable as the film in which Vanna White goes topless (much to her relief, the picture remains unreleased)...

Ross Hagen made a film about a fighting rooster around 1975 called *Supercock*. He gave lollipops as promotional give-aways and called them '*Supercock* suckers'. The film finally found some playdates under the title *Foul Play* (not to be confused with the major studio film of that title) ...

Lee Madden, who had a mainstream career as a TV and industrial film director, actually produced a picture which he called *Two Scared Niggers in a Haunted House*. By the time the film starring Sherman Hemsley was released as *Ghost Fever*, Madden wisely adopted the 'Alan Smithee' pseudonym approved by the Directors Guild for disowned films.

I have met or known all of the above, except Dixon, Esper and Sonney, and I can honestly say they were intelligent, articulate, charming men with a great love for the movies. Like Ed Wood, they could describe their films with such enthusiasm that you couldn't wait to see them; but also like Ed Wood their work simply did not measure up to their imaginations. They all pursued a demented muse; and if one were to make a side-by-side comparison it would be difficult to distinguish in any substantial way their films from Wood's.

Ed Wood did not bring a personal vision to his projects

In his nearly thirty-year movie career (from the late 1940s to the late 1960s), Ed Wood went from making B Westerns, to exploitational docu-dramas, to juvenile delinquency pictures, to science fiction, to soft-core and finally hard-core pornography. It is certainly no accident that his work moved along this path – it was the path of the low-budget picture through the same time period.

There is no doubt that Ed Wood was a big fan of the Westerns. Like his sometime collaborator and one-time room-mate Alex Gordon, Wood was an enthusiastic admirer of Buck Jones, Tom Tyler, and the other cowboy stars of the 1930s. Wood's first film efforts were low-budget Westerns, but the theatrical market for these films disappeared with the flood of oaters that hit TV in the early 1950s. Wood tried to promote a Western TV series in 1953 before abandoning the genre.

While Wood's fondness for cross-dressing may have made him an ideal choice as actor-director-writer of *Glen or Glenda?*, the film was an assignment and not a project that Wood originated. The prime force behind the picture was producer George Weiss, who sought to exploit then-current headlines about Christine Jorgenson's sex-change operation. The final result certainly had some Ed Wood 'touches', but it was also padded with stock footage from other Weiss productions and Weiss clearly shaped the final product for the screen.

Two of Wood's more successful efforts, *Jail Bait* (1954) and *Bride of the Monster* (1955), were derived from stories by Alex Gordon. Although Rudolph Grey insists that *Bride of the Monster* is really Wood's work, Alex Gordon tells me that Wood merely put his story into screenplay form and that the now infamous 'I have no home ...' speech that Bela Lugosi delivers was in Gordon's original[1]. Since there can be no professional advantage to be gained from claiming authorship of the speech (and because I've known Alex Gordon for many years), I'm inclined to believe him. Adding further critical support to Gordon's version of events, John McCarty asserts that *Bride of the Monster* is '... the nearest Wood ever came to making a cohesive – and coherent – feature film', suggesting that Gordon's story contributed to the relative quality of the screenplay[2].

Fig. 1. Edward D. Wood, Jr. (right) signs up some financing for *Bride of the Monster* (1955) as his only bankable star, Bela Lugosi, looks on approvingly.

Similarly, Wood's screenplay for *The Violent Years* was based on a story by the film's producer, Roy Reid. Although *Plan 9 From Outer Space* is an original, it is clearly patterned after other science-fiction films of the era.

Wood's many paperback novels and non-fiction pieces suggest he was a modestly competent hack-writer who wrote to order in rigidly established formulas. As often as not it would seem that any 'personal vision' Wood projected in his work represented the vision of others.

Even Wood's penchant for using down-and-out Hollywood old-timers seems to have been inspired by Alex Gordon. It was Gordon who introduced Ed Wood to Bela Lugosi (Gordon had been Lugosi's publicist on an English vaudeville tour in the late 1940s).

Ed Wood was not exploited by the system

Wood's career was spent in the marginal fringes of the Hollywood film industry making pictures for the so-called 'states rights' market. Under this system, completed films were sold to regional distributors for an advance against percentages. The territories and the prices to be paid by regional sub-distributors, who were usually exhibitors with small theatre chains, were established in the earliest days of the feature film – and did not change appreciably over the years.

In 1914 Frank Paret outlined the basic states rights formula for his employer, The California Motion Picture Corporation[3]:

'Herewith I am giving you the prices which a Standard Play may be expected to bring at the present time, if sold on a State-Right Basis, also the number of prints necessary for each territory.

New England States	(2 prints)	$3000
City and State of New York	(3 prints)	$6000
New Jersey	(1 print)	$1200
Eastern Pennsylvania, Delaware, Maryland, DC	(2 prints)	$3000
Western Pennsylvania, Ohio, Kentucky, West Virginia	(2 prints)	$2750
Illinois and Indiana	(2 prints)	$3500
Kansas, N. & S. Dakota, Oklahoma	(2 prints)	$2200
Texas	(2 prints)	$3000
Oregon, Washington, Nevada	(1 print)	$2000
California, Arizona, New Mexico	(1 print)	$3000
Colorado, Wyoming, Utah	(1 print)	$1750
Minnesota and Wisconsin	(2 prints)	$2500
Michigan	(1 print)	$2000
Dominion of Canada	(2 prints)	$2000
Southern States not included above	(3 prints)	$3500
TOTAL	(27 prints)	$41,400

This formula worked when producers like Cecil B. DeMille and D.W. Griffith were producing features for fifteen thousand dollars a piece, but as production costs spiralled upward it became clear that states rights distribution could not create enough revenue to make film production profitable, and the modern system of distribution came into existence with the establishment of Paramount Pictures Corporation in 1914.

By the 1930s the potential income from the states rights markets had not increased to any extent. To have any hope of making money on their films, independent producers were forced to keep budgets for non-Western features in the fifteen to twenty thousand dollar range, while the average Western was made for eight to ten thousand. The whole states rights market virtually collapsed in the mid-1930s as Monogram and later Republic Pictures created an elaborate house of cards whereby regional distributors (now called franchise holders) offered guarantees of payment on delivery for their territories, and the producers discounted the paper at the bank to raise production money. This worked as long as there was a demand for pictures in the theatres and as long as the producers could supply a steady stream of product. Television severely crippled the low-end theatrical market. As a result, Republic was forced out of production in the late 1950s after attempts at becoming a main-stream studio, while Monogram also tried to change its approach to production and distribution and managed to stumble along as Allied Artists into the 1970s.

The crumbling of the Republic/Monogram strangle-hold on the independent market created the possibility that independent production might once again flourish – but the economics were no better in the 1950s than they were in the 1930s.

One would expect the states rights formula to have changed drastically between 1914 and 1954, but the truth of the matter is that it remained relatively stable. Certainly California became a more important territorial component in the intervening years, and admission prices increased several fold – but overall revenues on marginal pictures did not increase in any substantial way.

Some random examples from distributors like Columbia Pictures and United Artists suggest the overall trend from the mid-1930s to the mid-1950s;

In 1937, the Columbia Western *Outlaws of the Prairie*, starring Charles Starrett grossed $72,750.00 in domestic film rentals. Fifteen years later, *The Kid From Broken Gun*, Starrett's last starring film for Columbia, grossed $75,000.00. Also at Columbia, the Three Stooges shorts were produced for about $18,000.00 and grossed about $33,000.00 in 1936 when they started and these figures remained virtually unchanged when they made their last two-reelers for the studio in 1958.

Similarly, figures for three United Artists science fiction releases show that films in this genre also played in a very restricted economic range.

Fig. 2. Lobby card for Wood's best known film, *Plan 9 From Outer Space* (1959).

The Creeping Unknown (1956), for example, grossed $244,932.00, and *The Monster That Challenged the World* (1959) brought $286,442.00 in domestic rentals. *The Four Skulls of Jonathan Drake* (also 1959) did a paltry $136,135.00 in rentals. These are films released by major distributors. Independent product with no ad budgets or recognized stars could not have done as well in the catch-as-catch-can world of regional sub-distributors[4].

Alex Gordon first came into contact with Ed Wood on Johnny Carpenter's *The Lawless Rider* (finally released by United Artists in 1952). Wood wrote the script for the picture with Carpenter and also served as production manager.

Through his brother, film broker Richard Gordon, Alex arranged for a ten-thousand dollar guarantee to be paid upon delivery of the finished picture which was to cost no more than seventeen thousand dollars.

According to Gordon, Ed Wood was a dear

soul but an inept production manager. Costs skyrocketed to fifty-seven thousand, and the investors put a lien on the picture in an effort to secure their investment. With the aid of attorney Sam Arkoff, Gordon managed to persuade the principal investor, a Mormon Bishop, into lifting the lien so the picture could be distributed.

Given this anecdote, it seems clear that what happened on Wood's own productions was a replay of what occurred on *The Lawless Rider*. He could not control the budgets, over-sold the pictures to investors, and ended up losing any financial claim in them. Rudolph Grey quotes Ed Wood as blaming financier Donald E. McCoy for being overindulgent and spending eighty-nine thousand dollars on *Bride of the Monster*, but Wood's accusation was self-serving and did not address the issue of his own pattern of profligacy. While eighty-nine thousand was a pittance by major studio standards in the 1950s, such a budget made a marginal picture like *Bride of the Monster* a dead-issue as far as potential profits were concerned in the states rights arena. The project simply wasn't worth that sort of expenditure.

Ed Wood's films did not find a wide audience

That Ed Wood has become well-known in recent years is one of the great ironies of film history, because in his own time Wood's films went virtually unseen. *Glen or Glenda?, Bride of the Monster, Plan 9 From Outer Space, et al.* received only limited theatrical distribution, and when they did screen they mostly played in grind houses and small-time drive-ins that did not cater to a discriminating clientele. TV made these films available to a wider audience than they ever found in theatres.

Several years ago, in the wake of the *Rocky Horror Picture Show* midnight-matinee phenomenon Paramount Pictures acquired *Glen or Glenda?* with hopes that it would generate similar audience response. It died. Audiences simply weren't interested after the initial curiosity. And the tradition continues with Tim Burtons's film, *Ed Wood*, which nose-dived with a resounding box-office thud.

While there are certainly devotees of rotten cinema (and there may be more of them now than ever before), they do not (and never did) exist in sufficient numbers to cause even a minor blip at the box-office.

Wood was energetic, if not gifted, and managed to hang around the picture business for quite a long time. By mainstream Hollywood standards, he was a hanger-on, a never-was, a loser, or as Sam Arkoff described him, a 'one-lung producer'. If Ed Wood's life and career are worthy of any serious critical or historical study, they need to be examined and measured against the economic and sociological context of the low-budget film market of the time. That Ed Wood has become something of a folk hero among students of film simply ignores the real man and his work and contributes to the general public's suspicion and lack of regard for the discipline known as 'critical studies'. ✪

Notes

1. Grey, Rudolph, *Nightmare of Ecstasy – The Life and Art of Edward D. Wood, Jr.*, Feral House, 1992, 1994. References to Alex Gordon's reminiscences are derived from informal interviews with the author over several years.

2. McCarty, John (editor), *The Sleaze Merchants* (New York: St. Martin's Griffin, 1995).

3. Letter from Frank Paret to California Motion Picture Corporation dated 1 July 1914, in author's collection.

4. The film rental figures quoted in this article come from Karl Thiede, a researcher who works in film distribution for 20th Century-Fox.

Film History, Volume 7, pp. 456–476, 1995. Copyright © John Libbey & Company
ISSN: 0892-2160. Printed in Great Britain

Joseph Lerner and the post-war New York film renaissance

An interview by Richard Koszarski

By the mid-1930s, New York City had ceased to be a factor in the production of theatrical feature pictures. Where Paramount alone had released 14 New York productions in 1931, the total for all producers by 1937 was close to zero. In other respects, of course, the city remained a powerful industry centre: cartoons, newsreels, documentaries and industrial films continued to flourish there, and experimental television broadcasting was just beginning. It remained the headquarters of distribution and exhibition, and housed the executive offices of America's great studios, whose factories were established in southern California, three thousand miles distant. But the number of theatrical feature pictures that would be produced in New York during the decade 1935–45 could be counted on one's fingers.

The reasons for this eclipse were economic, cultural, political, technological, and even meteorological. Whatever the explanation, when Ben Hecht and Charles MacArthur turned out the lights at the Astoria Studio in 1935, a filmmaking tradition which dated to the invention of cinema had essentially been snuffed out.

The most immediate casualties were mid-level creative talents unable to transfer their services to Hollywood. A few of the best technicians, like cinematographers George Folsey and Joseph Ruttenberg, were able to crash the west coast studios (and unions). Most were not. Those left behind could maintain their skills either in the non-theatrical or

short-film sector, or in the theatre (a major outlet for gaffers and scenic artists). But the longer the production drought continued, the more obsolete the studio facilities became, and the more the local pool of technical skills atrophied.

The most significant loss, however, was to the American cinema as a whole. Merely in terms of quantity, the disappearance of feature production in the east resembled the loss of a moderately-sized national cinema, not as expansive as Hollywood, but still capable of generating large numbers of first class features with A-list stars and directors. This was not just another product stream but, pace 'The Classical Hollywood Cinema', a different voice with an identifiably different agenda. Different production heads, different story departments, different talent. In fact, not just different, but rival.

When aware of this situation at all, most histories indicate a revival of New York production beginning with Kazan's On the Waterfront (1954) or Lumet's 12 Angry Men (1957). Some point to location films like The Naked City (1948), although the local contribution to films like these was minimal. No historian has investigated production in New York during the decade before On the Waterfront, and no history acknowledges the contributions of Joseph Lerner in helping to reconstruct this industry from the scraps that had survived after 1945.

Joseph Lerner is not mentioned in such encyclopaedic surveys as Sadoul, Sarris, Roud, Wakeman, Coursodon & Sauvage, Halliwell or Katz (where at least one of his credits is attributed to the unrelated, and remarkably better known, Irving Lerner). This is not the place to argue the merits of the four *noir*-tinged features he directed between 1947 and 1951. Because all are unusually hard to see (one, *The Fight Never Ends*, may no longer even exist), any claims made here would be rather hard to verify. Robert Porfirio, writing in Alain Silver and Elizabeth Ward's *Film Noir: an Encyclopedic Reference to the American Style*, offers one of the few modern commentaries on any Joseph Lerner film in his essay on *Guilty Bystander*. The film is not entirely marred by its budgetary limitations, he suggests, but somehow turns them to its advantage in creating an authentically grubby New York underworld – something which might be said about Lerner's other features, *C-Man* and *Mr. Universe*, as well.

The reason this interview with Joseph Lerner appears in an issue on authorship and *auteurism* is that Lerner shares more than he might have liked to admit with such non-conventional filmmakers as Oscar Micheaux and Edward D. Wood. Without direct access to established studio facilities, distribution systems, or means of financing, all these men had to invent the American cinema for themselves, making use of whatever was affordable and available. As writer-producer-directors they were the authors of their work in the fullest sense. Today this sort of filmmaking is often the rule rather than the exception, but working during the twilight of the 'classical studio system', Lerner was still busy helping deconstruct it.

In this interview Lerner discusses many of the currents which shaped independent cinema during the decade after World War II: innovative financing and distribution arrangements, the influence of documentary production techniques, the adoption of advanced technology (like magnetic recording) then unknown in Hollywood, and the return to what Janet Staiger might characterize as a neo-director-unit production system. In addition, he is remarkably candid about union problems, the use of blacklisted talent, the link between race movies and independent cinema, the 'devious' production realities which have always affected low-budget filmmaking, and his own inability to continue independent operations.

Lerner was born in New York in 1911. He worked on Broadway and in regional theatre during the early 1930s, and at RKO and Columbia in Hollywood from 1934–41. In 1942 he returned to New York, where he spent the war at the Signal Corps Photographic Center in Astoria, serving as writer, director and head of special productions. After the period discussed in this interview he continued to work in various areas of motion picture and television production in Europe and the United States. 'Planned Inspiration', a book on directing he wrote in the 1970s, remains unpublished. His wife, Geraldine Lerner, was a film editor who worked with him on all of his personal projects. She is the 'voice off' in this interview (indicated as GL), which took place in the Astoria Studio on 16 July 1987. The studio, which had once housed both Paramount Pictures and the Signal Corps, was at this time home to the American Museum of the Moving Image, which was preparing its renovation of one of the outlying studio buildings, a fact Lerner refers to in the interview.

JOSEPH LERNER

Let me tell you a few things about the beginnings, since it is on record that I am the first man, the first producer, the first writer, to make a complete film in New York. I got out of the Army looking for a job, didn't want to go back to California for whatever reasons, and I hooked up with Max Rosenbaum and we started a thing called Visual Arts Productions. Made a couple of shorts here for Universal, one with George Givot.

Where did you film the shorts?

On the streets. In somebody's house.

No studio?

No studio. I've got a thing about studios. It'd cost us six thousand dollars a piece, five thousand, four thousand, three thousand. There was a guy at Universal kinda liked me, and so he'd throw me a bone every once in awhile, and that kept Visual Arts Productions going for about seven or eight months.

The Fight Never Ends (1947)

One day a very nice black guy came in called Bill Alexander. Anyway, he says 'You Joe Lerner'? I say, 'I'm Joe Lerner'. 'You're from Hollywood aren't you'? I say, 'Yes I am'. 'Well, I want a movie'. I'll

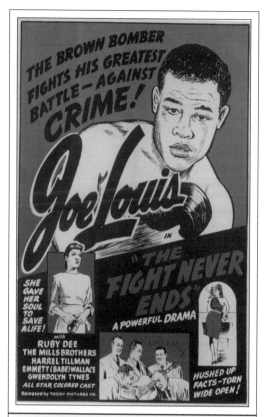

Fig. 1. One-sheet poster for Lerner's first feature, *The Fight Never Ends* (1947). [Courtesy of The Carson Collection.]

never forget that dialogue because that didn't make any sense to me. Because I'm from Hollywood doesn't mean I know anything about the picture business. He says, 'I've got $25,000 and I think I can get Joe Louis for a couple of days, I can get the Mills Brothers for a couple of days, and I'll get a bunch of people out of Harlem to do whatever the hell you're going to write about'. And I said, 'I don't understand'. He said, 'Make me a movie, you're a Hollywood guy, make me a movie'. He didn't ask me if I was a director, writer, gaffer or gofer, it didn't make any difference, 'cause I was from Hollywood, so I knew everything about the film industry. Well, Bill was very nice and very supportive, except [when] I said, 'Have you got a script?' He fumbled because he didn't quite know what I was talking about. Finally, with my backing off a little bit I thought, 'Hey, I've got an opportunity here to do something, and I don't quite know what it is he wants', I said, 'OK, I'll go home and write one'.

Well, I was living in a G.I. house in Cambria Heights, which is not too far away from here, and we had an unfinished attic with a couple of planks of wood over it, and we put a table up there, and a typewriter, and sat me down. I thought I would do a juvenile delinquency film. With Joe Louis and the Mills Brothers! And so Max, my partner, would go to Harlem and go to the YMCA and pick kids, and cast them. As he was reading the script he would cast them – we're talking rough drafts. Never a rewrite. God forbid! The payoff with Bill was that he said we could have all of the money we saved out of $25,000 and make him a feature. I had been exposed to quickie production in California for quite a few years, and knew about it, and knew how to handle it. I figured if I could make it in five days it would cost about $16,000 according to New York rates at that time. And so we, Visual Arts Productions, would make nine thousand bucks. [My wife] Geri would cut the film. She knew about sound editing because she was doing foreign versions here, in this place during the war. Probably in this room! And she did work in Hollywood at MGM doing foreign versions also. So she would do the editing, and we figured she'd get a thousand bucks to do the editing, that was $17,000. And she needed an assistant, so we got my sister, Mili Lerner Bonsignori, to be both assistant script clerk and assistant editor. And we would find a moviola someplace if we could promote it or get it cheap or whatever. I figured it would cost around 18,000 bucks to do the piece *if* we didn't shoot in a studio. So Max went out and found a warehouse for us in the 50s that was sending CARE packages to Europe. And it was dirty, and grimy, which was perfect for what I was writing about. We had a police station there in the piece, so we tacked an American flag up on the wall. And the entrance was the only door they had in this place outside of the main entrance, because it was a theatre that had been torn apart. And so that became the entrance to the police station. And because the floor sloped – we built our sets to fit the slant – all my dollies were going from left to right on one side and right to left on the other because it went down. To get a cameraman was interesting, because there wasn't anybody around. I looked and I looked. There were guys who had just gotten out of the Army but I couldn't trust them for quick shooting. Because I had to shoot 40, 50, 60 setups a day in order to make the picture.

Why couldn't you trust the Army guys?

Because they were too slow! Because I had worked with them here, you see. And they would take half an hour, an hour, to light a set, or light a close up. And here I am shooting on the basis of eight, ten setups an hour or else I can't make it, you see. So somebody told me about a man named George Webber. And they said, 'He's a little old, but he's *very* fast'. So I got to the union and called George Webber. And in came this guy – I swear, he had to hold on to the wall to keep from falling down. And at that time he told me he was 76. I found out later he was 84. And George was skinny as a rail, wicked kind of an eye. Looked at Geri and called her 'Girlie', looked at me and called me 'Sonny'. A cameraman doesn't call a director, especially a producer-director-writer, 'Sonny'. He says, 'Sonny, I'll make your picture for you, what's your schedule'? I say, 'Five days, fifty to sixty setups a day'. He says, 'No problem'. And they had told me he was very quick. He wasn't good, he was just quick. So I said, 'Fine, you're hired'. I don't know what we paid him, maybe $300 flat. His photography was gorgeous. I'd shoot a master and I'd say, 'I need a close up', and he'd grab a 750 in one hand and a 750 in the other, and he'd walk towards the subject, stop at a certain point, and say 'Ready, Sonny'. He would knock me out. I couldn't keep up with him, he was that fast. But I always felt if I wasn't close to him he'd fall over cause he was so old! Well we finished it on time, we made eight thousand bucks on it, I think. Geri cut it together, it turned out to be two hours and all we wanted was an hour and a quarter picture. We had so much footage. We had to cut it down. [Albert O.] Bondy, that's the name

of the old distributor, 723 Seventh Avenue, he had an office about half the size of this room, was the distributor for the race pictures. And Bill then called one day and said, 'You've gotta hurry up, we've got Loew's time, we're going to play Loew's'. I said, 'How do you know'? He said, 'They're buying it on the basis of Joe Louis and the Mills Brothers'. Well, I still have the notices for it, someplace. And they were really good. We played major theaters all over the country. With those notices I walked into the bank, Chemical Bank and Trust Company, and started a different company with Rex Carleton called Laurel Films. And then made *C-Man* and made a whole bunch of quickies for Astor, a whole bunch of garbage. This was under contract. But we made *C-Man* and [*Guilty*] *Bystander*, and [*Mr.*] *Universe* together before my partner decided to go to greener fields, as I did. It was very easy to raise money based on that $18,000 picture.

C-Man (1949)

It must also have been easy to raise the promise of distribution, too.

What happened was that a new company started called Film Classics, and Film Classics was very well financed by Chemical Bank. We decided on *C-Man* based on the fact that a friend of mine I'd known in Hollywood before the war had a completed screenplay. It wasn't any good, it was just completed. And *T-Men* had just come out with [Dennis] O'Keefe and was doing very well, and it was playing right across the street from the Film Classics office, at the Criterion Theater. And they were at the Paramount Theater. And I'm standing in Joe Bernhard's office, who was the president, and he says, 'I want you to make a picture for me. I've read those notices,

Fig. 2. Advertising art for the first Laurel Films production, *C-Man* (1949). This and all subsequent illustrations courtesy of Joseph Lerner.

you're pretty good'. He was formerly with Warner Bros., he knew his way around ... or was it Fox, I forget. And he says, 'You're gonna make a picture for us and what's the budget'? I didn't know what he was talking about. I said 'About $110,000'. He says 'That'll be fine'. This is a new company just starting up, and they were buying anything they could get their hands on to have something to sell. He says, 'What's the title of your film'? And I didn't know, I didn't have any, because the Bank said go over and talk to Bernhard, see what they think about ... We had nothing. And I looked across the street and there *T-Men* was playing. And I said, 'You see that picture across the street? Look at the people coming in there buying tickets'. He said, 'So'? I said, 'That stands for Treasury Man. We're doing something called Customs Man, *C-Man*'. All I could think about. So he says, 'Whatta helluvan idea'. He calls in his vice president in charge of distribution, and his vice president in charge of publicity. He says, 'Joe Lerner and his company Laurel Films is gonna do whatever they're gonna do, and it's a wonderful picture, a great idea'. He says, 'Look across the street, look at those people buying tickets'! He used all my words! And the payoff was that I left there with a picture called *C-Man*. The bank said, 'You've got yourself a deal. You raise 40 per cent, we'll give you 60 per cent of the dough'. We chased around, my partner chased around looking for money. Found some. We set a date for shooting on January – I'll never forget this. Am I boring you? On 3 January. And finally got Dean Jagger and John Carradine. I knew John before the war and he was in New York. I said 'You're in a picture', and he says, 'What do I get'? He didn't ask me what it was. And Jagger thought it was a wonderful script. He was on his ass. He didn't have a dime and there were no jobs for him. So I came in with Dean Jagger and John Carradine and a guy called Harry, who was gonna play the heavy. Harry Landers. I liked Landers, I liked his voice and I liked his cocked eye. He didn't have much to say, but he looked very menacing, and his voice was menacing. And Harry was the best thing in it. He was very good. Well, the payoff is that we said 3rd January, and Van Pelt and the bank said, 'Well, that's a liitle bit early, Joe'. We're now talking November or September. I said, 'Well, I'm committing to actors 3rd January', and left it at that. And we came into his office on

38th and Seventh about ten days before Christmas saying, 'We'd better have the dough now, because the boat leaves on 3rd January'. He says, 'Gee, we haven't even typed up the contracts yet'. I said, 'I've gotta make payroll the first week'. What we had was, if I remember the numbers, we had my salary deferred, my partner's salary deferred, the script deferred. Geri got paid so our kids could eat. We had about close to $40,000 in deferrments, you see. Which is money as far as the bank was concerned. And the other sixty was gonna be put up by the bank. So Van Pelt says, 'You've got your dough Joe, but don't start the third because it's gonna take four weeks to type this, and three weeks to get it approved'. He gave me a whole story. And I kept saying, 'The boat leaves 3rd January'. Well, my partner Rex was one hell of a chaser. He'd walk in in the morning, never say hello, go to his telephone and make calls, make his dates for the night, call up his girlfriends for the night. And once he got that organized, and got his afternoon joust organized, then he'd look up and say 'What's new'? Sounds funny now, doesn't it? I oughta write it. So I said, 'It looks like we ain't gonna get no dough for 3rd January'. He says, 'Whatta we do? Whatta we do?' And I said 'I don't know'. I won't mention any names, but she became very famous, she married one of the richest men in the country, and she was a model at that time for ... well, everybody he knew was a model at that time! And she was a gorgeous, gorgeous gal. And we said to her, 'Do us a favour. On the 26th of December walk into the Chemical Bank with your mink coat and nothing underneath, and we'll give you a little ribbon on which it says 'The Boat Leaves 3rd January''. She was one of these crazy gals that loved this kind of thing – high heels, stockings up to here, the whole business. We showed her how to get to Van Pelt's office, and she flings the door open – this is her story now – flings the door open and walks in and throws her mink coat off and stands there. And Van Pelt must have had a fit because five minutes after she did this he phoned. He says, 'What are you doing to me? We're a dignified bank. What the hell are you doing, Joe?' She did this every day – the 26th, the 27th, the 28th. On 3 January our girlfriend with the mink coat shows up at the bank with this ribbon, and on the ribbon it says, 'The boat has left'. By this time Van Pelt is sitting waiting for her to show up

Fig. 3. Edith Atwater, Rene Paul, Dean Jagger and Harry Landers (on floor) in *C-Man*. The television set at the left, rarely shown in Hollywood films at this time, is an example of early product placement. Rembrandt Television Corporation cross-promoted the film with displays in television dealerships.

every day. He's a sweetheart of a guy. And he says, 'Cover up and sit down'. And she covers up and sits down, she's already been primed. We knew he's gonna get comfortable after awhile. And he says, 'Where are they shooting?' And she says, 'Here's the schedule'. He says, 'Oh, my god'! And he calls the lawyer for the bank. And she says, 'And outside there is a limousine, a Carey Cadillac, waiting for you, to take you to the studio to see that the boat has left'. Those were her instructions and she remembered those lines word for word. The two of them dash up, jump in the car, sped across town, they get out and walk on the set, and there we are. And I looked up and said, 'Hi, fellas!' and I kept [going]. I think I was in my tenth or twelfth or fourteenth set-up by that time, it was like 11:00 o'clock. They turned right around, went back in the car and went back. And he started secretary after secretary typing the papers. Came Friday they didn't have all the papers typed and I had to make payroll. I said to the crew,

'You're not gonna get paid today'. I had quite a crew, and they were wonderful. They were in shock. 'Whattya mean? Whatya mean'? I said, 'The bank hasn't given us the money yet. Go to the bank'. Well, the [union] business agent came down. Every one of those guys went to the bank and were assured they would get their dough by Monday because they would type over the weekend. The bank, incidentally, charged us overtime for the typing. Deducted it from the 60 per cent. We were shooting at Reeves [studio]. And the reason we shot at Reeves was because he gave us a $6000 deferment if we would use magnetic audio tape instead of nitrate film. I didn't know what the hell magnetic tape was. I said 'What the hell is magnetic tape'? He said, 'Don't worry'. I said, 'I don't want to know about 'don't worry', I've got ten days to shoot it, tell me what it does'. He says, 'You'll love it'. But I needed that six grand because that six grand was a deferment for his studio, and our whole plan was to shoot all of the interiors in a room that was about four times the size of this, with a balcony around it. That was his so-called studio. It was an insert studio. And I needed that studio, because I had about four days of exteriors and six days of interiors, and we had, what, fifteen or eighteen sets, which we built sandwiched. And as we were finished with the smaller set – our schedule called for the smaller set in the front – we took it out, and we had rented a garbage dump truck, and it sat outside. We would have sent it to you if you had a museum then! So we started with the small set, and as we started throwing them out the sets got bigger and bigger, until we ended up with – what was it, a barroom or something. But I needed that six grand, so I said, 'OK. Let me hear that sound on the second day. If not we're gonna go back and Reeves will pay for the reshooting, and bringing the set back out of the garbage dump'. Because I was destroying three, four sets a day, throwing them out.

So you weren't waiting to see dailies?

Oh no, there was no time for dailies, no time for dailies. We saw dailies, but the sets were gone. You don't reshoot. We had one retake, I remember. We were out at the airport where the jewels were being smuggled in, and I forgot to shoot a close-up of Carradine, who was the bad guy. So I cheated the shot at the studio. I work very fast with actors, I've had a lot of experience with actors, up to that point a hell of a lot of experience with actors, as a dialogue director, as test director. So I knew how to get the performance I want very quickly.

I forgot to ask you about William Saulter, who was the art director on C-Man. William Saulter used to work for Paramount.

Sure he did. During the war he also built sets here. Bill was a very nice guy, a very sweet, sweet, sweet man, and a very giving kind of guy, to the point where you felt he didn't have any backbone of his own because he also wanted to give so much all the time. He did have backbone, really. He'd fight me a lot on the sets, 'cause he wanted to do more. And I'd let him, of course, if the money was there.

Did he come up with this idea of building the sets one inside the other?

He thought that was the greatest thing that ever happened to him. When I told him I wanted to sandwich the sets he didn't know what I was talking about. I've got news for you: I didn't know what I was talking about, either. I remember sitting in that little office of ours, and I took a whole bunch of little sheets of paper out of a yellow pad and tore them up, and said, 'This is the first set, put *it* here, put *it* there, put *it* there, like so'. And I said, 'Look what happens when you come down to about set 22', or whatever the number was. He thought that was out of this world. Incidentally , that whole stairway scene in *C-Man*, where he's walking upstairs and downstairs, going up someplace, where ever the hell he's going. I've forgotten now. That was all done at the stairway at Reeves. It was one flight of steps that we used. Same flight. I was going to move the camera upstairs? We had to schedule this shot last since all our props and furniture were stacked there for the whole picture.

Well, when we went into the projection room the next day – the sets are gone, of course – and listened to the sound it was fantastic. It was so wonderful. You could hear the rustle of a jacket as a guy unbuttoned it. You could hear everything. I was in seventh heaven. The problem was, how do you cut it, you see? They didn't know either. So Geri got into the cutting room to fiddle with it while we were shooting. Geri is always on the set with me, but in this case she disappeared, because of that piece of brown stuff ... All the Reeves guys were surrounding her saying, 'Show us what you're gonna do with it'. And she finally got to the point where she conformed it and ... she was cutting tape. My sister by that time was a full fledged assistant. We came in on schedule. No overtime. Incidentally, my cameraman was a guy called Gerald Hirschfeld, and this was his first job outside of the Army.

Did you know him from the Army?

Yes. And I was the guy that went to the union and got him his card, 'cause I liked what he did. His stuff was excellent.

Tell me a little more about that sound recording. Did you have any trouble mixing the tracks?

GL: Oh boy, that was my job.

Fig. 4. Filming on the streets of Astoria, using unfamiliar and even non-professional actors, lent an inexpensive veneer of reality to Lerner's film. Lottie Elwen and an unidentified extra in *C-Man*.

I'll tell you about Geri, I'll tell you about what a nut she is. She must have walked into the mix with maybe 15 tracks. She had a loop for every frame of the goddamn picture. And Vorisek, Dick Vorisek, who was the mixer, would sit there and say, 'My God, you're using up every pot in all of Reeves'! We did pre-mixes, and pre-mixes of pre-mixes, getting it all level. Because Geri's background had been sound, pretty much, editing sound for MGM and for this place during the war. And so to her the sound had to be excellent, as it always was for any of the films we made. And so she came in with a score, with a whole breakdown all lined up and laid out where to go. They had never seen anything like that before in this city, with a real MGM-like breakdown of all of the tracks and how they come in, and the footages and all that. You see, I run scared of her, which is one of the reasons I won't dub if I can help it. I do, because she's very tough on me, edi-

torially. Has been from day one. So I'm always looking for ways to satisfy her needs, be it picture or track. So as we tore one of these sets apart, I ran a piece of unmodulated on every one of these sets as we were pulling them out, because even the ambiance was changed as the size of the set was changed. So she would have a piece of what we called – what? – unmodulated – a piece of unmodulated for every one of those 35 sets. I wouldn't have done it that way, because it would take up one minute each time – about thirty minutes or more a day. But she wouldn't have it any other way. So finally every one of those sets had its own ambiance, silence, so called. And therefore, when it came to shooting exteriors, that's what I did as well. You'll find no dubbing in that picture at all. No extra sound effects whatsoever. All that stuff was shot live. And the same goes for *Bystander*, and the same goes for *Universe*.

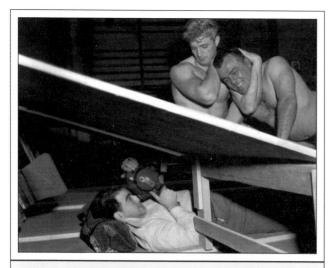

Fig. 5. The Bell & Howell Eyemo camera, popular with military cameramen in World War II, shoots an unusual angle in *Mr. Universe* (1951).

Was there any difference in the way they would mike the scenes?

Absolutely not. The men on the mike boom never held me up for a minute – one of the things I worried about when Reeves said I'd like you to use magnetic instead of optical.

There's a voice-over where Jagger is talking. And a lot of it occurs when you're looking at exteriors, which is what made me think that they didn't want to drag all that equipment out of the studio. But it was mobile? They had a van, a mobile car or something?

What we had was – I looked for a camera car in this town and couldn't find it. 'Cause they had no equipment. Remember, we were almost pioneers in this town. When we shot exteriors for *The Fight Never Ends*, what we did was get a convertible, put the top down, put a camera in the back seat, and shoot. And when we wanted to dolly on the street I just had a grip push the car so we got a dolly. We also used a baby carriage every once in a while. On *C-Man*, what we did was, Mr. Hertz, of rental car fame, contributed our so-called camera car. We promoted Hertz in exchange for a credit and got a Chevy convertible, took the hood off the front, and built a 3/4′ plywood platform type thing to sit there instead. It was very ingenious of Gerry Hirschfeld.

We had a built-in high hat on that thing. It got a little hot from the engine, but what's a hot seat if you can get a good shot? Did the same thing to the trunk, so that we had two platforms, and that became our camera car. We did the same thing on *Universe*, the same thing on *Guilty Bystander*. When we did the ambulance chase we rented a Carey ambulance with the proviso – they knew we were going to use it in the film – they gave it to us for nothing with the proviso we brought it back without a scratch. I was going to wreck that ambulance! So we had three prop men sprawled out on the floor of the ambulance, and when we had the accident they just flipped the doors open and we cut very fast. There wasn't a scratch on it when we brought it back. But when we brought Hertz's camera car back, the ad-lib camera car back – I remember this distinctly, the prop men were going crazy trying to put the hood back again, but it wouldn't fit. So they taped it and just delivered it. We never heard a word back from them. They just taped it shut. Isn't that funny. Why do I remember this?

What kind of cameras were you using on that picture?

Mitchells, mostly, We had an Eyemo handy. I don't like the Eyemo, it's too short a burst, for one thing. It's a different look for me.

I think if you look at that film again you'll see some Eyemo shots.

GL: You will, you will.
That's right, that came from the Chevy, because every time we moved the Chevy we could go any place with it.

GL: I don't know, I wasn't there when you shot that, but it seems to me to be hand held.

No, I'm pretty sure. Well, Arriflex hadn't come out yet.
GL: Well, on *Universe* you used a lot of hand held.
I used an Arri then. On *Universe* I used an Arri.

GL: Nobody was in that ring with the hand held?

Of course, with an Arriflex, but not an Eyemo. There was none of that fancy hand-held stuff, all of that nice Steadicam kind of stuff. We also had one guy, an assistant cameraman, a brute of a guy, who was wonderful. And he picked that Mitchell up and put it on his shoulder and operated it as if it were hand held.

A BNC?

A BNC, the whole cockamamie thing! Well, we looked at the picture in rough cut, and Geri said, 'Wouldn't it be nice if we had a real crazy score? Because the picture is just another picture, you know'. I don't know how good you think it is, but it's just another picture. We gotta have something to take it out of it's category, so why don't we get some wild, offbeat – none of this melodic stuff that we would settle for later on –

GL: No canned music.

We were going to put canned music in it because there was no restriction from the union at that time, they hadn't caught up yet.

You could use the library music free?

Oh yeah, sure. The Czechoslovakian Symphony Orchestra, the Hungarian Band, or whatever the hell they had. It didn't matter. Anyway, I don't know how we got to this guy, his name was Gail Kubik, and he was great fun. And when we met him and he looked at the picture he said, 'I can see it, I can see it, it's wonderful, I love the idea'! He made me think I'd just made *Gone With the Wind.* Geri got along with him beautifully.

Did you maybe know him from the Army, because he had done the scores for some of the Wyler films. Memphis Belle ...

I understand that, and that's what he showed us. But I spoke to Wyler some time after that when he used him for *Dangerous Hours,* a picture that he made at Paramount some years later, and Wyler had said to me that he would never have used Kubik for that film, with his crazy, way out kind of music, until he had seen *C-Man,* and thought that he had done such a beautiful job on it. We'd go to his place – he was in a brownstone, wasn't he, in the 90s somewhere – and he'd play us a piece of the score on that piano

and I thought that maybe he should play it on a garbage can cover, because it wasn't my dish of tea. But we both agreed that the picture would take on a tone of its own based on that sound. Whether it did or not, we were too close to know. When it opened at the Rialto the notices were kind of crazy. About 50 per cent of the notices, throughout the country, incidentally, were raving about the picture and its wild, 'incoherent,' that was the word, 'incoherent' music. And what we thought was, if they didn't like the picture, at least we bounced them out of their seats with that nutty score. But Geri loved it. And Kubik was wonderful. He'd go into the cutting room and he and Geri would cut and recut his ten piece orchestra score.

Also on magnetic tape?

Oh yeah, everything was magnetic. Reeves was in seventh heaven. I don't know if you knew Reeves at all, but Buzz was a tall, lanky, harried kind of guy with a kind of stutter, who would sit and regale you by the hour. He was a mixer actually, a sound mixer, and had his own little studio at one point, one room, two pots or something. And he would regale you with all the funny things he did with sound effects, like squeak a chair to get something done. He'd sit in that room and tap his feet for footsteps, that kind of stuff. This was before the war. And when he heard the score he said, 'Oh, God! What are you doing to my magnetic tape'! He was screaming. But he loved the whole idea of it. Kubik came in one day with a piece of railroad track, which he laid on the keys of the piano in order to get the sound he wanted. You know something? That was fun, those days were really fun, weren't they? We've never had that much fun since, have we!

So the budget of this picture was $100,000?

Actually, it was less. Our budget was ... I don't know if this should be for publication or not ... it's been so long it doesn't matter. Our budget was $110,000, of which we watered a lot of it, because nobody knew. The banks didn't know how much was one and one. And we were terribly careful with the money.

GL: How come we didn't see any of it?

I know, we never saw a dime on that picture. It did very well. Film Classics was in seventh heaven over it. Bernhard said, 'That's my railroad engine,

I'm going to sell everything based on that one'. They went out and sold like crazy. It paid off in about eight months, they thought it would pay off in 18.

What kind of distribution deal did you have with Film Classics? They didn't put up any front money?

No. If I'm not mistaken I think they put up the completion money. That didn't mean anything, because they all knew that the budget was watered. I think I told Bernhard that I was about twenty thousand over, that I might bring the picture in for ninety.

So did they take a percentage?

Thirty-five, if I'm not mistaken, and forty overseas, or something like that. As soon as we delivered this film they said to me, 'Make me another picture right away'. My God, we had put in all of our effort on that one, we hadn't even been thinking about anything else. We did get our office expenses back, and our overhead, and all that stuff that we had put in ...

GL: Did we ever get paid off on our deferments?

No. We cross-collaterized it with the next one. So I said to Bernhard, 'I've got a great film that I'm working on, soon as we're ready with it'. So I scoured the book stores – we had no sources for anything.

Guilty Bystander (1950)

[Zachary] Scott was interesting. I enjoyed working with Scott. I thought Scott was the ultimate Hollywood ... he was the ultimate superficial actor, was he not? He never felt anything. And yet on screen somehow he was projecting all kinds of things going on in his head. And the only thing he was worried about was the chewing gum in his mouth, because he chewed gum all the time. And when you said 'Roll it', he'd slide the gum in the back of his mouth and leave it there, and then play the scene. This drove me crazy. So after a while I'd go over and put my hand out and he'd give me the gum. Which I would return at the end of the shot. He was very cooperative. Well, our budget was $450,000. We got 60 per cent from the bank, we went out and raised the rest of the money. We did work the deferment business again, and Film Classics was vitally interested in that, because they

needed the engine again. And that was the engine, *Guilty Bystander*. Zach Scott, Faye Emerson, Mary Boland, Sam Levene. They had something to really sell, and they sold it even before it came out, it was really presold way the hell throughout the country.

GL: How come we never got our deferments on that?

Well we got some cash on that, not deferments. We kept eating. What was interesting about *Bystander* is Mary Boland played the first dramatic part she'd ever played in her lifetime.

You didn't use Howard Saulter on the picture.

No, because he was ill. I would have. And then there was another reason – Leo Kerz. I had seen something Leo did, James Joyce's 'Bloom in Love', way downtown, a little place, Houston Street, an upstairs theatre someplace, and the sets were just beautiful. The set. When we met he said to me, 'I heard about you, I'd like to do your sets'. I said 'Have you done any film'? and he said 'No'. And I said, 'Well it's about time I don't experiment anymore. I could do it with *C-Man*, but with a $450,000 picture I got to get serious, you know'. And he said, 'Well, let me read the script anyway'. I said, 'Alright'. He came up to the office. Now we had a fancy office. Wasn't it fancy though? I loved that office.

GL: It sure was!

We hadn't got any furniture in the office yet, just got an old desk until we got around to buying stuff. And he read the script and came back. He said one thing that was very interesting. 'She's a blue person, isn't she?' I said 'Who is'? He said, 'The character in the script'. I said 'She's Faye Emerson'. 'Yeah. She's blue'. I said, 'I don't know what you're talking about'. He said 'That's her overall color'. He said he sees the Thursday character [played by Scott] as a kind of dark brown. I said, 'I'm doing a black and white picture, I don't understand you'. He says, 'But that's what we're talking about. When he wears a seersucker suit, it should be against the color'. I said 'How do you know he's wearing a seersucker suit?' He said 'Because that's what he should be wearing'. And then he pulled out a couple of sketches and showed them to me, and I went hog wild for them. Everything had wild walls for me to do whatever I wanted with the camera. Everything was working as if he'd made fifty pictures in his lifetime as opposed to none. I could get any angle I wanted, I could do whatever I wanted with it. And I thought, maybe he ought to do it. And then he came up with ideas of wardrobe. When he came in with a set sketch he'd have swatches alongside his sketch, what the curtains would be like, what the people should be wearing, and everything about it seemed to work. The introduction to the flop house at the beginning – the rooms on both sides, and the camera's going down the centre hallway, and we look into every room as we're going through the whole thing – he had those rooms working so that I could just pull them away and keep working. Everything was mobile, it was just wonderful. I couldn't not give him the job. We fought like cats and dogs all the way through the picture. Because he put me in a place with the camera where I didn't want to be on occasions, and I'd scream and holler, etc. But we became very good friends.

Did you shoot this also at Reeves?

Oh, no, no. *Guilty Bystander* was shot at the old Fox studios on 56th. We had four stages working for us. We had the two stages at Fox. That little small studio at 57th and 10th. At Reeves we had two sets built for us. And downtown, the whole jail sequence was actually shot at 'the Tombs'. So we would go from one to the other. While one was being built we'd push to the other.

I talked just very briefly to Hirschfeld about this, and what he remembered was that at Reeves a set was built so close to the wall, to the edge of the studio, that he couldn't get his lights in, so he had to paint his shadows on the wall.

He did. That was *C-Man*. Yeah. Geri did exactly that. I think he did it on *Guilty Bystander*, too. He was a very good ... he was a very difficult man to work with, very difficult. I worked with him on maybe 500 commercials as well, later on when he was MPO [Videotronics]. I don't know if you know about that part of his life, or mine. Incidentally, I should send you some 16 mm [things] we did that were really very handsome, like all of the Buster Keaton stuff that was done for Ford. That's my schtick. I still have them, don't I someplace? Do you collect that stuff too? They won a helluva lot of awards, thirty or more.

Who did the location scouting? Because in Guilty Bystander the locations are very interesting, very novel.

I did.

You would do them, not Kerz?

Oh, no. For instance, I've never hired a unit manager, never. When I hired an a.d., I had the budget all done, I had the schedule all laid out, everything was organized, and then they came in. I did it myself. And I think the reason was that I couldn't see anybody else doing the producer's job – I was a co-producer as well. I always felt it was the producer's job to do all that stuff, and since my partners were actually money raisers, for the most part, I had to teach them about film. I couldn't see the actual detail done except by the director. I still see the director breaking down his own script, and still see him, maybe not adding up the money or anything, but I still see him searching the locations. For instance, when I worked with [John] Ford before the war, I know that Ford would go out and actually see the location, and then tell [Lou] Shapiro, who was then RKO's location manager, 'There's a place in this particular location ... go figure it out and see ... get me the east and the west and the north and the south look of it'. But he's already seen it. Because it doesn't make sense that the guy who's gonna shoot that thing, who's gonna lay it out and tell the story in front of it, is gonna let somebody else see it first, and pick three locations and say, 'Which one of the three do you want'? It doesn't make sense to me. Consequently, I think I may have boxed myself in a corner pretty much, and not been as productive, purely because I was fooling around with the detail as opposed to helping to raise the money, put other scripts together, and do whatever else.

There may not have been a lot of people in New York at the time whom you could depend on to do the work.

Yes there were. You could instruct them. When I was doing commercials, for example, that didn't bother me. You could always send a guy out and give him a polaroid, and say, 'Knock me off something like this and bring it back', because I wasn't serious about commercials at all.

Fig. 6. Faye Emerson and Zachary Scott in *Guilty Bystander* (1950). To art director Leo Kerz, Emerson was 'a blue person', Scott 'a kind of dark brown'. This view through two rooms and a corridor suggests Kerz's ability to create a believeable space with meager resources.

What was your shooting schedule on Guilty Bystander?

22 Days, 23 days.

Mr. Universe (1951)

How many takes would you usually have to make of a scene?

I don't know. Put it another way. I was shooting 7 or 8 to 1, 10 to 1 tops. And if a take went sour, in many instances I would print it because a piece of it could be used. So we'd make a notation to Geri in the cutting room saying, 'Check on the piece where he says, or she says ...' And then I go and reshoot it again, but then I'd usually change the angle, so I'd get a different look at it. So the point

was, feed the cutting room as many accents and camera set-ups ...

How many of those takes would you print?

Oh, an average of maybe, tops, two. For instance, you know the bed scene in *Universe*, where they're all clustered around in the hotel, remember that one? That was one take, all the way through. I rehearsed it from 9 until about 12. I had Gerry make sure she was on the set. The whole scene took a few feet less than a full roll of 1000 feet, ten feet less maybe. We shot that twice. Reloaded and shot it again. Looked to her and said, 'The timing is off'. The two of us agreed the timing is off here, is off here, is off here. She says, 'Don't worry about it, I'll jump it'. That was one take all the way through. Almost eleven minutes. And all she did was get her scissors and jump a little piece here and jump a little

Fig. 7. Ray Julian, Harry Landers, Kay Medford and Zachary Scott on an especially stylized staircase in *Guilty Bystander*. Like the German masters, cameraman Gerald Hirschfeld was not above painting shadows on his walls when necessary.

piece there which you don't see. To this day no one has seen the jumps, and I'm afraid that now you will look for it. But there were four or five jumps in that piece to just keep the comedy timing right.

Was that also for Eagle Lion?

Actually UA. We had a great adventure with *Universe*, incidentally. [Film Classics] sold out to Eagle Lion about the first week of shooting of *Universe*, and without our knowing what the hell went on. The bank then decided that they wanted a better deal for us both if we signed a new contract with Eagle Lion than they had with Film Classics. Because we were in the driver's seat because Eagle Lion said that we were again the engine to pull their whole year's product. I don't understand why! Bill Heinemann, who was the sales manager, would come down every day and say, 'Joe, you gotta make this one, because this is the one, and all that shitty product that we've got ...'. 'Wait a minute,' I said, 'You've got *Bystander* doing very well'. 'That's

different', he said, 'but this one ...' In the middle of it, I forget what the reason was, they turned around and sold out to United Artists, and then we got the same pitch from the UA people, because they were in great trouble. We were in the middle of the motion picture depression. TV was keeping the theaters empty. We thought, because of our contract, we did not have to go to UA, and we got an offer from Columbia to go with them. They had just made another picture with [Jack] Carson and wanted to use this one to hook on. It was called *The Fuller Brush Man*, and they wanted *Universe* for some reason, I forget. They offered us a fantastic deal. And we could take it, according to our contract, so we came to the bank, 'Look what we can do. Columbia Pictures will pay off the nut completely, even before it hits the theatres'. That's $507,000, which I suppose today would be $10 million, the way they spend money. And they were gonna give us $507,000 in cash. We had about $80,000 owed to us in that 507, Geri and I, plus our pieces and plus god knows

Fig. 8. One of the few *noir* comedies, *Mr. Universe* is the story of a body-building champion (Vince Edwards) taken up by a fast-talking wrestling promoter (Jack Carson). The corruption of the wrestling racket, and the connivance of television in promoting rigged fights, is pictured with a completely cynical eye.

what. And my partner Rex had whatever he had coming to him, I don't remember exactly what he had. The bank wouldn't let us do the Columbia deal. And we fought the bank to see if we could do it. So what we did was hide the negative.

You thought that the bank was going to seize the negative?

Yes, because they said, 'If you guys don't go along with our U.A. deal, we'll never finance you again, Joe'. Which was a lot of bullshit. 'And we won't do this, and we won't do that. And besides that, all your negative is at Deluxe [laboratory] so we can just take it'. I said, 'Go ahead, you just try and find it'. We had taken ten reels of negative, this is work print negative, and hidden it. I don't know if you know about laboratories, but if you walk out with a can of film you've got 14 security guys looking at

you saying, 'Give me the pass, where's the piece of paper, what roll is this', etc. So we got a devilish idea. We were filed under M – *Mr. Universe* – under M in their vaults. So we walked into their vault, which we were allowed to do because you couldn't get out of the building anyway, and we picked up ten reels of negative and put it under T or something. Just stuck it in there. We misfiled ten rolls of negative. We knew where it was, but they didn't. Well, they followed us all over the place. They came to our house, they came to the office, they looked in the cars, they could never find those ten rolls. And all this time we're saying, 'OK, if you guys go along with us you can have your ten rolls'. 'Well come on Joe, you know we can take you to court, we can put you in jail for 400 years. You stole our product. Hang you from the nearest gibbet ...' And all this time we're fooling around with them. And we lost.

Fig. 9. J. Edward Bromberg (right), once an important character actor in Hollywood, was one of many blacklisted actors to appear in New York films in this period. With Harry Landers and Zachary Scott in *Guilty Bystander*.

We finally agreed to give them back the negative. In the meantime Geri's cutting the picture, the work print. We didn't have safeties in those days, one work print went. Today they make five work prints.

GL: Every time I needed a piece of film, if it tore, we had to order up another piece.

Anyway, we finally lost, so the bank finally convinced me. Van Pelt, who was our mentor at the bank, took me to the Republican Club for lunch, up in the penthouse where all the fancy go, where he says, 'You are now sitting in the seat of Mr. Wilkie'. And I said, 'Gee, I'm really ...' He said, 'Joe, you've gotta be a good boy, we're good to you, anything you want'. I said, 'Whatta ya mean good to me, you guys are taking away my picture'. He says, 'We'll finance the next five, just change the name of your company because it is marked lousy. Call it anything you like'.

GL: Why were you marked lousy?

Because we had stolen the negative, you know. Anyway, the payoff to this was everything came out all right. It did very well, incidentally.

GL: I still want to know why we didn't get more money.

Don't you remember the swindle, Geri. The swindle the bank's lawyers pulled. Swindling all of the producers? There were fifty producers that were hosed because the contract read if it were not paid off in eighteen months from the date of the loan they'd foreclose on our film. And they spent $250,000 advertising it and then foreclosed on it. It was worth half its budget just to advertise it, that's how they thought of it. It did very well. Another producer had five films that were stuck in there. They shafted all of the producers and the lawyer formed his own TV distribution company.

Were all these producers tied in with Film Classics?

No, no no. They were all over the place, all distribution companies. And what happened was they were forming a TV distribution company. They saw that some other smart fellow had bought the Warner Bros. library, and was making a fortune distributing them to television at that point. And so the lawyers decided that they wanted to form a distribution company. Now they had no film, all they had was a law office, and so as the loans hit the 18th month they would foreclose. Normally it was easy, they'd give you an extension of another year. We never needed it before, because we were paying off very fast. *Guilty Bystander* paid off in less than 18 months. So we were looking forward to profits, and *Universe* was foreclosed! That got us fairly disgusted, Geri and I, because the truth of the matter is we were looking toward making something that we wanted to make, as opposed to making something that sounded like commercial product in the accepted sense. I had an option on a story that I wanted to do, a science-fiction film. It was just a beautiful, beautiful story. And I figured that that would be it. I wanted something off-beat a little bit that would show my hand, because I thought I was getting to be a fairly good director. I thought that now I could show my performance handwith actors more than in those things I was kind of knocking out. The truth of the matter is, those three films ... when push came to shove and there was a problem of schedule, a problem of budget, and a problem of script, that many times I didn't shoot the script, I shot the budget, or I shot the schedule. And I thought, just about now maybe I should do something decent. We were sure the two of us, Geri and I, could do fairly well at it. But it didn't work, and so we just walked away from it. We went into whatever was around. I became a whore. The only difference was I didn't peddle it in Eighth Avenue. When they waved a buck in front of me I lay down and hollered 'Roll 'em'.

You were telling me you made these films for Astor. Were they all race pictures?

No, they were all just speed up things. They were playable, but the less said about them the better.

In general, when you were making features in New York in the late 1940s, what were some of the problems? Were there permits you had to get in those days? Everyone I talk to says there were police payoffs. Is that true?

Sure. These days there was no city motion picture office. Its much better now.

Was that just the average cop who walked by, or did it seem to be organized?

And then the sergeant would drive up, and the lieutenant would drive up, and you smeared them all. We had an item in the budget, the first budget I handed to the bank, I had an item in there called 'schmear'. And the bank said, 'Come on now, you can't put that item in'. I said, 'Alright, put grease'. So finally they gave me a number called 'incidentals'. So you'd put in 'incidentals'.

Was there a way of getting a shooting permit? Where did you have to go?

Way down town someplace. Usually the a.d. went down and got them.

They really did help you. For instance, Astoria Boulevard, the widest street here, we needed the whole goddamn street, because the action in *C-Man* was where Landers jumps out of something, grabs the car, pulls the driver out and does whatever he does. Then [the] ambulance comes down, the whole thing going on with seven or eight or ten cars going back and forth underneath the El, I forget. We had to close up everything for the whole day. We loused up traffic pretty bad.

Many of the features that were made in New York at this time, by you and by other people, I see are employing a lot of actors who are blacklisted in Hollywood at this point – Paul Henreid, Franchot Tone ...

Joe Bromberg.

GL: Well he hadn't been called yet.

Oh yes, oh yes! So was Eli. Eli Sullivan lived next door to me in Hollywood long before I met Geri. He was a sweet guy, a wonderful guy. Sullivan is one of the mugs in *C-Man*. He was called up by this McCarthy thing. And Joe [Bromberg] I knew when I was an actor in the early 1930s. We worked very much alike, Joe and I, as actors. And he always said, during that time, that if he saw me at a casting session he knew I was going to get the part and he wasn't, because I could out-read him. He never admitted I could out-act him, just out-read him. And Joe was very much in trouble at that point, and called me. As did Lee Cobb. Lee called and wanted to play the lead in *Bystander*, and Lee was a fairly big name at that point. And Lee had talked. I couldn't see putting Lee in anything, as much as I used to like Lee as a person. But when Joe called me and said, 'Whattya got, I'll take anything', and this was a guy who was doing so well in Hollywood ... He was under contract to Fox, he was one of Zanuck's favourite actors. One of mine. I put him down on the list and didn't say anything, and he was approved.

Approved by whom? By Eagle Lion?

No, I think it started with Film Classics.

They had cast approval?

Not all cast, but just top names. And I don't remember whether his name ever came up at all, whether they ever brought his name up. I don't remember now. I on purpose put Eli down. I knew there wasn't a decent part for Eli, he just played a hood, and I made a deal with Eli, and with Joe. And I said to them, 'Look, you've got five days work, whatever it is, and you're getting paid whatever I can pay you for it. Just do extra work all the rest of the picture whenever I need you. Be there, but stay the hell out of camera. Keep your back to camera'. Which he did. He was paid for it every day of the shooting. We were on the streets a lot with *Guilty Bystander*. We were in studio a lot, too, but whenever we needed extras, he was there. Bromberg also, if I remember correctly, took about ten days of that extra work stuff, 'cause he needed the money. And there were, I would guess, seven or eight other people who were getting extra work who were actors who were ...

It almost seems to me that so many of these people drifted to New York, where they could continue working for a couple of years.

They could try. I can tell you about Eli, because I used to see him a lot. If I had a lot of money I would have put him on salary to us, if I could have afforded it. When I ran into him the first time, when he came

to a casting session ... Elliott Sullivan is who we're talking about ... we even gave him a credit, didn't we. He said, 'This is what I'm selling'. And he stuck his hand into his pocket and took out a paint brush. And on the paint brush was a little piece of plastic or something. And he says, 'It's this little piece of plastic that keeps this paint brush nice and soft. So after you've used it it doesn't get dried out'. I said, 'That's what you're doing'? He says, 'Yeah, house to house'. He said somedays he makes as much as three dollars, or two dollars. Whatever the number was. It was dreadful. The guy was married, had a kid, was a good parts player in Hollywood. When I knew him in Hollywood before the war he was making five, six, seven thousand dollars a year, which was ... bread was a dime, gasoline was a dime. Joe, on the other hand, who was living high off the hog, all of a sudden woke up and found himself flat on his ass. His wife was out doing ... I don't know what. Do you remember what Goldie was doing? I think these guys were all in shock. I knew a lot of the Hollywood people who were involved. Lester Cole, who was a writer at Metro, probably one of the highest priced ones. Got $2000 a week at that time, that was *money* money. All of a sudden dropped colder than ... [Leonardo] Bercovici the same, Eddie Dmytrytk the same.

Do you think it's true that they were able to work a little more easily in New York?

Well they knew they damn well couldn't work out there at all. And Joe, incidentally, died on a ship going to England because there was nothing here for him, and he figured he could go to England. Carl Foreman went to England and was picking up a job every once in awhile. At the beginning, though, England was allowing work, Italy was allowing work. I'll tell you about Tone. Tone had a problem. I knew Tone. Not well, but I knew him. I knew him when he was part of the Group Theater. He was heavily loaded, moneywise, and one of the financiers of the Group Theater. He was one of the few actors I've known who didn't have to look for a job, purely because he had so much dough he could finance himself in anything he wanted to do. He was that loaded. But he was mixed up with a whole group of 'radicals,' namely the Stella Adlers and the Luther Adlers, and Gadge [Kazan], and the rest of the people at the Group Theater, Julie Garfield

Fig. 10. Zachary Scott and Elliott Sullivan struggling near the tracks in Brooklyn's deserted Court Street subway station for *Guilty Bystander*. Note the minimal lighting and improvised mike stand at left.

and the rest of them. I knew them then because I was an actor then. As a matter of fact, I played a second lead in the first play that Kazan ever directed, his first directorial job, something called 'The Young Go First'. I knew them all, and they were all tarred with that brush. Some of them just literally got up and walked away from it, never acted again. Gadge and Lee talked. It didn't help them very much. It took them three, four, five years to get back after that. Gadge to this day and I talk about that, because we're both on the council of the Director's Guild and we see each other a lot. I keep saying that I don't know how I would have reacted if I was part of that. I was never a member of the C.P., although I was so goddamn close to being one that ... I just wasn't a joiner, that was what saved me, I think. Because I was very well known. I directed plays for the Hollywood Anti-Nazi League on radio, I knew all those people. And I felt that they were

tarred with the wrong brush, I think. But I felt that in New York City they may have had a chance to do some theatre, but they wouldn't get film work.

The last question is this. You stopped making films in New York, and these other producers stopped making films, and it all happened around 51, 52.

Universe was distributed about that time. And we said, 'The hell with it', because we had been caught up with that foreclosure thing.

I wonder whether that had something to do with it, or the fact that there didn't seem to be the opportunity for small producers to get a guaranteed distribution for their product anymore?

Getting distribution was comparatively easy. It was not as tough as it was before the war. Before the

Fig. 11. Joseph Lerner (centre) with two of the stars of *Mr. Universe*, Jack Carson (left) and Dennis James. James, playing himself in the film, was a local sportscaster notorious for breaking chicken bones off camera to suggest bodily injuries. Lerner's growing disillusion with the film business at this time seems mirrored by the film's casual acceptance of corruption and racketeering in the world of televised wrestling.

war it was impossible. You had to be Sam Goldwyn before you could do anything.

After the Consent Decrees there was a big push to find some independent product, to say that you were open to independent films.

Yes. You've done your homework, haven't you?

Well, I'm trying to find out why this flourishes for five years and then goes 'poof'.

Well the reason it went 'poof' with us is because we felt that we were ... If you didn't get it out of the budget, you'd never get it, in other words. Remember the guys that were on the set that were so feeble they were falling apart? They all came out of retirement for this. Local 52 had nobody. We had a propman who I said to as a joke, because I knew about prop men, 'I'll tell you what I'll do, Danny. I'll

give you $10 a week over scale (that's 175 bucks), if you go 50–50 with me on your payoffs. He answered, 'I can't do that, Joe, 'cause I've got to make a living'. (laughs) I'll never forget it. There was that there was no way for the producer, forget the director, there was no way for the producer to make any money unless he was getting his cut out of the budget in various ways. Because you weren't making it out of the profits of the picture itself. And yet my pictures were doing well. *Universe* paid off in 14 months, after they foreclosed. *Universe* was sold to CBS alone, where they played it 18 times. 18 times at – take a number, $1000, $2000, $5000 for every run. Now they're getting certainly much more than that. Would pay off its budget again and again and again. And that was only one station, CBS New York. And yet they foreclosed. We could have come out ... with our percentage, I owned 37 per cent of *Universe*. That 37 per cent of *Universe* could have feathered our nest for maybe three, four hundred thousand dollars. I'll give you an example of that. When were we in India? 72? 73? *Universe* was playing downtown Bombay. That's our money it was playing for, and we never saw one rupee.

That sounds like an old Hollywood story, where the small independent gets squeezed out by the people who were controlling the money.

There really weren't many of us, we were quite unique. And if the assistant directors and the few gaffers and the few propmen didn't have commercials coming up about that time, and didn't have a documentary once in awhile, they would have starved.

A number of people also moved into television. Somebody like Frank Satenstein, who wound up with Jackie Gleason.

Yeah. But remember what happened then. What was going was that 'Big Story' started up in the Bronx, and 'Man Against Crime', and then a lot of them were coming into town and shooting quickie – five days, six days, seven days, they were doing it. I can tell you about 'Man Against Crime'. William Morris Sr. came to us at Laurel Films, we were on 57th and 6th, and William Morris was 55th and 7th, I think. And Bill Morris, Jr. himself came to our office trying to get us to do 'Man Against Crime' and we said no way, we had no interest in it, it was television, we weren't going to do that, we were in the big money. We were making half-million dollar pictures, you know. Which was a big mistake. And there was a big piece of propaganda that Hollywood was putting out, that if you came to New York to shoot you'd get squeezed, you'd get hosed, you'd get cheated, swindled. There was that propaganda. It wasn't true. Not at all.

GL: There were also rumours that there were not good technicians here.

That's right. And they were stretching the day's work. Well, I never saw it happen. What is interesting is that at that particular time there were other things happening. Commercials started up. We came back from Europe in '56, after working there for three years. We looked around for something to do and Hirschfeld met us at the ship. He was

involved in commercials. We hadn't seen each other in three years, and the first thing he said was, 'You gotta go into commercials'. I didn't know what the hell a commercial was. I said 'Fine, where do I get my first job'? Seventy-five bucks a day, take it. That was good money in 1956. I started making commercials. The whole industry, United Artists, the guys I knew, would say, 'Oh, you don't wanna make 'em here, go to Hollywood'. I didn't want to go to Hollywood. I wanted to stay in New York. And I started making commercials. I must have gotten thirty awards for the commercials. I made 2,000 of them. Hirschfeld started up with a group called MPO. And MPO was grinding them out like crazy, with seven stages. Imagine that. You wanted more than two stages for a feature, you had to go all over town to get them. They were all housed in one place.

That was another problem why there was no feature industry in New York: there weren't enough stages.

Oh without a doubt, without a doubt.

They rehabilitated things like the Biograph Gold Medal Studio, and the Vitagraph plant, which I understood were really bad studios.

You couldn't walk the floor, the floor would give under you.

Do you think that the union situation, the problems between NABET and the IA, had anything to do with New York's problems.

The IA's biggest mistake, I think, was they allowed television to get away from them, whereas the producers, the big Hollywood studios', biggest mistake, was they allowed television to escape as well, and become deliverers of merchandise for television, as opposed to controlling it. They could have had their own tv stations. I remember a meeting of the Directors Guild, sometime before the war, where the directors were begging the Harry Cohns and the Zanucks to start up tv stations, and they were being told it wasn't their kind of business, it was a shitty medium, a six inch picture, who was going to look at it ... That was their attitude towards it. Not realizing what it was going to do. Who's going to stay home and see movies? They go to a theatre for that.

You bet! ✪

Back issues of Film History – volumes 1-6 (1987-94)

'A Good Emotional Hook': Selling *Sign of the Pagan* to the American Media

Forty-five Years of Picture Making: An Interview with Cecil B. DeMille, by George C. Pratt with an Introduction by Herbert Reynolds

The Hammond French Film Script Archive at New York University, by Robert M. Hammond

Volume 3, Number 3, 1989

Hollywood Censored: The Production Code Administration and the Hollywood Film Industry, 1930–1940, by Gregory D. Black

Emile Reynaud: First Motion Picture Cartoonist, by Glenn Myrent

The First Cinema Shows in the Czech Lands, by Zdenek Stabla

Introducing the 'Marvellous Invention' to the Provinces: Film Exhibition in Lexington, Kentucky, 1896–1897, by Gregory A. Waller

A History of the Boxing Film, 1894–1915: Social Control and Social Reform in the Progressive Era, by Dan Streible

Tom Daly's Apprenticeship, by D.B. Jones

Career in Shadows: Interview with Charles Van Enger, by Richard Koszarski

Volume 3, Number 4, 1989

The Worst Location in the World: Herbert G. Ponting in the Antarctic, 1910–1912, by Dennis Lynch

Liebe Macht Blind and Frans Lundberg: Some Observations on National Cinema with International Ambitions, by Jan Olsson

The German Film Credit Bank, Inc: Film Financing during the First Years of National-Socialist Rule in Germany, by Wolfgang Muhl-Benninghaus

Sources for Archival Research on Film and Television Propaganda in the United States, by Richard Alan Nelson

An Industry in Recession: The Italian Film Industry 1908–1909, by Aldo Bernardini

Volume 4, Number 1, 1990

In The District Court of the United States for the Southern District of New York:

United States of America v. Paramount Pictures, Inc., *et al.* Equity No. 87-273

Ammended and Supplemental Complaint, November 14, 1940

Final Decree, February 8, 1950

Findings of Fact, February 8, 1950

Volume 4, Number 2, 1990

The Exhibition of Films for Japanese Americans in Los Angeles During the Silent Film Era, by Junko Ogihara

Harry Buckwalter: Pioneer Colorado Filmmaker, by William Jones

Disaster Spectacles at the Turn of the Century, by Andrea Stulman Dennett and Nina Warnke

Effects of Censorship Pressure on the New York Nickelodeon Market, 1907–1909, by Robert A. Armour

Shooting the Great War: Albert Dawson and The American Correspondent Film Company, 1914–1918, by Ron van Dopperen

Fascinating Youth: The Story of the Paramount Pictures School, by J.B. Kaufman

Casablanca and United States Foreign Policy, by Richard Raskin

Fighting for What's Good: Strategies of Propaganda in Lillian Hellman's 'Negro Picture' and *The North Star*, by Brett Westbrook

Volume 4, Number 3, 1990

Cecil B. DeMille and the Lasky Company: Legitimating Feature Film as Art, by Sumiko Higashi

The War of the Wolves: Filming Jack London's *The Sea Wolf* 1917–1920, by Tony Williams

Fritz Lang's *M*: A Case of Significant Film Variation, by Joseph Garncarz

History and Historians in *La Marseillaise*, by Leger Grindon

Forty Days Across America: Kiyooka Eiichi's 1927 Travelogues, by Jeffrey K. Ruoff

Synergy in 1980s Film and Music: Formula for Success or Industry Mythology?, by R. Serge Denisoff and George Plasketes

Volume 4, Number 4, 1990

The Postwar Economic Foreign Policy of the American Film Industry: Europe 1945–1950, by Ian Jarvie

Fritz Lang Outfoxed: The German Genius as Contract Employee, by Nick Smedley

Regionalism in Disney Animation: Pink Elephants and *Dumbo*, by Mark Langer

The Nightingale and the Beginnings of the Alco Film Corporation, by Steven Phipps

D.W. Griffith's *Intolerance*: Reconstructing an Unattainable Text, by Russell Merritt

Volume 5, Number 1, 1993

Fritz Lang's Trilogy: The Rise and Fall of a European Social Commentator, by Nick Smedley

The Invisible Man behind *Caligari*, by Uli Jung and Walter Schatzberg

Cecil B. Demille writes America's history for the 1939 World Fair, by Allen W. Palmer

Rin-Tin-Tin in Berlin or American Cinema in Weimar, by Jan-Christopher Horak

The Erotic Melodrama in Danish Silent Films 1910–1918 by Marguerite Engberg

The Roots of Travel Cinema. John L. Stoddard, E. Burton Holmes and the Nineteenth-Century Illustrated Travel Lecture, by X. Theodore Barber

Witness to Hollywood: Oral Testimony and Historical Interpretation in Warren Beatty's *Reds*, by Leger Grindon

Showmen and Tycoons. J. J. Murdock and the International Projecting and Producing Company, by Martin Sopocy

The Missing Reel. The Untold Story of the Lost Inventor of Moving Pictures, Review by Alan Kattelle

Volume 5, Number 2, 1993

Animatophilia, Cultural Production and Corporate Interests: The Case of 'Ren & Stimpy', by Mark Langer

The Invention of Plasticine and the use of Clay in Early Motion Pictures, by Michael Frierson

Before Snow White, by J. B. Kaufman

Phenakistoscope: 19th Century Science Turned to Animation, by Richard J Leskosky

Toontown's Reds: HUAC'S Investigation of Alleged Communists in the Animation Industry, by Karl Cohen

The View from Termite Terrace: Caricature and Parody in Warner Bros Animation, by Donald Crafton

'That Rags to Riches Stuff': Disney's Cinderella and the Cultural Space of Animation, by Susan Ohmer

Reviews: Women & Animation: A Compendium, by Maureen Furniss

The Illusion of Life: Essays on Animation, by Will Straw

Felix: The Twisted Tale of the World's Most Famous Cat, by Mark Langer

Volume 5, Number 3, 1993

Editorial: Film Technology and the Public, by John Belton

Bringing Vitaphone Back to Life, by Robert Gitt

The Space Between the Object and the Label: Exhibiting Restored Vitaphone Films and Technology, by Steve Wurtzler

The Archeology of Cinerama, by Fred Waller

Sponable's CinemaScope: An Intimate Chronology of the Invention of the CinemaScope Optical System, by Stephen Huntley

The Aesthetics of Emergence, by William Paul

Volume 5, Number 4, 1993
Editorial: Institutional Histories

In the Belly of the Beast: The Early Years of Pathé-Frères, by Richard Abel

Early Alternatives to the Hollywood Mode of Production: Implications for Europe's Avant-Gardes, by Kristin Thompson

Belasco, DeMille and the Development of Lasky Lighting, by Lea Jacobs

Passions and the Passion Play: The Theatre, Film and Religion in America, 1880–1900, by Charles Musser

Intimate Theatres and Imaginary Scenes: Film Exhibition in Sweden Before 1920, by John Fullerton

Advertising Independence, by Charlie Keil

Fiction Tie-Ins and Narrative Intelligibility 1911–18, by Ben Singer

Volume 6, Number 1, 1994
Editorial: The Philosophy of Film History, by Paolo Cherchi Usai

Out of this world: theory fact and film history, by Stephen Bottomore

Film history: or history expropriated, by Michèle Lagny

The place of rhetoric in 'new' film historiography: the discourse of corrective revisionism, by Jeffrey F. Klenotic

The power of a research tradition: prospects for progress in the study of film style, by David Bordwell

Re-reading Nietzsche through Kracauer: towards a feminist perspective on film history, by Heide Schlüpmann

...film in a lifeboat? by Barry Salt

Anyone for an aesthetic of film history, by Eric de Kuyper

'Don't know much about history', or the (in)vested interests of doing cinema history, by Richard Abel

Restoring history, by Jonathan Dennis

Animal and other drives of an amateur film historian, Tom Trusky

Volume 6, Number 2, 1994
Editorial: Exhibition, by Richard Koszarski

'New theatres a boon to real estate values', from *Record and Guide*

When a dime could buy a dream, by Linda Woal

'You can have the Strand in your own town', by Kathryn Helgesen Fuller

The 'Theater Man' and 'The Girl in the Box Office', by Ina Rae Hark

Helping exhibitors: Pressbooks at Warner Bros. in the late 1930s, by Mark S. Miller

Hub of the system, by Robert Sklar

Film journeys of the Krzeminski brothers, 1900–1908 by Malgorzata Hendrykowska

Telling the tale, by Vanessa Toulmin

Motion picture exhibitors on Belgian fairgrounds, by Guido Convents

The creation of a film culture by travelling exhibitors in rural Québec prior to World War II, by Pierre Véronneau

'Cinefication': Soviet film exhibition in the 1920s, by Vance Kepley, Jr

Reviews: *The American Film Institute Catalog: feature films 1931–40,* by Richard Koszarski

Hermann Hecht, Pre-Cinema History: An Encyclopaedia and Annotated Bibliography of the Moving Image Before 1896, by X. Theodore Barber

Volume 6, Number 3, 1994
Editorial: Exploitation film, by Mark Langer

Resisting refinement: the exploitation film and self-censorship, by Eric Schaefer

White heroines and hearts of darkness: Race, gender and disguise in 1930s jungle films, by Rhona J. Berenstein

The woman on the table: Moral and medical discourse in the exploitation cinema, by Felicia Feaster

MAKE LOVE MAKE WAR: Cultural confusion and the biker film cycle, by Martin Rubin

The trope of Blaxploitation in critical responses to Sweetback, by Jon Hartmann

Reviews: *Animating culture: Hollywood cartoons from the sound era,* by Susan Ohmer

Volume 6, Number 4, 1994
Editorial: Audiences, by John Belton

The world as object lesson: Cinema audiences, visual culture and the St. Louis World's Fair, by Tom Gunning

The taste of a nation: Training the senses and sensibility of cinema audiences in imperial Germany, by Scott Curtis

Forgotten audiences in the passion pits: Drive-in theatres and changing spectator practices in post-war America, by Mary Morley Cohen

The K-mart audience at the mall movies, by William Paul

Stepin Fetchit: The man, the image, and the African American press, by Charlene Regester

Enemies, a love story: Von Stroheim, women, and World War I, by Lucy Fischer

Reviews: *Hollywood's overseas campaign. The North Atlantic Movie Trade,* by John Belton

Correspondence, from Janet Staiger

UPCOMING ISSUES/ CALL FOR PAPERS

Cinema and Nation
edited by Mark Langer
(in press)

Films of the 1950s
edited by John Belton
(deadline for submissions 1 October 1995)

Cinema and Nation, Part Two
edited by Kristin Thompson
(in press)

New Trends in Film Studies
edited by Paolo Cherchi Usai (in press)

FILM HISTORY encourage the submission of manuscripts within the overall scope of the journal. These may correspond to the announced themes of future issues above, but may equally be on any topic relevant to film history. It is the journal's policy to publish non-thematic contributions in future issues.

FILM HISTORY

Back issue and subscription order form

PLEASE SUPPLY:

.... Subscription(s) to *Film History*
at Institutional/Private rate (please specify)
Surface/Air Mail (please specify)
.... Back issues of the following volumes/issues
....
....

I enclose payment of £/US$ ....
Please send me a Pro-forma invoice for: £/US$ ....

Please debit my Access/Master Card/Visa/
American Express/Diner's Club credit card:
Account no...Expiry..........

Name ....
Address ....
....
....
.... Zip/Postcode ....

Signature ....Date ....
(This form may be photocopied)

SUBSCRIPTION RATES & BACK ISSUE PRICES

Institutional Subscription rates:
All countries (except N. America)
Surface mail   £85   Air mail   £95
N. America
Surface mail   US$151   Air mail   US$172
Private Subscription rates (subscribers warrant that copies are for their PERSONAL use only):
All countries (except N. America)
Surface mail   £33   Air mail   £44
N. America
Surface mail   US$59   Air mail   US$79
Back issues: All issues available – Volumes 1 to 7:
£12/US$20 each number.

JOHN LIBBEY & COMPANY LTD,
13 Smiths Yard, Summerley Street,
London SW18 4HR, UK.
Tel: 0181-947 2777 – Fax: 0181-947 2664

FILM HISTORY

An International Journal

Aims and Scope

The subject of Film History is the historical development of the motion picture, and the social, technological and economic context in which this has occurred. Its areas of interest range from the technical and entrepreneurial innovations of early and precinema experiments, through all aspects of the production, distribution, exhibition and reception of commercial and non-commercial motion pictures.

In addition to original research in these areas, the journal will survey the paper and film holdings of archives and libraries world-wide, publish selected examples of primary documentation (such as early film scenarios) and report on current publications, exhibitions, conferences and research in progress. Many future issues will be devoted to comprehensive studies of single themes.

Instructions to Authors

Manuscripts will be accepted with the understanding that their content is unpublished and is not being submitted for publication elsewhere. If any part of the paper has been previously published, or is to be published elsewhere, the author must include this information at the time of submittal. Manuscripts should be sent to the Editor-in-Chief:

Richard Koszarski
American Museum of the Moving Image
36–01 35th Avenue
Astoria, New York, NY 11106, USA

excepting for submissions to thematic issues directed by one of the Associate Editors.

The publishers will do everything possible to ensure prompt publication, therefore it is required that each submitted manuscript be in complete form. Please take the time to check all references, figures, tables and text for errors before submission.